TRYSTE AND THE SEA

Tryste And The Sea

The Last Two Voyages

Val Haigh

Order this book online at www.trafford.com
or email orders@trafford.com

Most Trafford titles are also available at major online book retailers.

Note for Librarians: A cataloguing record for this book is available from Library
and Archives Canada at www.collectionscanada.ca/amicus/index-e.html

Printed in Victoria, BC, Canada.

ISBN: 978-1-4251-8659-3 (sc)

Our mission is to efficiently provide the world's finest, most comprehensive book publishing
service, enabling every author to experience success. To find out how to publish your
book, your way, and have it available worldwide, visit us online at www.trafford.com

Trafford rev. 9/28/2009

By the same author

CHASING THE DREAM

Front cover design by Carol Haigh

Copy Editing by Nicola Haigh

Maps by Ernest Haigh

All photographs by Ernest and Val Haigh

 Trafford
PUBLISHING®   www.trafford.com

North America & international
toll-free: 1 888 232 4444 (USA & Canada)
phone: 250 383 6864 ♦ fax: 812 355 4082

Dedication

This book is for our daughters, Janet, Carol, Anne, Susan and Nicola, and the grandchildren: Dana, Corrin, Rhiannon, Caitlin, Christopher, Kendra, Guy, Eryn, Lee and Hannah, and all the rest of the ever- expanding family.

My thanks go to Ernest and to all our children, who have given me so much of their time and attention whenever the book, or I, needed it. They all helped with editing, spelling, punctuation or advice at one time or another, as did Anne's husband, Russ. Janet helped me enormously with the photographs and with technological computer knowledge, and no one ever said, 'Sorry, I don't have time'. Ernest, the instigator of the voyages, gave me all the nautical and navigational advice I needed and much support.

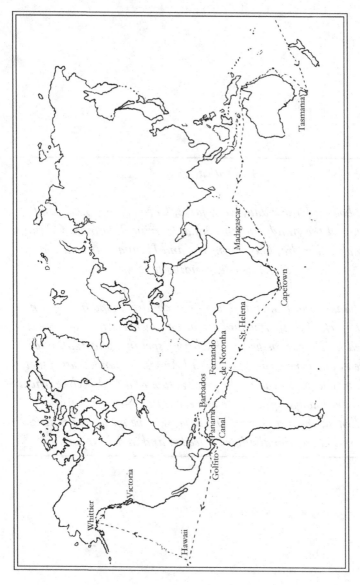

The World. Tryste's second circumnavigation 1981-1983

Contents

INTRODUCTION:

EMTEESS

'Friends! You blew my mind!' Ugo Conti wrote us exuberantly in a letter from California, near the end of 1983. Ernest and I had met Ugo in June of that year in Hawaii's port of Hilo, after the completion of our second circumnavigation aboard *Tryste*. We had anchored and tied stern-to in Hilo's Radio Bay after a slow forty-day passage of nearly four and a half thousand miles from Golfito in Costa Rica, too exhausted to take much notice of the strange outsize inflatable that was the vessel to starboard of us.

In the morning we looked with more interest at this unique 28 ft. ship, *EMTEESS*, with its cabin, leeboards, tubular superstructure and 30 ft. mast topped by a flotation device, never dreaming that it had been sailed all the way from California: yet both we and Ugo had started our voyages from North America. We had left from Canada's west coast, in July1981, planning to sail west-about around the world aboard *Tryste* for the second time, while he had left from Morro Bay two years later in May of 1983.

Ugo had left with two aims. The first was to resolve his mid-life crisis by sailing totally alone, downwind to Hawaii; the second, after enjoying sailing among the Hawaiian Islands for a few months, to ship his boat back to America. To this end he had designed this large inflatable sailboat primarily for downwind sailing and in components that could later be taken apart and packed into a crate only twelve feet long.

Having successfully sailed the 2,400 miles in just over 24 days, and before sailing around the islands, Ugo prevailed upon us to rendezvous with him outside Hilo Harbour, so that we could photograph *EMTEESS* under sail 'at sea,' with Mauna Kea in the background, for an article he was writing for *Cruising World* magazine. We could hardly refuse, since for one full day he had driven us around Hawaii in his rented car to explore the island and see the volcanic activity.

Although he downplayed his expertise in creating this unusual sailboat, and claimed to have 'just read a few books' to calculate the stresses and tolerances necessary for the main structure that he designed to hold together the mast, leeboards and floorboards, he had advanced degrees in both electrical engineering and geophysics and had worked at U Cal, Berkeley since 1967. With his dark ragged hair, greying beard, Italian nose and slightly European air, Ugo quite looked the part of the mad scientist.

'He's a brain', Ernest said, after our day out in the car, when Ugo had given us a comprehensive and mostly comprehensible explanation and world overview of the extraordinary El Niño weather we had encountered both off the coast of South Africa and in the Eastern South Pacific.

Ugo, we discovered, was a romantic as well as a scientist. Not only was he hoping to re-marry his divorced wife on his return, there was also the matter of the name of his boat, *EMTEESS*. This was his spelling of MTS, which stood for *Morituri Te Salutamus*, the Roman gladiator's salutation to Caesar on entering the arena: *'We who are about to die salute thee.'*

The day we were ready to leave, we met *EMTEESS* outside Hilo's long mole, and once the photography session was completed and we were ready to head offshore, Ernest nudged *Tryste* alongside *EMTEESS*, so that I could hang out and hand Ugo his exposed film; but he refused to take it. He insisted that we should keep it and send it to him when we had had it processed in Canada, since we ought to be home in about three weeks. That was his mistake.

Three weeks later we were not safely home in Canada, but at the end of a towline, nearing Alaska's Prince William Sound, with our mainmast thousands of miles astern and two miles deep, and with our starboard hull broken off and destroyed. We wondered then if we should have named our boat *EMTEESS*.

This book is the story of some of the adventures and misadventures that brought us to this end in the 'good old days' when life for cruising sailors was easier, with less restrictions and regulations (and costs) and when all navigation was still celestial (before GPS or even Satellite Navigation) and of how we could not resist pushing our luck with 'just one more voyage with *Tryste*'—well two—a year's voyage to New Zealand and back, in 1977/78, and our second circumnavigation in 1981.

CHAPTER ONE:

A TELEGRAM FROM HOME

Back in July 1977 Ernest and I had left Saltspring for our 12-month cruise to New Zealand and back on our own. On all our previous voyages we had had daughter crew, first four and then, after leaving Carol and Anne, then 19 and 18, in Australia, only the two youngest, Susie, 16, and Nicky, 14. Our eldest daughter Janet, now 27 and married, had never sailed offshore with us and was happily settled in Victoria.

After three years working we could just about afford to go. We were off again, in search of that indefinable something that we could not find on land. We knew that it could never be the same without the family, and we also wondered how well we would manage the boat, just the two of us; but the bad times at sea of fear, danger and worry had faded from our memories, while the extraordinarily good times, when each day was full of its own particular sense of living life to the full, had become burnished and treasured and yearned after.

Our minds filled with memories of blissful nights in the trades when *Tryste*, with her running sails set, rushed headlong downwind through the darkness, seeming to come alive under the soles of our bare feet, while the warm tropical wind caressed our skins. We remembered how the roaring roadway of flashing phosphorescence of our wake would signal to a group of dolphins that a boat was speeding through their domain, and how they would explode around us leaving long glittering trails like comets, noisily blowing out great gasps of air as they curved and twisted beneath *Tryste's* bow. It was because of memories like these that we were prepared to turn our backs on Saltspring, home and family, and head out again.

When, three years earlier, we had returned from our family voyage around the world, Ernest had carried out his plan, formulated in our last year of family cruising—somewhere between South Africa and Saltspring—of turning the shell of the boat shed, where we had built *Tryste*, into a house with a hip roof, to be called The Barn.

I had found the last few months of the voyage extremely stressful and had lived apart from Ernest for a year. Nicky had lived with me and she and I moved back in with him before Christmas the year Nic graduated from high school. Susie was living with Anne, now a single parent, who had rented a house near Ganges, Saltspring's main village, with her baby, Dana. When Ernest and I moved back aboard *Tryste*, Anne and Dana moved into the Barn.

Susie, who was working in the Saltspring hospital kitchen as well as doing leatherwork crafts, rented a house in Ganges where Nicky joined her. She too was soon working in the hospital kitchen, as was Carol for a while.

Although Ernest expressed some concern about submitting *Tryste* to another long voyage (since we had had considerable constructional problems when there were the six of us aboard) we both felt that with only the two of us, and with all the work Ernest had subsequently done to strengthen her, *Tryste* would be perfectly fit to go deep sea. We planned to sail from Victoria and head roughly 100 miles offshore, as we had done in 1969, and, as then, our first destination would be San Francisco. After that we hoped to cruise through the South Seas to New Zealand before sailing home by way of Japan (perhaps), the Aleutians, and Alaska. We were realistic enough to know that in future our voyages would always be circular, with home and family as the ultimate destination.

We wondered if the thrill of new places and faces, the wildlife, and the unpredictable weather would be enough for us now—or would we discover that we did not really want to spend long periods at sea enclosed in a floating wooden box with only one other, oh-so-well-known, companion. A year would surely be long enough to find out.

We had an easy start to the passage, motoring out of the mouth of the Strait of Juan de Fuca 'towards San Francisco' with virtually no wind. As night fell and the lights faded behind us we saw the night sky, like a black curtain speckled with stars, right down to the horizon. We soon turned the motor off, and gradually drifted back with the tide, almost to Cape Flattery, and had to motor away again for another hour. At daylight a light southeaster came in, and at last we could set sail.

Coming on deck on our second morning out and looking round the horizon we saw—absolutely nothing. We had almost forgotten what being *at sea* was really like, how there was nothing at all to see but an endless line of water, stretching in a silken ring around us. It was cold, but it was beautiful, and when the sun came out it was like being reborn. We felt that we had returned to our natural element. We two, with our boat, were an island of peace and tranquility and the outer world could now impinge on us only if we invited it in by means of a short-wave receiver, the sole piece of radio equipment we carried.

That was the good side. The bad side was that we had to come to terms with there being just the two of us aboard. We had expected to miss the girls as friends, but had shrugged off how different it would be as the only crew, when we were used to there being four of us to share the watches and deck work, as well as to do the cooking and the cleaning-up chores.

Ernest discovered that he had almost forgotten how to do celestial navigation and had to give himself a quick crash course. As for me, I endured my usual first three days of I-wish-I-were-dead-seasickness, writing in my diary, 'I don't think I want to go to Alaska on the way home. Being sick and scared is only tolerable if you are warm.' We would experience many more plan-changing thoughts before we reached Saltspring again a year later. Meanwhile a visit from a Hawaiian Island Laysan albatross told us that we were heading in the right direction—south to the Tropics!

We had ordered two new tan sails, main and genoa (sometimes called 'the genny'), from Lucas and Sons in England before we left B.C. Ernest had come up with the bright idea of picking them up in the States from the brother of a Saltspring friend as a 'Yacht in transit' to save the import duty, which was why we were making San Francisco our first port of call. Remembering that the most expensive part of going cruising is always when you hit port, I doubted that we would end up better off, but Ernest overrode my arguments.

Three days out from Victoria we were only two thirds of the way down the coast of Washington State, about 115 miles off Gray's Harbour. We picked up a coastal forecast of north to northwest wind, 15–20 knots, a knot being speed measured over a nautical mile (1.1516 statute miles), which would be perfect for *Tryste*. By nightfall the promised wind had hurried in under a clear moonlit sky and Ernest was happily writing his old standard: 'Moving along nicely' in the log. Only a day later *Tryste* was revelling in a building northerly gale. We felt as if we had been at sea forever.

We had our poled-out running sails set on the forestay—one of the original pair of twin jib sails hanked onto the stay, with the genoa sail set flying—a superb downwind rig, right up until the moment we had to hand both sails in too much wind. We left it too late, until *Tryste* was occasionally surfing at 15 knots, and when Ernest dropped the genoa in a rush both he and the sail almost went overboard.

It was only when we had smothered both sails, had tied the wheel to weather and were lying ahull (with no sail set) that we realized just how much wind we had. We decided to make the best of it by trying to catch up on our sleep, but the wind's howling, the revolting motion and the stuffy air below, all made sleep impossible. Ernest and I both soon had headaches. 'A horrible night,' says my diary.

We lay ahull all that night as the gale built and then peaked. The next day, with Ernest anxious to be under way, we set sail too soon. I failed to respond to my orders fast enough which resulted in a torn twin. Ernest was furious but he had to remember that he was now blessed with only me to be the three-person crew he was used to, and that I did not react as quickly as those smart sailor girls, Susie and Nic, had done. He soon forgave me (he would have a lot of practice), and a few days later he was saying fondly, 'You're a good old tit in a tight spot'—probably not everyone's idea of a compliment.

Even after sailing around the world I could never be described as a born sailor. Although sometimes when we were working together on the heaving foredeck and Ernest was being incredibly patient, I would really enjoy it and would think to myself, 'This is wonderful!' but it never lasted, and there were other occasions, even at this early stage, when I would confide to my diary, 'I love Ernest and I love *Tryste* but I won't go to sea again after this voyage is over.' Some people never learn—I would still be sailing offshore with Ernest twenty years later.

Over the next two days of this first passage the wind gradually eased until we were almost becalmed. Ernest turned the motor on because we needed to charge the batteries but soon turned it off again. We were supposed to be *sailors,* for heaven's sake, and impoverished ones at that.

It had always been a part of our subsistence living not to expend fuel unnecessarily.

At noon on our eighth day out, we were nearing the California coast in a heavy overcast with a light nor'wester. For the second day in a row it was impossible for Ernest to take a noon sight although he had managed to catch a quick sight of the sun earlier in the morning. This, together with a faint signal on the Radio Direction Finder, from the radio beacon on the Farallon Islands, gave us a reasonable fix of 30 miles from Point Reyes, itself 30 miles from the mouth of San Francisco Bay. Apart from the depth sounder, the RDF was the only electronic navigational aid we carried.

Two migrating land birds visited us that day: a handsomely marked plover and a fluffy, cheeky little nuthatch that gradually became increasingly tame before settling on Ernest's shoulder.

By morning of the last day we were wrapped in thick fog. Now we understood why we had not seen the strong light on Point Reyes overnight, although the chart claimed it was visible for 26 miles. At last we picked up the sound of its foghorn and shortly after that, the fog thinned enough for us to see the misty shapes of two freighters heading out to sea from the Bay.

Passing Drake's Bay, where the six of us had sheltered so gratefully from a gale on our first ocean passage ever, we tipped our metaphorical hats to it. The wind soon died completely and we handed sail and motored in under the Golden Gate Bridge in wispy fog, anchoring off Sausalito mid-afternoon after an eight day passage of 848 miles from Cape Flattery.

Following author-sailor Eric Hiscock's version of Murphy's Law— that you always make port either at the weekend or on a public holiday when all the offices are closed—by the time we were anchored it was too late on a Friday afternoon for us to clear Customs and Immigration. It would be a glum weekend if we could not go ashore to look for family letters because we had not cleared in. Anchoring off the Sausalito Yacht Club after this first passage, as we had done eight years before with the children, was a mistake, making us remember how new and exciting it had all been then. We had hoped to re-live those heady early days in 1969 when we, and most of our new friends, were neophyte cruisers who had just completed their first offshore passage.

Although the Yacht Club made us reasonably welcome, there were no other overseas cruising yachts anchored there, since Marin County, where Sausalito lies, was suffering a bad drought. There would be no visitor's showers or laundry facilities. But we were in the right place for collecting the sails since the ferry across the Bay to San Francisco docked nearby.

A quick dinner was over by seven; the sun set at eight and we fell into our bunks and slept ten and a half hours. Early next morning Ernest sneaked ashore and, to his pleased surprise, found the post office open and a long letter from Anne in General Delivery. Our weekend was saved. We phoned home to Anne later and asked her to spread the word: that we had arrived safely and were leaving again in about a week. Carol and her partner Gerry were also living there, in a tent in the garden for the summer. They had bought a 26 ft. sailboat, *Nomad*, and were working on the boat while sharing the Barn's amenities with Anne and Dana.

After the weekend we were cleared by Customs and Immigration, and set off to collect our sails. We found our way to the San Francisco Customs House with its imposing white marble hallways. After visits to four different offices all the forms were filled in and all the questions answered satisfactorily. It only remained for us to go over to a warehouse nearby and collect the sails—or did it? Suddenly the appraiser changed his mind. He thought that we had to pay duty after all, either that or we could apply for an import permit—which might take weeks. No one seemed to have heard of duty-free 'Yacht in transit'.

Afternoon office hours were running out while the appraiser spoke to his supervisor. We were sent to see this supervisor, with all our papers, passports and friendly hopeful faces. We found him phoning *his* supervisor. They could none of them see a way out of our paying duty—which they said would be, 'A considerable sum'. It was office-closing time 'Please come back tomorrow.'

We left the city and took the ferry back to peaceful Sausalito with Ernest fulminating and me just plain tired. Next morning he went off alone and returned a few hours later triumphant. The 'considerable sum' turned out to be only $36. 'If I'd known that,' Ernest told them, 'I'd have paid it yesterday.'

Having achieved our main objective, we decided to leave next day, just as soon as we had collected our hoped for mail from the Post Office.

That morning, which was a Friday, I took the last load of laundry to the laundromat while Ernest collected the mail. There were letters from Janet and Carol and a telegram. At that time telegrams were often bad news but Ernest assumed this one would just be saying 'Bon Voyage.' When I got back to the boat he told me deadpan, 'I've decided we're not going today after all.' This was so out of character for Mr. *Time-to-be-moving-on* that I gaped at him. 'What on earth are you talking about?' Then he handed me the telegram:

'PLEASE CONSIDER LEAVING SATURDAY. BRINGING FRESH VEGETABLES DOWN FRIDAY. LOVE CAROL AND COMPANY.'

Our crazy Saltspring daughters, Nicky and Carol, with Gerry and two friends were driving Gerry's old '52 Chevy, *Gertie,* the best part of a thousand miles to bring us garden vegetables and to visit, when we had expected that they would have been glad to see the back of us and get on with their own lives. They arrived before lunch on Friday, with the one missing letter from Susie. Carol had phoned U.S. Customs and found that the only types of 'garden produce' that were forbidden entry were potatoes—and pot—so they had brought us lettuce and green onions, beets, carrots, broccoli and chard from the garden we all shared at the Barn. They thought visiting *Tryste* was a lovely excuse for an outing to California.

The Sausalito sun shone as we all lolled on *Tryste's* broad decks and watched local children race small sailboats, heeling and almost capsizing in the fresh breeze. In the evening I cooked a massive beef stew with dumplings to feed our visitors, and we all cleaned our plates. They were either too hungry or too polite to mention that some of them preferred to be vegetarians. After that Swensen's was still open nearby, offering us a choice of 31 flavours of ice cream for dessert.

Next morning we put them ashore at 6 am with cups of early morning tea, and sailed *Tryste* back out under the Golden Gate. More tears! It had been heart-warming to see them but now we were miserable again.

Chapter Two:

BRIEF ENCOUNTERS

Our passage to Hawaii turned out to be remarkable for two reasons: an excruciating lack of wind and encountering another yacht at sea.

Once our visitors were safely ashore, we motored under the Golden Gate and optimistically set sail, but soon accepted that there really was no wind, handed sail again, and motored the 25 miles offshore to the Farallons. This group of rocky, bird-whitened islets and photogenic rock arches is home to thousands of cormorants that feed offshore each morning before returning home at dusk.

We did not fancy the Pilot Book's recommended anchorage there, which is exposed to the northwest, but decided to lie off to the east of the islands instead and wait for wind. Ernest swam after lunch. He would probably have thought twice about it an hour later when we were joined by large quantities of the biggest moon jellyfish that we had ever seen. Their light brownish-khaki caps, about ten inches across, had short frills around and masses of thin, kelp-coloured tentacles 5 or 6 feet long hanging under them. Certainly he would have thought more than twice a few years later when the Farallons became the haunt of great white sharks.

By dinner time we were debating whether to motor off for a couple of hours or try anchoring, when a zephyr sprang up from the west, which soon had us moving along at 3 knots. We kept moving indolently forward all night, with the night skyline of San Francisco lying comfortingly astern and the Farallon light sweeping across us, allowing Ernest on his watch to see that we were surrounded by millions of tiny fish.

Four days later we had made good less than 200 miles and were becalmed in a high-pressure area with the barometer still rising. With not a breath of movement in the air, the telltales lay slack against the shrouds while our breakfast eggshells tapped companionably against the hull. Weather reports from Hawaii spoke of 5k winds everywhere. What hope had we? The huge swells lifted us up and slid us down, over and over, in a smooth mesmerizing manner. A keelboat would have been rolling from side to side; our much-maligned trimaran provided a perfect raft-like platform over the gentle slopes.

'Why are we doing this?' Ernest asked, 'For pleasure?' Already he was bored, irritated and frustrated, but he stopped yelling imprecations at the wind gods long enough to launch the dinghy, row away from *Tryste* and take a series of photos of her disappearing down to the top of her 40 ft. main mast between the oily swells.

There *were* compensations. Lying side by side on the foredeck, the hot sun searing our brown backs, we looked down through the safety nets into the cool depths of the clear cobalt water between the hulls to where a thick soup of life surged endlessly in the swell. Animals like sandy combings from a hairbrush, as well as red and blue protozoa the size and shape of punctuation marks, caught the light as they turned and twisted. Tiny white medusa jellyfish hung and swung like miniature parachutes, while white snowflake copepods moved effortlessly through the water sideways.

When we tired of watching these microscopic multitudes beneath the surface, we stood up and looked for activity among the hundreds of blue velellas on top. These small by-the-wind jellyfish that are related to the larger, showier Portuguese man-of-war, are only two or three inches long, with a gas filled sail which acts as a buoyancy mechanism. They seemed to be able to set or hand their sails at will and seeing them— flaccid and collapsed on the silken ocean—we knew that it was useless for us to try and get under way. When they filled their gas bladders and sailed off over the sea like a scattering of soap bubbles, we hopefully sent up our new small homemade chute (part of an army-surplus nylon parachute.)

With a year's cruising ahead, our slow progress would not have mattered if only Ernest had remembered '*Look not thou upon the wine when it is red*', that last day in Sausalito.

'How many days to Hawaii, Dad?' Carol had asked then. Nicky, who had sailed with us all the way home in '74 and remembered the windless Pacific High Pressure Area, might have been ready to suggest 'twenty' since it was over 2,000 miles, but Ernest answered negligently, 'Oh, fifteen.' It was the wine speaking. Admittedly, in theory at least, it was a downhill run, but we never, ever, estimated more than a modest average of 100 miles a day. A week later, as we wallowed in the sunshine in the placid, oh-so-pacific Pacific, we both cursed Ernest's indiscretion.

'I'll never touch the stuff again.' He vowed, pouring himself a stiff pre-dinner scotch.

The following day was the first time that we had ever met another yacht out at sea. Since we were moving along gently under sail at the time, we excitedly changed course to meet her. The crew of the sloop, *Carenage*, white-haired captain, partner, and large German shepherd dog, bound for L.A. from Yokohama, were in no mood to stop and chat after four and a half thousand miles. Landfall, to them, must have seemed just over the horizon.

'It's been twooooo months!' The bearded skipper shouted as the two boats closed and parted again.

That evening at sunset, as we lay becalmed with all sails furled, irritated by the occasional cat's-paw rippling the water from dead ahead, we saw the tiny triangle of another yacht's sail on the southern horizon. We knew that they would not see our bare sticks against the dark sky, so we turned in, only to turn out again at midnight for a breeze and then crossly hand our drooping sails once more.

Our noon position on the fifth day showed us five miles back east from the previous noon. We were both disgusted. The afternoon was breathlessly hot. Standing on the cabin top in search of cooler air, I scanned the horizon.

'I don't believe it!' I said. 'Sail Ho!' Was this a yacht highway?

'Let's ask them to take a letter for us,' I suggested, and went below and hastily scribbled a note about our lack of wind. 'Good idea,' said Ernest as he started the motor and headed towards them. As with *Carenage*, the couple doing a yacht delivery of the attractive blue ketch *Azulao*, sailing from Lahaina to Long Beach after the Transpac race, could smell land only a few days ahead and wanted to keep going. But first we circled one another and I handed over our letter, which the smiling mate promised to mail.

'Where do we run into the wind?' She asked hopefully. 'There isn't any.' I said. 'What about the tropical storm?' 'No sign!' 'There's no wind left in the world!' Ernest shouted, as the two yachts drew apart. We were left with a feeling of profound relief that we had sent off our message. We had been becoming more and more worried about the family being anxious about us.

Mid-morning next day Ernest, who was on deck, shouted in amazement,

'My God! It's a spinnaker!' From never seeing another yacht at sea we had graduated to three in as many days, not counting the one we had seen as a sunset silhouette. By now we had found the yachts so blasé and unresponsive that since we were actually moving slowly but steadily on course we just kept going.

'Hang on,' Ernest said, 'they're dropping their spinnaker. Ease sheets and we'll motor-sail over and meet them.' Far from being unresponsive, the four young people who were delivering *Celox,* a sleek sloop with a blue and white spinnaker, to Long Beach after the Transpac, were as excited at meeting another boat as we had been three days earlier.

'How about a glass of plonk?' Ernest called, forgetting his resolution again. 'What's plonk?' asked one of the girls. 'The cheapest possible wine,' I yelled back. Within minutes, the two vastly dissimilar boats were rafted together with every available fender jammed between them. When two hours later, a nor'west breeze began to fill in a little, we reluctantly parted from our new friends. Walt, *Celox's* skipper, brought out a wilted lei, which he cast into the ocean as a joint offering to the gods for more wind. With cries of 'Aloha!' the two yachts headed off roughly east and west. Amazingly soon we were alone again.

Our twenty-sixth wedding anniversary fell on the next day. We celebrated with smoked oysters and by making good 100 miles noon to noon for the first time since we left San Francisco. At last the wind changed to northeast and we had some good trade wind sailing, with the wind blowing 20 – 25 knots and rising at times. By the next night, *Tryste,* with the staysail and old genoa set wing and wing, was running downwind in the moonlight, her three silver wakes merging into a jumbled highway of foam as the water swished away astern. On either side, giant waves, their crests 40 feet apart, rose, crested and hissed away like a thousand invisible snakes. As each wave lifted *Tryste* from astern she surfed dizzily ahead at ten or eleven knots, checked at the end of her run, then hitched a ride with the next passing comber. We enjoyed this glorious sailing with the helm lashed and *Tryste*'s twin wind vanes doing excellent work steering, although occasionally, when the wind gusted up over 30 knots, we needed to be on hand to rescue her, as the waves built up and flung her off course with a wild flapping of sails and banging of poles.

Bemused by wind and sea and movement, we allowed ourselves to succumb to a feeling of euphoria. Sailors' memories are so short and our living always so immediate, that we could almost persuade ourselves that the whole passage had been like that.

'I don't know what you were worrying about,' Ernest said cheerfully, 'I told you the wind would come in, in the end.' I gasped, remembering the bad times of his total black despair. On one of those nights—perhaps it was on the day we had made good only 24 miles—as we crawled onward at a knot and a half, Ernest had wordlessly shaken me awake at the end of his first night watch and, in complete silence, had lain down on his bunk, turned his back, and pulled the bedding up over his head. Where, I wondered, was the usual report on the last four hours, the friendly chat and the few words about the next watch?

In the last week we clocked up almost 1000 miles. The evening we made landfall we were within 20 miles of Hawaii at sunset. Although the distance tables in the back of Mixter's *Primer of Navigation* told us that Mauna Kea should be visible 121 miles off, it was not true for us. All we could see in the direction we believed Hawaii to be was the enormous cloud of a big black rainsquall. But once it was dark we picked up a golden glow below the clouds, which over the hours turned into the orange lights on Hilo docks. We motored around the long mole that protects the outer harbour and into Radio Bay about 0200 in brilliant moonlight. I dropped the hook where instructed by my Captain who then motored *Tryste* astern, delicately squeezing her in between two sleeping yachts. It did not take long after that for us to make our stern lines fast to the wharf and gratefully go below to sleep.

Longing to turn in, I did not use my normal care taking out my contact lenses and dropped one onto the heather-mixture carpet under the table, where it immediately became invisible.

'Ernest!' I cried. 'Help!' As we crawled, almost naked, on the saloon floor searching, a brisk voice from the dock hailed us. 'Hullo there! Where're you from?'

I cowered, half-hidden under the table, while Ernest supplied the few necessary particulars to the container dock's guard, who was just checking us in.

We fell asleep to the sound of dockyard Martians peeping, moving containers around on 'our' dock, and to the sweet smell of pink frangipani blossoms, after twenty-one days at sea—an average of 100 miles a day.

CHAPTER THREE:

FANNING ATOLL AND
THE SEARCH FOR *WISHBONE*

By the time we left Saltspring in 1977 all our daughters, except Janet, had embraced a more relaxed, alternative lifestyle than the way we had brought them up. This included more permissive parenting as well as a leaning towards health food and vegetarianism. In vain I assured Ernest, 'Vegetarians are people, just like us.' 'Like you, maybe,' he growled. In spite of this attitude, we both had accepted that some of the family had now departed from our old-fashioned 'meat-and-two-veges' lifestyle, and only Janet and Jerry ate what we considered to be 'normally'. To keep us healthier on our voyaging, Carol and Gerry made us a huge cardboard carton of rich, organic granola, full of good things like wheat germ, flax and sunflower seeds, nuts, dried fruit and coconut. This large carton would accompany us most of the way to New Zealand. We made only a small dent in it ourselves, sailing from Saltspring to Hawaii and on to Fanning Atoll, but from there on it would at last be properly appreciated.

Ever since reading about Fanning in Eric Hiscock's *Sou' west in Wanderer IV,* and Miles Smeeton's *The Sea was our Village,* I had wanted to visit this northern Line Island, 1,000 miles south of Hawaii. Both accounts made it sound beautiful and rich in birds, with a safe peaceful anchorage. The atoll, 33 miles in circumference and 12 miles across, lies at 3°51'N, 59°22'W, near the meeting of the west-going South Equatorial Current and the east-going South Equatorial Counter Current, in an area of predominant but unreliable southeast trade winds.

14

Captain Edmund Fanning, sailing the brig *Betsey* out of Stonington, Connecticut, discovered the low-lying northern Line Islands in 1798. He had already sailed out to the Cape Verde Islands where the crew had re-rigged the *Betsey* as a 'ship' (square-rigged on all three masts), had sailed the length of South America to the Falklands to load seal furs, rounded the Horn and called at Juan Fernandez Island, off the coast of Chile south of Valparaiso, before heading out across the Pacific.

Captain Fanning was obviously adventurous, and apparently decided not to take the usual sailing route directly to China but to explore a little on the way. He visited two of the Marquesas Islands; in the first of which, *Le Dominique*, as Hiva Oa was then known, he narrowly escaped having his ship taken over by the Marquesans. From there, seemingly still undaunted, he went on to discover the northern Line Islands. These low-lying atolls are a difficult place to navigate through, and also, as we found later, to search amongst. Sailing among the shifting and unpredictable currents, that we later experienced, he was lucky. In May, in daylight, he discovered Washington Island, which he called New York, presumably finding, as we did, no safe anchorage there. A few days later, a premonition during the night (or was it just good seamanship?) made him decide to heave to, which saved the *Betsey* from running onto the submerged reefs off Palmyra atoll, 119 miles to the northwest of Washington. The *Betsey* was still in the Line Islands area on June 11th of that year, when at 0300 the lookout spotted the glow of breaking surf ahead. They were only a mile off the atoll that took his name. It appeared to be uninhabited, although they discovered several burial cairns. After these two close calls Captain Fanning decided that it might be more prudent to rejoin the known shipping route—and headed off for Canton.

In September 1977, Ernest and I sailed *Tryste* south from Hilo to Fanning atoll. The Pilot Book led us to hope that we would carry the fresh northeast trade winds to 10 or 12°N. To our disgust we soon discovered that this year the doldrums lay exceptionally far north. Only two days out at 15°N we lost our lovely trades. For a week after that we were either becalmed in oppressive heat, or suffering squalls from every possible direction; by the end of the week we were only at 8°N having covered just 450 miles.

That morning Ernest called me out on deck. 'Listen!' He said. 'Can you hear it bubbling and burbling?' The sea was full of swirls and eddies and little breaking waves like tide rips. Small bubbles constantly came popping to the surface and we felt sure it must be the edge of the Counter Current.

The passage was never to be easy. For most of the time the wind remained light and variable. Showers and black squalls made celestial navigation difficult, although Ernest took both sun and star sights whenever he could, heeding the Pilot Book's warning:

> *'The currents round Fanning Island are strong and variable; every opportunity should be taken to fix the ship by astronomical observation when in its vicinity.'*

Like Captain Fanning we were cautious the night we approached Fanning Island, with light trade winds carrying us towards it. Three fuzzy star sights gave us a reasonable fix, which put us closer than we expected. A large black beetle suddenly appeared in the galley sink. It must have flown aboard.

'I don't like that beetle,' Ernest said, 'they can't go to windward worth a damn. We'll hand sail until daylight.' As we lay off, we both suddenly picked up the intoxicating tropical scent of land. At dawn we set sail in a faint south easterly. As the sky lightened, Ernest suddenly said, 'Hand me the binoculars! Land Ho!' Fanning lay only ten miles off.

Nearing the atoll we saw that a freighter seemed to be standing close in, north of the pass into English Harbour where we had to enter. 'Isn't there something wrong with that ship?' Ernest asked. We looked again. There, right up on the reef with its good side towards us, was the wreck of one of the Bank Line freighters, the *Lindebank*. Later we saw a huge, gaping hole in the other side.

Once we had been cleared by the officials at English Harbour, we moved across the wide entrance passage, where the current ran at 5 knots, to anchor behind Cartwright Point on the other side. Here at last we were totally relaxed, and could swim, have tea, swim, have drinks, swim, have supper; all in a calm, palm-tree-lined bay where maroon and orange coconut crabs scurried amongst the roots of the trees and frigate birds wheeled jaggedly high overhead. We could stay there, I thought unrealistically, for weeks—unrealistically because of Ernest's restless nature. But still, there was much to explore. Maybe, just maybe, I could keep him in one place for a little longer than usual. That dream was shattered the next day.

We had arranged to go back over to English Harbour, to see Mike Ross, a skinny young New Zealander we had met the day before. He had been crewing until he became sick, on Canadian-registered *Wishbone,* a heavy displacement gaff-rigged ketch, and had been on Fanning for a month, recovering from his illness. He was living part of the time in English Harbour in the house of Bill Frew, the Australian manager of the copra plantation, and the rest of the time in one of the houses five miles up the coast at Napari. This was the old disused cable station (closed in 1964) that now housed PERL, The Pacific Equatorial Research Laboratory, and the weather station, both run by the University of Hawaii. He had offered to take us round the village at English Harbour, where all the Gilbertese copra workers lived.

We pulled the dinghy up on the white sand beach and tied it to a wild almond tree. Mike was outside the little yellow radio shack listening to Bill Frew, who was on the short-wave radio to Washington Island, about 70 miles away, talking to Ted, the manager there. The news was puzzling. *Wishbone* seemed to have disappeared!

The yacht's French owner, Dr. Claude Detouillon, was understandably distraught. He and his crew, Beatrice, had sailed to Washington a few days earlier and had wanted to spend their last night there ashore (where Claude had been doctoring some of the inhabitants by pulling teeth). He had arranged for three of the Gilbertese islanders to care-take the boat, since anchorage in the open roadstead was too dangerous to leave the boat unattended. The idea was that if they had any trouble, they could call up on *Wishbone's* CB radio. Now the boat had apparently dragged its anchors, and been swept away on the currents. One anchor warp floated uselessly on the surface, still attached to an anchor, but the other was missing. Claude demanded that the U.S. Coastguard in Hawaii send a plane to search for *Wishbone.* He wanted Marty, who was the head of the Napari station and at present in Hawaii, to make representation to them.

Ensnared by the sense of unfolding drama, we stayed by the radio shack waiting for news. Word came that the coastguard said that *if* they were to send a plane, they would want one of the yachts in the Line Islands to go into the search area. Ernest, naturally, volunteered

Tryste, and said that we would pick up Claude from Washington Island on the way.

Claude, on the radio, demurred. 'I'm not sure I should leave Washington! Zee coastguard should send a plane!' Then the clincher, 'Zey do not have a radio on zis boat!'

It was true that we did not have a transmitter, but we had a good receiver and Bill provided us with a CB radio for close work (a 'talkie-walkie' as Claude endearingly referred to it later). If Bill was prepared to transmit messages to us on a regular schedule, we could keep in touch. Mike would come with us and when we picked up Claude from Washington, they could give us extra fuel. Claude still seemed reluctant to leave Washington, apparently feeling that he had a better chance of persuading the USCG to take an interest, from there. He also suggested that if we found *Wishbone*, Mike could sail her back. Faced with this possible responsibility, Mike, who had not learned celestial navigation but had already experienced the fickle local currents, sensibly said, 'No thanks!'

We were off within half an hour, gunning *Tryste's* motor to get us through the pass against the flooding tide. Our attitude at that time was coloured by the opinions of Bill Frew, manager Ted on Washington, and apparently Claude: that these three simple Gilbertese had drifted away in this big, unmanageable boat and that they were in danger of floating around helplessly until they starved to death. Not that there was much immediate fear of that since *Wishbone* was loaded, ready to sail next day, with supplies for Bill Frew on Fanning, including flour, sugar, rice and cases of beer. Perhaps all the Caucasians (us included) still had an unfortunate paternalistic attitude to these 'simple islanders.' Yet, at the same time, Ernest and I did query whether these island men *would* be so helpless; would they not have a feeling for the sea, and an innate sense of direction, wind and currents?

We certainly asked Claude, once we had him aboard, whether the three men would be knowledgeable enough to get the sails up (Claude said he did not think that they could manage *Wishbone's* gaff-rigged main) and whether they could run the motor. Since the eldest of the three was the island mechanic this seemed very likely, but *at the time*, Claude did not appear to think so. Perhaps he was just too upset to think clearly. He argued that these men had come from the Gilbert Islands, 2,000 miles away by freighter years ago, and had never been off Washington Island since. Our focus was thus on rescuing the poor helpless islanders, but did knowing that there was beer aboard influence us; making us wonder if Dutch courage might have played a part in the disappearance?

These doubts partly explained Ernest's reaction to Claude's unwillingness to join *Tryste*. 'Tell him,' he said to Bill, on the CB as we went out through the pass, 'that if he does not come with us and we find *Wishbone* we will take off the islanders and let the boat go.' (Which of course he never would have done.) Bill tactfully passed on this message in slightly modified form.

We reached Washington at sunrise next morning, and lay off in the open roadstead, without anchoring, since we wanted to be away again as soon as possible. Combers curled in onto a surf-scoured sloping beach, while not far away, on the southwest corner of the island, lay the rusted wreck of a salvage boat which had come several years ago to take a load of lead from the earlier wreck of the *South Bank,* another Bank Line freighter, and had itself been wrecked. It looked a highly questionable place to leave your boat overnight.

An aluminum skiff soon came zooming out through the surf to take our diesel cans ashore to fill, and to put Claude aboard. He was hardly a typical French yachtsman. A tubby, 29-year-old with short black hair and a stubby rusty moustache, he looked more like a successful butcher, lacking only a blue and white striped apron and a boater. He clutched almost all he had left in the world, a carton of cigarettes. Everything he owned, collected over the last ten years, was aboard *Wishbone.* Ernest could not help but feel sympathetic.

'I'm sorry about your boat, Claude,' he said, 'but it's the Gilbertese I'm really worried about.'

'So am I', said Claude.

'I wanted you to understand that,' Ernest said, 'do you still want to come with us?'

'Yes, I will come.' The men shook hands.

While waiting for our diesel we experienced a strong set to the northwest. This was to be one factor in Ernest's decision where to search. Assuming *Wishbone* to be drifting helplessly, we decided to head northwest for 50 miles, which would take us through the probable area of drift and keep us within radio range, while waiting for the coastguard plane to appear.

As we sailed and motored northwest in a light sou'westerly we constantly scanned the horizon from deck level, and from time to time hauled Ernest up the mast in the bosun's chair for better visibility. On our first official schedule with Bill, we listened to a link-up between Washington, Fanning, and Christmas Island, 150 miles to the southeast, the main Gilbertese administration centre of the Line Islands, where the D.O. (the British District Officer) resided.

He was languidly unimpressed with the islanders' plight.

'There's nothing much out there, is there?' He drawled. 'I don't suppose we'll hear anything more until they bump into something. They'll probably turn up in Penang or somewhere.' We found his bored lack of concern irritating. Neither he nor the US Coastguard (1000 miles away in Hawaii) seemed at all concerned about the men's safety. It was true that they had plenty of food and water aboard, enough for a few weeks, and were not in any immediate danger, but if not soon found they could be at sea for months drifting helplessly in the unpredictable currents.

By nightfall no Coastguard plane had been sent, nor was there news of one coming. When the south westerly freshened we handed sail and lay ahull, hoping to drift in the same direction as *Wishbone*, fearing to pass them in the night if we kept sailing. To our surprise we drifted only eight miles due west. A full moon encouraged us to keep a good watch all night, but we saw nothing. Claude suggested going another 40 miles north-west to look in at Palmyra Island, the only remaining piece of land before the wide empty expanse of nothingness, but Ernest felt that this would use up too much time, take us out of radio range, and, still concerned mainly with the men's safety, reasoned that if the boat reached Palmyra, the men would be safe, rather than lost at sea.

The two captains then agreed that having done our fifty-mile leg northwest without success, we should turn east, since if *Wishbone* had gone this far and set sail, with the southwesterly blowing she might be further east. The chances of finding the boat were lessening fast, but we were still hoping for the Coastguard plane that would transmit us a bearing on the yacht *if* they managed to find it. After all, they had asked us to be in the area. Claude still had the utmost faith that a plane could find *Wishbone*, if only they would look. But would they? We heard on the 1000 sked that they had no serviceable aircraft nearer than Guam 4,000 miles to the east. But they had contacted a freighter in the area that was going to search. Now we had something else to look out for; surely we would see something as big as a freighter!

On this sked too, our friend the D.O. referred to 'This Canadian trimaran.' He said wearily that he thought it was 99.99% against our being lucky, but, 'No doubt they feel better to be doing something.' In spite of this damning assessment we continued to search, scanning the horizon, our eyes on stalks, our necks aching, seeing—nothing. It was now the third day of fruitless searching. Ernest's plotting chart was a maze of position lines and fixes, as he took sun sight after sun sight, and star sight after star sight, to be sure that *Tryste* was not being carried off in an unexpected direction by the currents.

The 1600 schedule brought the news that a commercial DC 6 from Hawaii bound for Christmas Island, to the southeast, was being diverted and would do a limited search of the area that evening. Another chance, we thought! But they never glimpsed *Wishbone* or *Tryste* and *we* never even heard the plane. We learned that on the morning of that day, the promised freighter had stood close in to Washington Island, given two toots and headed north, but they found nothing. We never saw the ship either but we were cheered to think that there was someone else out there searching. Claude, who had a volatile temperament, was elated and *sure* that they would pick *Wishbone* up on their radar. He and Ernest huddled over the chart to compare the freighter's search area and ours.

That afternoon the weather worsened. The southeast trade which had been light to non-existent for most of our passage to Fanning now blew steadily and we plugged into it. The sky clouded over, limiting visibility. We could no longer see the horizon clearly from deck level, and it was too rough for Ernest to go up the mast. Whitecaps stretched across the sea and there was little chance of picking out a white sail. Claude was depressed and disheartened and had almost given up searching. Even when it was technically his watch, he sat, sunk in melancholy, gazing unseeingly at a *Wishbone*-less future. That night we again handed sail and drifted, this time in short, steep, confused seas. Both Mike and I were seasick.

After a couple of hours of this, Ernest and Claude conferred and decided that we should head back to Washington. With the southeasterly heading us we would be close-hauled, making wide tacks across the section that both we, and the freighter, had probably missed. It would be one more area covered, and if there were still no news next morning we could put Claude ashore and head *Tryste* back to Fanning to await developments there.

I was annoyed to think that we were giving up so 'easily'. Yet at the same time, now that we had been out there, I could see how hopeless the task was. One could search for ever. The variables of wind, current, counter current, motoring, sailing, beer and the men's intent, were limitless. We had bet on the one chance in a hundred and it had not come up. The D.O.'s odds now seemed realistic. If the coastguard was not going to send a plane there was no point in our staying in the area.

As well there was our growing acceptance of the probability that the boat had not drifted at all. Claude now told us that the mechanic had worked on the engine and then he and Claude had circumnavigated Washington. If only we had known this in the beginning! Perhaps it had all seemed so easy and pleasant that he and his friends had thought that they too would like to be ocean voyagers. We learned later that only one of the three had close relatives on Washington, and he was living apart from his wife.

There were so many unanswered questions. The line to the anchor floating off Washington suggested that the boat had drifted, but then where was the other one? Why had the men not kept in touch with Claude with the CB on board as arranged?

Much later we heard that *Wishbone* had at some time after a week (where were they till then?) put in to Palmyra Island, but had headed out again in a hurry when some young Americans who were subsistence living there on their own yacht, had questioned their ownership of the boat. The Gilbertese must have been able to read the charts aboard, and they apparently had both the confidence and the know-how to enter what, years later, Ernest and I found to be a fairly tricky pass. Perhaps they were just lucky.

Meanwhile back on Washington atoll it was Sunday and all the friends and relations of the missing men, who believed (or pretended to) that they had drifted innocently away, were in church praying for them, praying that the DC6 would catch a sight of them, and praying for us aboard *Tryste* too. At daybreak on our fourth day out we were about 30 miles from Washington and there was still no news of a plane.

We beat our way south, still hard on the wind, arriving off Washington at 1530, sad, disillusioned and feeling we had let everyone down.

On the 1600 schedule Bill asked us to stay anchored off Washington overnight. There was word that there was a chance of a plane tomorrow or the next day. Ernest said, 'Sorry, no.' I agreed. It was just a waste of time; we no longer believed in the possibility of a plane. (We were right, none was ever sent. Was one ever intended or were they just stringing Claude along?)

We wanted to be well away from Washington by nightfall, and as soon as the boat came out through the surf we bundled Claude ashore. He was a strange conflicting mixture but we had grown to like him. We felt that he had been crazy to leave his boat overnight, but he had paid a heavy price. It seemed unfair that while he was so genuinely fond of the Gilbertese people and had spent time and money doctoring them, that they had repaid his kindness with treachery.

Our trip back to Fanning was agony. We were loaded down with a tremendous deck cargo from Washington: cartons of soap, sacks of rice, flour and sugar, tea chests and taro, as well as innumerable odd-shaped parcels for Bill Frew and his wife, Marina. We also carried two Gilbertese passengers, a slim copra worker and the heavily-built pastor Yotiba, both of whom had sailed to Washington from Fanning with Claude and were now anxious to return home. Because of our deck load, we were unable to set any sail at all and had to motor into both sea and headwind. *Tryste* winced as she hit each wave—and so did we.

After 24 hours of this we came in through the pass, which was lined with warm welcoming waving brown arms. Once *Tryste* was unloaded and the anchor down behind Cartwright point we could at last relax and enjoy Fanning's gentle peace and the scent of frangipani and wood-smoke drifting across from English Harbour. Although we felt that we had failed and let so many people down, everyone seemed truly grateful to us because we had tried.

Over two months later, *Wishbone* reached Utirik Atoll in the Marshall Islands, nearly 2,000 miles northwest of Fanning, a voyage that under normal conditions *Wishbone* would have sailed in less than a month. The three men were apparently so glad to be there and so hungry and thirsty, that they rowed ashore in the tender without anchoring the yacht. Later she washed up on the reef and was soon stripped of everything of value by the inhabitants.

Like most cruising boats at that time, *Wishbone* was not insured. Claude and Beatrice lost everything, although later an American yacht took them to Majuro, capital of the Marshall Islands, from where they were able to reach Utirik atoll on a trading ship and re-possess a pathetic few of their possessions.

The three Gilbertese returned to Tarawa, capital of the Gilberts, as heroes. Apparently the fact of their scurrying guiltily out of Palmyra with *Wishbone* had never become known. During a radio interview of these supposed heroes, the interviewer briefly left the room, inadvertently leaving the tape recorder running. The Gilbertese congratulated one another on having fooled everyone and got away with it. Their guilty voices on the tape were eventually discovered, and they were charged with stealing *Wishbone* and found guilty. The older man received a ten-year sentence and the two younger ones five years each.

Back in Cartwright anchorage on Fanning after four days away, Ernest and I began to recover. Food and drink softened the sharp edges of our distress, and the companionship of the new friends we found in the anchorage helped. Wendy and Harold Goddard had built their ketch-rigged Wharram catamaran, *Kiskadee*, in Vancouver. They were sailing her westward around the world to Barbados, their island home in the West Indies, with their two young boys, Kevin and David, 10 and 8 years old. The boys made us feel nostalgic for our own cruising family and Harold, swimming over with a bottle of white Barbados rum, cheered us up considerably.

Mike borrowed a jeep and bumped us all up the coral road five miles to see the launch of a weather balloon at Napari where the buildings of the old cable station still stood. One of the old staff-houses was the temporary home of Cathy, a pregnant California 'flower child' who had been brought from Palmyra atoll by one of two American boats now anchored in English Harbour. We assumed that she had sailed to the atoll aboard the 'hippie' boat that was rumoured to be tied up to the wharf there.

Ernest enjoyed talking to her, sitting at the top of a long flight of steps that led up to 'her' house. She was a sweet ingenuous girl who told him wide-eyed, 'I've never been, like, pregnant, before. It's all, like, you know, a new experience for me.'

We finally saw the village at English Harbour next day, and found those essentials, Post Office and Port Captain. We had not gone far before Yotiba, the solid Gilbertese parson, popped out of his house and invited us to come to dinner, to thank us for bringing him home. Bill Frew's gratitude was expressed by pouring us most of the beer that had been in the deck load that we had brought back for him from Washington. As well he gave us an 18-inch-high brass shell case from an old World War I gun up at Napari. Nowadays this case holds the fire irons on the hearth at The Barn, home on Saltspring.

A few days later it was time to sail. We had done all the necessary maintenance work, like filling and fiberglassing a small patch under one wing where the plywood had started delaminating, and master-cleaning the deck after our return from Washington with our messy deck-load. We hated to leave lovely Fanning and all our new friends, but the *Kiskadees* too were leaving shortly, bound for Samoa and the Fijis, while we were heading for Suvarov in the Cooks, over 1000 miles to the southwest.

Mike was looking for a boat to join. Wendy and Harold offered to take him as crew to Samoa, if we could help out with some extra stores. We were glad. Not only was Mike good crew, but the whole family would find him fun to have around. We could certainly spare them the few stores they needed. One of the things we could easily spare was plenty of Carol and Gerry's granola. Mike had enjoyed it while crewing aboard *Tryste,* and we knew the *Kiskadee* family all liked granola too. From Fanning on, this exceptional cereal would finally come into its own.

CHAPTER FOUR:

TOM NEALE'S KINGDOM

After a picnic ashore on Anchorage Island, Ernest and I were happily back aboard *Tryste,* and I for one felt supremely content. This deep happiness engulfed me in spite of the fact that my whole body was throbbing with sunburn, my lips were swollen and burnt and my nose was really painful. As well, one thumb, elbow and knee were grazed and sore from tripping over my feet and rolling down the hard coral beach, and my back ached from rowing the dinghy around while Ernest tried to shoot reef fish for dinner with a spear gun. This, I decided, was sublime happiness.

For three days *Tryste* had been anchored off Anchorage Island, Suvarov atoll, in the Cook Islands: 513 miles north of Rarotonga, and 200 miles from the nearest inhabited Cook island of Manihiki. Anchorage itself, half a mile long, 300 yards wide and only 15 feet at its highest point, is the largest island on the northeast reef of a huge coral ring enclosing a lagoon roughly eight miles by twelve, shaped like a distorted circle.

Suvarov, we called the atoll at that time, with an 'a' in the middle, while the Pilot Book more correctly called it *Suvorov,* the name of the Russian ship whose Lieutenant Lazarev discovered the atoll in 1814.

We had sailed the thousand miles from Fanning in nine days, lured here by the chance of living on an uninhabited island. We had heard through the grapevine that New Zealander, Tom Neale, who had made this island his own, had been taken off to Rarotonga for cancer treatment earlier in the year; but we did not know if he had returned. We did know that other yachts were beginning to make Suvarov their destination but we still hoped to have it all to ourselves if Tom was not there.

The passage, after an irritating light-wind start, had been wild and rough with frequent showers of driving rain. At midnight on the eighth day, with only about 35 miles to go, we handed sail and lay off. We would very much have liked a star fix but, predictably, a low overcast covered the whole sky. At first light when we set sail again with genoa and mizzen, the wind was blowing easterly force 6 and the sea was still grey and rough. We soon found that on our present tack we would just fail to clear the northeast point of the atoll's reef, on which stood the small motus of One Tree Island and Fanu.

Ernest turned on the motor. 'I think we'll give the old girl a hand,' he said. It was a good decision. With the help of the engine we crept past the northeast point on that tack; we were still close-hauled down the eastern reef and past Anchorage Island to the pass into the lagoon.

When at last we had picked our way cautiously through the passage, between huge stretching coral patches which lay, pink or blue or cream, below the clear green water, we found to our delight that there was no one in the anchorage or on the island. There was only Tom's sad notice to passing yachts, written seven months previously, attesting to the fact that he left still hoping to return. Later, in New Zealand, we learned that he had died in Rarotonga before the end of the year at the age of 75.

To whom it may concern

I am obliged to leave here to go to Rarotonga
for medical attention and will probably be away
for at least one month. I earnestly hope that
any visitors will respect my property.
The gate to the fowl yard will be tied open for the fowls
to be able to fend for themselves. Any eggs they may lay,
people are welcome to them. I may state that I am virtually
forced to leave everything here. You name it, it's here.
Also I would appreciate it if visitors left a note stating
the duration of their stay here. Thank you!

Tom Neale: March 11th 1977

As we stowed the sails and set anchors fore and aft we had time to absorb the peace, sunshine and near silence. The only sounds were the wind rustling in the palm trees, the boom of the distant surf on the outer reef, the waves slurping on the shore, and the calling of the seabirds. We were finally alone on a desert island.

Before we could even begin to take it for granted, a squall rocketed across the lagoon, turning it from a lucent clear blue to steel grey. The squall lasted two hours with heavy rain. Delightedly we scurried round and filled all *Tryste*'s water tanks and cans. We had no idea that ashore beside Tom's house, we should find six large tanks overflowing with fresh water. When the squall passed and the sun emerged we rowed ashore. We grounded the dinghy on the newly washed beach in the shelter of a broken-down, bleached coral jetty, in front of the boatshed where Tom used to take his evening cup of tea and watch the sunset. As we walked up the path to the house his cat met us, well but thin, meowing hopefully, and a scurry of chickens disappeared, clucking and agitated, into the bush. Later we found that there were only seventeen left, out of Tom's one-time flock of forty or fifty.

At the top of the path we came to his old tin-roofed shack, which had been left behind by the wartime coast watchers of WWII, who had kept an eye open for ships and aircraft in the area and reported them by radio. The accommodation was fairly spartan, with a hard-looking narrow bed; and with a separate cookhouse, Polynesian style, in the shade of a big breadfruit tree. Purple bougainvillea arched over the house, crotons and sweet scented *tiare tahiti* (white gardenias) lined the path, as well as pink frangipani trees and parau trees with yellow hibiscus-like blossoms.

We wandered across the island past the 'fowl yard' and the fenced garden with papaya trees and bananas, to Pylades Bay. This was the shallow rocky fishing area on the east coast of the island, where Tom had speared many different types of fish, chief among them parrot fish and cod, and hunted 'crays' (as he called the local lobsters) in holes in the reef and under rocks. Perhaps we could take over where he had left off. First we would fulfill one of his last requests, tacked up in his house, and cut open coconuts for the chickens.

For the next few days as we strolled near-naked around the island under the soughing palms, collapsing into the milky tepid sea whenever we felt too hot, disturbed only by the occasional 'clunk' of a falling coconut, we were euphoric. An evening meal on the beach, after a Technicolor sunset, cooking small reef fish over a fire of coconut husks, did nothing to disabuse us. White-capped noddies, disturbed at their rest, scolded us from the tops of tall palms under which we had our fire, and the Tilley lantern lit up the undersides of the palm fronds and turned them into a jet black necklace across the throat of the night sky.

We took time out from this exhausting life to row half a mile away, along the reef to the north, to a small motu called Whale Island. Here we found terns, noddies and bosun birds nesting in low bush or on the bare ground, while the white terns, passing low over the lagoon, picked up the aqua blue from the water to be unfairly jeered at as 'terncoats' by Ernest.

Returning to *Tryste* at Anchorage Island we flung ourselves into the sea to cool off; drifting in over the coral heads watching fish, until that in turn became too, too enervating and we swam ashore to lie wallowing languidly in the warm water of the shallows. Obviously Tom Neale's energetic life of self-sufficiency was not for us.

When Tom, then in his fifties, first settled on Anchorage Island in 1952, he expected soon to live off fish, crays, coconut crabs and fruit (such as bananas, papayas, coconuts and breadfruit) as well as roosters, chicken eggs and seasonal tern eggs. He took with him from Rarotonga: tea, coffee, sugar, salt, flour, rice, onions, butter, and beef fat, a few tins of bully beef for treats, and a 40 lb tin of that Polynesian staple, Cabin Bread— at 4" x 4" square, as solid as a dog biscuit. He also took kerosene for his lamps and a good supply of matches.

The coast watchers had had a garden until 1945, but when Tom arrived seven years later the soil had all blown away. He had to start again from scratch, carrying over a hundred sugar bags of poor soil—all of which he had to sift to remove coral stones—from a patch he found on the south side of Anchorage.

Tom had roamed the Pacific for thirty years picking up work whenever he needed cash: either as a fireman on one of the old inter-island tramps, or settling down on land for a spell, clearing bush or planting bananas. In 1940 while living on Moorea, Tahiti's sister island, he met Andy Thompson, captain of the sailing schooner *Tiare Taporo*, which traded through the islands. Three years later Andy told him about a job available in Rarotonga as relief storekeeper for the Cook Islands. Tom took the job and, based on 'Raro', did that until 1952.

During his first year on Raro he met the American writer Robert Dean Frisbie, who had lived on, and written about, several South Sea Islands. Tom listened enthralled to Frisbie's tales of Suvarov where he had been living a year earlier, during World War II, with his four young children. There were also five coast watchers there then—three New Zealanders and two Islanders. In the extreme hurricane of 1942, Frisbie had saved his children's lives by tying them to forks of tamanu trees, which bent, but did not break, when the tidal wave following the hurricane swept across the island to a height of six feet.

Having listened to Frisbie's stories, Tom knew that he wanted to see Suvarov, probably to live there, but it was 1945 before Andy could even take him to have a look—aboard the *Tiare Taporo*, as 'engineer'. Tom was hooked and immediately started collecting up basic necessities, but had to wait until 1952, when another trading schooner, passing on a supply run to different islands, dropped him and all his Robinson Crusoe gear on Anchorage Island, for a passage price of thirty pounds.

On the whole Tom was successful at living off the land. We were a lot less so, although I did have one fresh egg. On one of our first days there, a hen laid an egg beside the path up from the beach. Ernest walked straight past it, so it was mine by right of 'finders-keepers'— and besides, I was the one who was longing for a soft-boiled egg.

It was the only fresh egg that we found, although on our walk to Pylades Bay we had noticed that there was a broody hen sitting on a clutch of eggs by the henhouse. Ernest brought one of the eggs back to *Tryste* to test. It floated ominously. When I cracked it over the side of the boat I found that it contained a distressingly well-developed embryo. But that had been a day earlier; I had had time to get over it by the time I found my new brown egg, and I cradled it lovingly in my hands as Ernest rowed me back out to the boat.

Apart from the egg, our only successes in living off the land were catching fish and eating coconuts. We were used to being offered a refreshing drink of coconut milk by Pacific Islanders, and now carried a machete to open our own. We liked the coconut meat but never learned to enjoy *uto*, the spongy white insides of a coconut that has fallen from the tree and been left to sprout. Even Anne and Russ, who sailed to Suvarov years later with their own far-more-food-adventurous family said, 'We tried *uto* fresh from the nut but none of our crew really took to it.' We had all enjoyed coconut cream made from grated coconut though. Anne had bought herself a proper coconut grater in Tahiti in 1970, but aboard *Tryste* in 1977 Ernest and I had to use a cheese grater which was less efficient and often resulted in grated knuckles.

When we reached Suvarov's Anchorage Island it must have been in much the same state as when Tom first arrived: with the coast watcher's shack and water tanks still usable, but the garden a wreck; although after he had reclaimed it he was able to grow tomatoes, shallots, kumaras and pumpkins, as well as the bananas and papayas we had found there.

Tom spent a total of over six years alone on Anchorage Island. The first time he left, after two and a half years, it was because he ricked his back so agonizingly badly that, as he put it, his whole body seemed clamped in one vast torturing vice. As he lay paralysed on his narrow bed for four days, despairing of rescue, a yacht sailed into the anchorage, only the second yacht to call there in the two and a half years. The two Americans aboard *Mandalay* stayed for two weeks to help him, and then went on to Samoa where they contacted the High Commissioner in Rarotonga, who stopped the next passing trading schooner to pick him up for treatment.

Once he was well the administration would not give him permission to go back, on the grounds that he might get sick again and they would have to divert a government ship to rescue him. At last in 1960 a yachtie took him back. He stayed another three and a half years, in which time six yachts visited, but he had started to think about the fact that he was getting on and that he did not fancy the idea of a lonely death on the island, when the invasion of eleven large, cheerful, noisy pearl divers to his peaceful island, destroyed his peace and helped to speed his decision.

Tom's book, *An Island to Oneself*, came out in 1966 and was well received. Only a year later another small yacht took him back to the atoll, and Sir Albert Henry, by then Premier of the Cooks and a friend of Tom's, appointed him Postmaster of 'Suwarrow' as the island's name was by then spelt and known officially. Tom sold a few stamps to passing yachts—and then had to ask them to take their letters elsewhere to be mailed. He stayed there for another ten years.

Although for Tom living on Suvarov was living in the most beautiful place in the world and his life there, as long as he had his health, totally fulfilling; for us it was different. Although we revelled in the beauty of Suvarov, where the sun shone almost all the time and the trade wind blew and at night, stars that were the biggest and brightest in the world shone out of a dark sky, it took us only a week on Anchorage Island to realize that 'an island to oneself' was not for us, or perhaps we were not for it. The all-pervading heat was too much for us and besides, we were poor hermit material; we missed the family too much.

One day we had set to work and cleared the fallen palm fronds off some of the paths through the island, and had done our best to clean up the beach where it seemed that every party of pearl divers had made a fire in a different spot. This was dirty, heavy work and we began to appreciate the fact that holidaying in a place like Suvarov and actually working at living there were two different things. It *was* paradise, and perhaps in our thirties or forties we might have wanted to take on the hard work that living in paradise entailed, but unlike Tom, in our early fifties we rather thought not. Perhaps the knowledge that Susie would soon be flying out to the Tongas to meet us made us restless too.

We went ashore and put out some raw fish for the cat—we had found that it preferred not to have its fish cooked. We cut open plenty of coconuts for the chickens, before bathing in lots of lovely fresh water for the last time. Then, without a backward glance, we were off in a fresh northeast breeze for the Tongas, the next kingdom to explore.

CHAPTER FIVE:

TOGETHER AGAIN

Back in 1974, at the end of our family circumnavigation, arriving back at Saltspring had obviously felt like *reaching home* for all of us, and we knew that from now on our family crew would mostly be pursuing their young-adult lives there. But now that Ernest and I had left, it did not surprise us that both Susie and Nicky still yearned after the sailing life aboard *Tryste* and planned to join us somewhere along the way on our present voyage.

Susie, together with her boyfriend Greg, scraped together the fare to Neiafu on Vava'u in the most northerly Tongas group. Here they would join *Tryste* and sail the roughly two week (1,279 mile) passage with us to our 'second home' of New Zealand. Nicky, last seen in San Francisco, planned to fly directly to New Zealand later, and meet us there. Then we would all cruise *Tryste* around some of the lovely bays and beaches of New Zealand's north island.

As we soon discovered when we reached Neiafu, in 1977 you needed a lot of patience to connect with people who were arriving by plane to join your yacht. Not only was this pre-internet and pre-email; in the Pacific islands at that time, apart from Tahiti's bustling city of Papeete, phone communication was often dodgy—time-consuming and expensive, while telegrams were frequently lost or mutilated. We did not want Susie and Greg to have to pay for accommodation while waiting for us, nor did we want to arrive too soon and sit in port waiting for them. Although we knew when they were leaving Canada, we did not know the exact date that they were arriving in the Tongas, as they were stopping for a few days in the Fijis on the way. Ernest always worried too much, so that inevitably we reached Neiafu days too early.

Leaving Suvarov, we had expected light winds and adverse currents. Instead we had enjoyed a steady trade wind passage of less than six days for the 735 miles. Now we were happily anchored off the one big hotel in Neiafu, socialising with other cruising boats' crews, some of whom we knew already, like Geoffrey and Ruth Goodman on the Australian bilge-keeler *Karloo*—the only yacht we ever met with wallpapered bulkheads.

Geoff, who sported a fringe of white beard, like Snow White's dwarf Doc, liked gadgets. He had designed a viewing box with a glass bottom, and helped us set our anchor away from any patches of coral by peering into it over the stern of his dinghy.

Once safely anchored we could only wait and enjoy the scent of the hotel's white and gold frangipani trees, and wonder where our crew was. Their plane would be arriving at the south end of the island chain (while we were at the north) on the reef-fringed island of Tongatapu, which boasted the capital, Nukualofa, as well as the palace of King Taufa'ahu Tupou IV. Arriving at the airfield there, they would have to find a plane, or perhaps a boat, to Neiafu. As it turned out we arrived twelve days before them, which was eleven days more than Ernest's normal patience quotient.

Large, well-attended churches of various denominations dominated the harbour of Neiafu. We wandered the dusty streets of the village, where swarms of schoolchildren in royal blue uniforms ran and chattered and smiled shyly at us. The small wooden shops, often colour-washed a pale blue, reminded us of Mexico, and the goods available were similarly dated. Sometimes they were old enough that—as in so much of Polynesia—you could still find things like laundry blueing (to make whites whiter) big yellow blocks of laundry soap, and scrubbing boards with legs; things that were almost unobtainable in North America.

We haunted the handsome brown and yellow wooden Post Office and the small sleepy Telegraph office, hoping for word. One early morning Ernest noticed that an inter-island steamer had come in overnight and thought that Susie and Greg might have arrived in Nukualofa and come up on the ship, but had not yet found us where we were anchored. At 6 a.m. he went to see if he could find out. He spoke to a smiling Tongan deckhand. Were there any *palangi* (white) people aboard? Yes there were, three. Were two of them a young woman with long hair and a young man with dark hair? 'Yes, yes'. Oh those agreeable friendly Tongans! They want so much to please!

When we met the solo passenger later he told us that the pair traveling together, identified by the deckhand as Susie and Greg, were elderly missionaries from New Zealand. Well that's how it is with *palangis*— they all look alike.

At last there *was* a telegram for Haigh. Our crew would arrive next afternoon. By now our seven-day clearance had expired and we had to go to customs and immigration to extend it by another seven. That posed no problem, but when we requested permission to go for a little cruise among the islands when our passengers arrived, the response was, 'No, I can not give you permission.' What? Why not?

It was not as final as it sounded; it simply meant we had to go to the top—and see the Postmaster at the Post Office who was also the Collector of Customs. He had a large dusty office at the back of the building; a charming older Tongan, tall and grizzled, he agreed to give us permission to go to a specified island for two days, to leave on one particular day and return the next.

We left the office proudly bearing our piece of paper, typed slowly by the Collector himself, which said:

Customs Dept, 3/11/77
Capt. Ernest Haigh.

Permission is granted to leave from Neiafu to the island of Kapa on 5ᵗʰ November 1977 at 10am for vacationing purposes only and will be returning to Neiafu on 6ᵗʰ November1977 at 1700 hrs and the Captain of said yacht must be reported to the Collector of Customs by the time of his arrival at Neiafu on 6ᵗʰ November at 5 pm. You are also warning here not to do any smuggling things etc.

Collector of Customs   3/11/77

As we were getting ready to go to the airport outside Neiafu, the next afternoon, Susie and Greg suddenly materialized on the beach below the hotel. We were delighted to see them, not only for themselves, but also for the end to the tedious waiting.

In the morning we all headed out to our permitted island of Kapa, but stopped off en route at famous Swallows Cave, still on Vava'u, where we rowed the dinghy in and looked up to an opening about 60 ft. high in the rocks, and watched the chattering swallows fly in and out around the long clumpy limestone stalactites. The water was clear and still, like aqua stained glass, and *Tryste* lay outside in brilliant sunshine framed by the dark rocky entrance. Most of the Vava'u group are fascinatingly under-cut chunky limestone islands and several have interesting caves.

A little further on we anchored off Mariner's Cave. Here Ernest and Greg swam over to a crevice in the steep cliffs of the island and dove down to the underwater entrance to the cave, while Susie and I stayed aboard. The swim in under the rock of the island to the cave was not far but they were relieved when they surfaced in a cave full of mist, although the pressure made their ears pop. The experience of coming up in this large, empty cave smelling so strongly of sea and seaweed was fascinating, they said, but they were not tempted to stay long, and after they had swum back against a strong surge they advised Susie and me not to attempt it. Half of me was sad to miss the experience, but the half with a strong tendency to claustrophobia was relieved.

It was not far after that before we reached Kapa Island. Here we anchored in peaceful Port Maurelle, which had a sand beach, good holding, photogenic palm trees, coral to swim over and little fish to catch. The following day we sailed to another small, uninhabited island with sand beaches all around, where we paddled, swam, looked for shells and sun-bathed. In the afternoon we had a superb sail back to Neiafu in time for Ernest to report to the Postmaster that we were back and had not done any smuggling things. Two days later, we bought several locally made handsome brown-and-white round baskets with lids, the sort of baskets that would delight the heart of any snake charmer, and wrapped them in old pieces of tan sailcloth and mailed them as presents to all the family in Canada.

By now it was the second week of November and Ernest was beginning to worry that it was getting late in the season to sail to New Zealand. Only twenty-four hours later we had loaded up with fresh fruit and vegetables from the market, cleared *Tryste* out from officialdom and sailed out from the sweet- smelling religious Tongas.

We hoped to stop off on the way out of the harbour for a last swim, but the anchorages we tried were too exposed to the fresh trade wind. After two of these abortive attempts to anchor in coral, I was becoming anxious to get away from land, while Ernest, as always, was worried about wasting an unexpectedly good wind so late in the season. Susie just wanted to be on her way to New Zealand aboard *her* boat, while Greg, who would almost certainly have liked to stay in the Tongas longer with its lovely warm swimming water, beaches, constant sunshine and cute little chunky islands covered in coco palms and bush, was having his first taste of seasickness and was not expressing anything much except, 'Yeeuch!' a sentiment that Susie and I both echoed later.

The second day at sea we all felt better although Greg was still a bit delicate. It was a great pleasure to have the two of them aboard and by teatime we felt well enough for a game of *Scrabble* in the cockpit in the sunshine, while *Tryste* sailed herself with a steady wind. By noon next day we had made good 142 miles. The wind fell light in the afternoon and we had to steer, but that was no problem now that we had crew.

The day after that was a very bad day indeed. All our lives inevitably deteriorated as Ernest spent all morning wrestling with the blocked-up marine head, something that every sailor dreads. He had known for some time that a valve needed replacing, but had hoped to reach New Zealand before that. The other three of us worked the boat and kept out of the way. Greg, perhaps nudged by Susie, was tactful silence itself.

The next morning Ernest, listening to WWV (The US National weather and time signal) on the radio, discovered that a tropical cyclone named Pam was only a few hundred miles away due east of us, and reported to be increasing in intensity and speed and heading our way. Ernest started to worry. Should we change course? Would Pam change direction? This time the worry was short lived. A few hours later we learned that Pam was no longer dangerous.

When that scare was over it was time for Ernest to prepare Greg for what to expect on this, his first offshore passage. In spite of the easy sailing we had enjoyed up to then he warned him that: 'You have to be prepared for at least one bad gale on the voyage, since you always hit filthy weather off the coast of New Zealand.'

Greg at that time was more interested in the here and now: in being at sea and in the magic of celestial navigation and in being aboard *Tryste* and sharing Susie's old life style. Susie, herself, was on top of the world, able at last to show Greg many of the wonders she had told him about. Frustratingly we had seen only distant dolphins so far, but on the tenth day she could write in the log, 'Dolphin visitors at last!' About a dozen Common dolphins came leaping over the waves out of the late afternoon sun to welcome *Tryste*, putting on a real round-the-boat display: weaving, jumping and diving, and staying long enough for Greg, out on the leaping bow, to spend plenty of time with them. Meanwhile Susie and I tried once again, and failed once again, to get just one good dolphin picture.

That same afternoon Susie caught a ten-pound tuna and on the following one we saw a huge white albatross with such a tremendous wingspan that we decided he must be a Wandering albatross. These giant birds' wing spans can run to 11 ft—although ours was probably not quite as big as that. Ernest and I recalled the fourteen-year-old Susie in the early 1970's, with her joyous albatross-sightings cries of: 'Alby's back!' Now our log was scattered with her unique comments like 'Going well enough at last to keep our albatross interested,' 'Poddly but perfectly pleasant,' and 'Good Progress, yes sir!'

When we were only a few days away from New Zealand Ernest came up with his second prediction for Greg: 'There's one good thing about this passage. We're entering in Opua, in the Bay of Islands, sixty miles north of Whangarei, which has this amazing landfall, the headland of Cape Brett on the south arm of the Bay. You can see the light on it for 25 miles, and we've even picked up the loom of it on occasion, from nearly 40.'

Neither of Ernest's predictions came true. We never had the 'inevitable' gale-force bad weather, and we never saw the superb light on Cape Brett. The voyage could best be described as placid, as day followed uneventful day of mostly satisfactory sailing, a bit slow for *Tryste* (and Ernest) but easy for the rest of us—the 1,297 miles from Neiafu taking us just under twelve days.

On the day before we made landfall, noon sight put us only 71 miles from Cape Brett. Luckily Ernest had also taken good star sights and so was doubly sure of our position. 'Luckily' since overnight fog swathed the coast, so that we never even saw the Cavallis, a dangerous group of rocks and islands about a mile and a half off the coast, as we crept cautiously past them. Nor did we ever see Cape Brett's high headland; the whole Bay of Islands was locked in fog. Since we had no radar and no GPS, it was only by watching the depths on the sounder that we managed to squeak safely in. Ernest was pretty sure he knew where we were, but as the fog thinned slightly we were suddenly aware of the rock pinnacle—the Ninepin—looming close to starboard in the darkness. We had entered the Bay. The first glow of lights we located were from Paihia, the small tourist town on the western side of the bay. Oriented by these lights, and by the confirming depths, we finally spotted the small navigation beacon on Tapeka Point on the eastern side, by which time we were in Veronica Channel, which fed us safely into Opua, our old familiar port.

We tied up at Opua dock at 0800 on November 21st. A little yellow car came screaming down the wharf and our physiotherapist friend, Celia Reed, jumped out to take our lines, while our other long-time Opua friends, Ted and Molly Leeds, who had waved as we passed below their house, were there almost as soon. Customs and Agriculture came aboard at once. Celia left for a few minutes, returning with milk, bread, butter and a newspaper. It was great to be back. Our friendly Scottish Agriculture man let us keep our remaining bananas from the Tongas, after inspecting them for mealie bugs. We had to have a narcotics search and Angus, a female black Labrador, patiently endured being lowered from the high dock overhead, poor dog. Once we had been searched Celia lent the officials a hand to haul Angus up. She was so hugely strong that a startled Angus flew through the air and up onto the dock faster than she had ever gone before.

Soon Ted told us the welcome news that he had a mooring for us to use, and that Nicky had phoned, having arrived safely in Whangarei to stay with her school friend Bev, and was coming up at once by bus. Such a homecoming!

With so much of the crew back together aboard *Tryste*, Nicky and Susie were soon hamming it up, nostalgically singing one of their favourites, 'Together again, my tears have stopped falling,' learned from an Emmylou Harris tape. It was, as comics love to say, '*Déjà vu* all over again.'

For the next few weeks we cruised around the Bay of Islands, visiting *Tryste*'s special places from our two spells of living in New Zealand. We introduced Greg to the small towns of Russell, Paihia and Opua, as well as to our friends. We anchored off the wide golden sand beaches of Urupukapuka, Moturua and Motukiekie islands, walked their wonderful green hills and inhaled the scents of manuka and cabbage trees in bloom. One day we anchored off Roberton Island (Motuarohia) and walked up the hill to the big Pa site (Maori fortified settlement) where we could look out over the islands dotted in the clear cerulean sea all the way to Cape Brett.

Several times we gathered the small, flat shellfish called *pipis,* as the receding tide uncovered them. We ate them boiled, dipped in butter. We caught snapper off Roberton Island's jagged black rocks, as well as out in the bay. Many of the islands' shores and headlands flamed with the brilliant red blooms of pohutukawas, the New Zealand Christmas trees, while at night we heard with delight the calls of the little nocturnal owl: 'Morepork, morepork,' and other native birds. 'Was that a kiwi?' Someone asked hopefully. 'Probably not.'

Back in Opua in the middle of December both Susie and Nic came down with flu, Susie first, so that she was beginning to feel fit enough to sail when Nic was still feverish. I did not think we should move while Nicky still had a sore throat, headache and fever, but Ernest was eager to go. Later I was pleased that we had moved. We sailed round to Oke Bay, on the northeast coast of the Cape Brett peninsula, where we three healthy people had our best-ever Bay of Islands experience.

Three dolphins came into the bay and spent a couple of hours circling the anchored boats (most of which were closer inshore than *Tryste)* jumping, playing and interacting with the swimming humans. Then they came out to us. Ernest and Greg both swam with them and were ecstatic. As the only female crewmember well enough, I finally plucked up the courage to swim too. The water was so cold and/or I was so scared, that I thought I was going to die. But I struck out towards the two dolphins that were coming to investigate me. Together they dived and swam, a few feet under me, looking at me interestedly as we passed one another. Their grey backs looked almost black and clearly delineated from their white undersides. They were much, much bigger than me, smoothly muscled and glossy and overwhelmingly beautiful—sentient, curious beings. The nearest one rolled a little on his side to look up at me with a bright, intelligent eye—and then they were gone. 'Come back! Oh do come back,' I begged, but no, they were on their way to some new amusement.

Tied up in Opua, gearing up for Christmas, we found a telegram from Carol's partner Gerry, saying that their expected baby, a girl, had been born on December 19th at home. The home in question was Susie and Greg's rented house 'Kumonin' on Drake Road in Ganges, where Carol and Gerry were living while Susie and Greg were away. Though happy with the good news, it was a little hard for the five of us to enthuse about the *name* of the new baby as we had no prior knowledge of their choices and the telegram distorted her name to 'Rain onion.' Poor Rhiannon!

We saw the New Year in anchored off Russell, where the local inhabitants at that time liked to celebrate a raucous New Year by breaking beer and wine bottles until the narrow shore-side street, normally one of Russell's main attractions, was dangerously littered with broken glass.

In Opua once again, the crew left *Tryste* for Whangarei. They planned to camp around Northland until mid-January, when Susie and Greg would fly home from Auckland and go back to work, and Nic would visit her friends in Whangarei for a while before rejoining *Tryste*. As they walked off up the steep hill at Opua with their heavy backpacks, to catch the bus at the crossroads at the top, Ernest was surprised that I was tearful to see them go.

'You'll be seeing them all again in six months,' he said bracingly, 'and Nicky will be back here with us in a few weeks.' I was too choked up to explain why I felt so bereft. It seemed to me that we had only just regained the warm family circle back aboard *Tryste* and now it was broken again. It was just one more example of how hard it was to divorce ourselves from the dear demanding bonds of family.

'Do you really think,' I asked Ernest, 'that when the time comes that we are nearing Canada, that we shall manage to sail past the entrance to the Strait of Juan de Fuca and on up to Alaska?'

'I don't see why not,' he said.

Well yes, I thought, that *was* the agreed plan, but after all being so happy in New Zealand 'Together Again,' I couldn't really see either of us wanting to carry it through.

CHAPTER SIX:

SILICA SANDS AND KAURI DAMS

In the New Year, after Susie and Greg had flown back to B.C. and before Nicky was back aboard *Tryste*, Ernest and I decided to visit some of the northern anchorages on the North Island's east coast. Two places in particular appealed us (or to be more truthful, to Ernest); Rangaunu, where, as he pointed out happily, there was an eight mile length of navigable river for *Tryste*; and Parengarenga, the northernmost harbour in New Zealand, less than seven miles south of North Cape, notable for a shallow bar entrance, sand cliffs and a long white ocean beach. These harbours were at each end of the narrowest part (only about six miles wide) of the 30-mile-neck of peninsula that widens out to form the northern tip of New Zealand. Nearly all of these 30 miles are edged by rolling sand hills from 100 to 300 feet high.

After spending the night in Mangonui, about 15 miles southeast of Rangaunu, we sailed out early in brilliant sunshine into a fresh easterly. We soon handed the main, and with only mizzen and genoa set, still enjoyed a wild wet ride that had us covering the ground so fast that there seemed hardly time to identify each rocky cape or headland before it was behind us.

To enter Rangaunu Bay we had to round the high cliffs of Cape Karikari where the steep, confused seas beat back with a loud roar. We thought that they must be left over from cyclone Bob, which had passed to the north a few days earlier.

Before long *Tryste* was screaming across the bay on a broad reach and rapidly approaching the headland that formed the western point of Rangaunu Harbour and the entrance to the Awanui River. Off this entrance we could see white water leaping skyward. Ernest ducked below to check the chart leaving me to obey his flung-over-the-shoulder order of, 'Keep well off the point' which had two off-lying rocks. Muttering, 'How far off is well off?' I tried, but he was soon back and grabbing the helm to force *Tryste* further offshore against fluky gusts and the push of massive green swells. Once we safely cleared the ugly black rocks awash, we were able to gybe the mizzen and head in beside a shallow sand spit that ran two miles out into the bay.

With an onshore wind, the water at the entrance seethed. To starboard pale green swells rolled in and broke over the sand spit in great plumes of sandy spray, while to port breakers swept across shallow water and random dervishes of spray leapt and spun and fell. Two small stick markers stood in the middle of this wide expanse of breaking water to show the channel entrance, while green water smoked across the gap between them. We could not turn back. With wind, tide and swells behind her *Tryste* could only go on. Ernest started the motor in the hope of gaining more control. When a swell picked us up and hurled us onward we were surfing close to 20 knots and in great danger of broaching. As *Tryste* flew between the markers, the water was breaking on either side of the fairway but the middle was clear.

We were now in a channel in a flat estuary area across which the wind blasted unrestrictedly. Ernest clawed down the sails, which slightly slowed our progress and made it easier to pick out the few tiny markers ahead in the twisting channel, but even with only the wind pushing us our multihull windage still had us going too fast. Suddenly we saw the masts of a ketch inshore and realized that she was anchored in the lee of some sand dunes, well off the fairway. Should we try to anchor nearby and wait for the tide to rise and perhaps the wind to drop? No sooner had we thought of it than we were past—long before we could locate the channel that would take us safely through the shoals towards the yacht—but at least it was low tide; we could see the channels between banks of sand and shingle.

At last the wide estuary was behind us and we entered the more sheltered mouth of the Awanui River, passing strange greenish flats alive with wading birds, then banks of low-growing mangroves, then bush, then farmland.

We saw a jetty ahead and in trying to reach it, ran aground on thick, black mud. For a little while it was heaven just to stay in one place. I felt utterly exhausted, as if I had been beaten. Ernest launched the dinghy and checked the depths around the boat with a boathook while for one brief blissful moment I sat wedged up against a pile of cushions on the saloon settee, still in my oilskins, and did absolutely nothing. Soon the tide began to rise and we moved slowly, sluggishly (and smellily) forward, through and out of the mud, stirring up a dark cloud in the water behind us.

Motoring past the jetty in a narrow winding channel between high mud banks, we soon misread a single, ambiguous marker and *Tryste* took the ground for a second time. We decided to anchor, have tea and once more wait for the tide to rise. While we were enjoying our tea and incredulously re-living our wild introduction to Rangaunu, the yacht we had seen anchored at the mouth of the estuary came up behind us and passed.

As *Tryste* had floated off we prepared to follow and make use of 'local knowledge', but before we could get the hook up the ketch went on the mud herself. Before long the skipper rowed over to see us.

'We couldn't believe it!' He said, referring to the sight of *Tryste's* tan sails appearing through sheets of flying spray at the harbour entrance. We were relieved to learn that conditions had been exceptional.

He had built his big steel ketch, *Lady Oh,* near the head of the Awanui River, where we hoped to anchor. She had a centreboard in a three ft. wide keel box, which allowed her to take the ground comfortably, but she did it rather more often than he wished, as she drew four ft. instead of the three and a half ft. as designed. *Lady Oh* soon floated off but then dragged into the bank, so we went past and they followed. The river channel was not well marked; it had last been surveyed in 1852 and some of the markers looked to be of that vintage. When the marks became too confusing we let *Lady Oh* pass in a wider part of the fast-narrowing river and then followed, stopping twice to wait when she went aground.

Moving along the winding river, it was as if the wind was cut off completely; as if we were in a different world from that wild bar entrance only ten miles back. The riverbanks were not high, and on either side of us we saw hawks, ducks, rushes and flowers, sheep, cows, horses and water meadows. Ernest was ecstatic. Later we learned that cargo barges used to sail right up the river to Awanui. We tried to imagine them, with their big red sails, passing silently between the green banks of the river. Finally *Lady Oh* went aground in the entrance to the side creek where she had her mooring and we passed her and anchored in front of a low road bridge in the centre of the village of Awanui. It was farming country and as old farmers we felt right at home. I thought perhaps we could just stay there with *Tryste*, anchored beside the bridge, with only the cows for company, for the rest of our lives.

Although I was quite, quite sure that I never, ever, wanted to try another New Zealand bar harbour, Ernest still had his sights set on Parengarenga. We had heard about this amazing place the first time that we had sailed to New Zealand with *Tryste*.

In 1971 the barque *Monte Cristo* (renamed *Endeavour II*) out of Vancouver, BC, had been tragically unable to beat out of this bar harbour in a strong northeast gale after she ran out of diesel for her engine, and had been wrecked. At the time of the shipwreck it was low tide and only eleven feet covered the bar—the *Endeavour* drew thirteen.

The crew of one woman and thirteen men had tried to save the ship by anchoring, but when their two anchors dragged several hours later, the *Endeavour* was swept onto the southern sand spit and later pounded to pieces. Both their larger life raft and their ship's papers had come ashore safely already; the life raft inflated, and let go by mistake. The crew donned life jackets and tied themselves together with nine feet of line between each and one end attached to a smaller life raft (containing the captain, with a broken arm, and the woman crewmember, suffering from exposure). They all floated safely ashore to a crowd of rescuers standing chest high in the breakers ready to help them.

Before we were prepared to try this tricky entrance therefore, we wanted to be sure of fair weather and sat in a delightful anchorage at Houhora, 25 miles down the coast from Parengarenga, patiently waiting for an offshore wind. In Houhora's small general store we met a friendly fisherman and asked his advice about entering Parengarenga. He sketched out the entrance for us on a brown paper bag and assured us that if we followed his instructions we should be fine. We put his sketch in *Tryste*'s chart table drawer with the handsome green New Zealand charts, and when the time came we navigated by chart and brown paper bag.

Next day the forecaster was calling for fresh westerlies, but since by noon there was no sign of fresh anything even I was prepared to face the short passage to Parengarenga. Out at sea we found a brisk south westerly and had glorious sailing, romping north beside a low coast backed by sand hills edged with miles and miles of empty sand beaches. Soon we were eating up the ten miles of Great Exhibition Bay that curves away south of the huge sand spit, composed of the world's purest silica sand, that forms the southern headland of Parengarenga Harbour.

By late afternoon we were nearing Parengarenga, but turning inshore we found it extremely hard to be certain of our position in such a featureless landscape of sand, sparsely daubed with patches of dark brush. We handed sail and proceeded cautiously under power. Finally Ernest picked out one of the two leading marks our fisherman had mentioned—a square beacon on the beach at Ngamaru Point, the northern inner entrance arm—but the triangular one, that was supposed to be higher up among the sand hills and which would give us our line in, was missing.

The entrance channel to the harbour lay between two shallow mile-long spits of sand, extending out to sea. The Pilot Book said that entering directions could not be given owing to '*the shifting nature of the bar.*' Luckily we could rely on our Houhora friend's recent grocery bag update.

We located Dog Island, the mark he had given us to keep off the northern sandbank, which was the one people usually went aground on, since the sea breaks more obviously on the southern one. At last the sand hills began to close in either side and, in spite of the late afternoon sun shining in our eyes, we could easily pick out the angry lines of breakers over the fast-shoaling bar, in the pale green water. We watched the depth sounder going steadily and a little unnervingly down; but we crossed the bar at 10 ft. which was nothing to our two and a half ft. draft. We were soon past the inner entrance point and within the wide entrance of the deep inner bay.

Turning south we cut the motor and set the genoa. With a dying breeze we ran down a deep channel called Te Keao, between miles of sand hills to seaward and low lying cliffs inshore, to anchor off a yellow-green beach of cockle shell, mud and mangrove shoots. It was one of those still, silent places where we ghosted into our anchorage under sail and Ernest said very, very quietly, 'Let go,' and when I did, and the anchor chain ran out, I felt that I should apologize for making so much noise.

Later, Kiwi friends in Opua, perhaps influenced by the newspaper stories about *Endeavour II*, asked us why on earth we had gone to Parengarenga. 'What did you go there *for*? There's nothing much there except sand, is there?' No there's nothing much there except sand: not unless you count nesting Caspian terns and their newly hatched chicks, the remains of a petrified forest, odd metal outcrops like the rusting oxidized skeletons of car engines, tall toi-toi perched high on hillocks eroded by wind and water, strange lengths of dune grass like heavy sea-wrack, and tiny wind sculptures. No, there's really nothing there but great heaping mounds and long plains and endless hills of glaring white silica sand; waiting to be shipped off south to the Auckland glassworks. We never saw a soul in the whole huge bay, although we did hear the gentle drone of a far off farm tractor and we did see a speedboat on the distant, opposite side of the bay.

The day before we left, we tramped the burning hills and plains that lay between our little creek and the open ocean: then swam in the warm breakers of a silver beach which stretched emptily south for miles and miles; emptily that is except for hundreds of migratory Bar-tailed godwits—*kuaka* to the Maori—collecting on the gleaming wet edge of the sand ready for their annual holiday in Siberia. At our approach they rose like an aerial corps de ballet and soared up into the blue sky; keeping such perfect time that as they caught the light all their backs and breasts flashed grey or white in unison.

That evening, as we made a fire on the inner beach beside our channel, and picnicked on beer and cockles, three black swans flew overhead heading north like the godwits. It looked like the way to go. In a month or two we would do the same.

But first we took *Tryste* back to Whangarei to pick up Nicky for some more back-home-aboard-*Tryste* time. The three of us were eager to sail to Great Barrier, a handsome green island that lies about twenty-five miles off Cape Rodney on the east coast, to the north of Auckland.

Our first night was spent in a less than perfect anchorage at Boulder Bay in the Hen and Chickens (a small group of islands a few miles off the coast). This would give us a ten-mile-leg on towards Great Barrier Island to the southeast. 'Bloody cold and wet,' was Nicky's log entry after a miserable, two-hour passage of sailing discomfort heading into a left-over northwest swell with a fresh southwest wind and constant rain. The holding in our anchorage among boulders the size of ostrich eggs proved to be better than we had feared. It was well tested early next morning when a violent windy thunderstorm raged over us.

Once the storm passed, leaving only light sou'west winds in its wake, we were soon on our way. The sun came out, the grey sea turned blue, the wind died and we motored the last three hours to anchor in Nagle Cove on Great Barrier's northwest coast in the late afternoon. Here we all immediately stripped off and swam in crystal clear water in the shelter of handsome Oyster Island, whose one stark Norfolk pine dominated the bay. That evening we dined on a delicious roasted chicken, which we had bought frozen in Whangarei and which had kept perfectly under the remains of a $1.50 bag of party ice. From now on we expected to live off the land, or rather the sea.

Ernest was up early next morning setting an extra anchor as the wind had come up and was blowing into our anchorage. It was still blowing a few hours later and he thought we should move to somewhere more sheltered, but then he noticed that the floor of the bay was, in part, carpeted with scallops. He dived for a small bucketful, which took care of that night's dinner. It was only much later that we, ignorant Canadians, found out that scallops were out of season.

For the next few days we moved around among pleasant recommended-by-friends anchorages where we were sheltered from the occasional breezes. The sun mostly shone and the swimming was always heavenly. Snapper fishing was as good as it used to be in the early days when we were all living aboard *Tryste* in the Bay of Islands, and we kept many legal-sized snapper and threw back a few illegal ones. One day Nic hooked a huge grouper. We knew it was really very large because we all saw it when it surfaced, before it broke the leader and returned to the deeps. We did catch enough fish (without the grouper) to have fresh fish for most of our meals.

We paid a visit to Port Fitzroy, Great Barrier's main village-sized town where float planes and coastal vessels both docked; and we had a good walk up the hill from the ferry dock. The island's gravel roads and proliferation of dead cars reminded us of early days on Saltspring. We noticed that, like Saltspring, recycling was in full swing, an improvement on most of the places we knew in the North Island, where recycling seemed to be in its infancy.

'I wouldn't mind spending a whole winter here,' Ernest said, admiring the laid-back feeling of the island. We had already discovered that there were so many bays and coves all round the coast, that shelter could be found from every wind direction simply by moving. We all felt strongly attracted to the island, which reminded us of home, of rural mainland New Zealand, and in its scenic emerald, rocky beauty, of the Marquesas.

After a few days we moved over to Kaiarara Bay on the north side, where we anchored and dug in the bigger Danforth anchor so that we could leave *Tryste* with peace of mind, since the weather, even though warm and sunny, featured squally williwaws. We had come to walk to the two enormous kauri log-moving dams further up the mountain. The walk, even to the lower one, was quite steep, often crossing and re-crossing mountain streams. The dam consisted of huge kauri logs about 60 ft long spanning the canyon, and the structure itself stood about 50 ft high with a gate, which opened at the bottom to let the build-up of water and logs rush through. Once we had admired it and kicked ourselves for letting the cloudy weather earlier persuade us to leave the camera at home, it was not hard to come up with a unanimous decision to abandon the hot uphill walk to the upper dam. We planned to return (with the camera) another day.

Only a few days later, anchored in yet another splendid green anchorage with sand beach, Ernest, who had been doing boat jobs and wanted a break, decided to go ashore for a walk saying, 'I'm going to see if I can penetrate the bush. It looks a bit impenetrable.' Nicky and I were both happily settled down to being lazy aboard, and declined the invitation to go with him. 'I'll take you ashore, though,' Nic said, and was soon back aboard and deep into her latest book. Only a few minutes later a shrill whistle came from the shore.

'I'll go,' said Nicky. She was back shortly with Ernest with blood pouring from his foot. As she told it later, as she approached the beach she called out, 'Was it impenetrable?' 'Far from it,' said Ernest as he scrambled into the dinghy, 'it penetrated my foot!' He had stepped squarely onto a spur of broken ti-tree (manuka), and it had gone straight through the thick rubber sole of his thong-sandal into the sole of his foot.

Nicky administered first aid in the shape of copious disinfectant, and held his foot well up, to slow the bleeding. Later we bound it up and persuaded him to lie down and put his foot up on a cushion, but, always a rotten patient, he would not stay there and when Nicky and I went fishing from the dinghy he insisted on coming with us; obviously a mistake. By the time we returned his foot had, as Nic said, 'swole up somefink 'orrid,' so we soaked it in warm water and Epsom salts, which seemed to help.

Next morning it was worse again, red and swollen, and had kept him awake at times during the night. We wondered if we were going to have to sail to Fitzroy and get help from the Red Cross nurse there, who was a friend of our Opua friend Molly Leeds. As a last resort before that we tried the Epsom salts cure again, this time in painfully hot water. Nicky held 'the foot' down while the patient squirmed. After that we bound it up with a hot fomentation. This seemed to do the trick and it gradually began to improve, but four days later when we left the island, there was still no question of him going for any walks. We never did see the upper kauri dam.

CHAPTER SEVEN:

STEER DUE NORTH

Nicky flew home from Auckland the third week of March. We were on our own again, facing up to the voyage home to BC, which at times would be against both wind and current, and thinking about which way to go. One common route was by way of Tahiti and Hawaii, making a relatively easy trip that could be divided, by stopping at both, into three passages of roughly 2,500 miles each. But we intended to go duty-free shopping in Fiji, before heading homeward, and decided to take an alternative, more westerly route across the Pacific. I had read several National Geographic articles about the Carolines and wanted to go there. Ernest reluctantly conceded two stops, at the eastern islands of Kusaie and Ponape. We would start with a voyage to the Fijis, and then, instead of taking the recommended route in the Sailing Directions from there to: '*Steer due north to cross [both] the equator and the parallel of 18° N on the 180ᵗʰ meridian...*' we intended to stay east of the meridian and visit outlying Rotuma. This island is administered by the Fijis but lies over 400 miles north of them at 12°S, 177°E, and the inhabitants are mostly Polynesian, not Fijian. After visiting Rotuma we hoped to call at two of the nine Ellice Islands, which used to be half of the British-administered Gilberts and Ellices (Now Kiribati and Tuvalu).

From the Ellices we would head off to the northwest to Kusaie and Ponape. The reason Ernest had stood out against this for such a long time was that we would eventually have to beat back again against both the north-east trade wind and the west-setting north equatorial current; but we had discussed our route with our Whangarei friend Noel Barrott of *Masina* and he had had strongly recommended this western option (which he and his wife Litara had taken) and in particular visiting Kusaie.

Once Nicky left we were ready to sail, even though it was hard to part with all our good friends like Ted and Molly Leeds in Opua, Colin and Marjorie Edwards of the British cutter *Harrier*, first met in the Marquesas and now new Kiwis in Whangarei, and Dawn Hayes, a real estate agent from the office where I had worked in 1970. Many of them came to see us off, bringing us treats for the voyage: cakes, fruit, vegetables and home-grown honey.

Customs cleared us out at 1400, surprised to learn that we were actually leaving right away. We intended to anchor in Urquhart's Bay down at the end of the Hatea River, but if they guessed this they did not ask and we did not volunteer. Probably, at that time, their only worry was that we might sell off some of our duty-free grog, something we had *absolutely* no intention of doing. Nowadays rules are much stricter all over the world, even in New Zealand, and anchoring in one of the bays at the mouth of the river is totally verboten, either on the way out or even on the way in, in a state of extremis, after battling a brutal sea-state and storm force winds for four or five days—when all you want to do is drop the hook and get your head down.

By our third day out we were well on our way, most of my seasickness was behind me and by my night watch we were, as Ernest put it, 'Going like the clappers,' on a broad reach with a fresh east southeast breeze. At noon we were almost 200 miles offshore and it was time for our regular log entry of 'Bumpy!'

'Fish!' I yelled, soon afterwards. I had glimpsed a flash of a totally golden body. 'I think it's a dorado!'

'It can't be,' he said, 'it's too close to New Zealand!' But it was—ten pounds of the best eating. It was definitely time to hold on tight, as we hauled in the liveliest fish we had caught in a long time. As we cleaned up the mess it had made, our minds were delightedly fixed on delicious meals of *mahi-mahi*.

The next day we made good 162 miles with our lovely trade-like wind. A day like that, with such perfect sailing, cast doubt on our firm 'unalterable' decision that this would be our last voyage. We found it harder and harder to remember why we had agreed about this in the first place. Maybe it was because we sometimes had so much trouble getting along, and were involved in so many tiring verbal skirmishes.

But now peace reigned as we reached our way at six knots over a clear blue sea towards the Fijis with the temperature becoming marginally warmer each day. As the wind gradually rose Ernest wrote 'ESE 6' in the log. I checked my notes for force 6 on the Beaufort scale pasted into the back of my journal: '*Large waves begin to form, white crests more extensive.*' Yes indeed! That exactly described the busy scene around us.

The passage from Urquhart's Bay, Whangarei, to landfall on Cape Washington's light on Kandavu Island was just over 1,100 miles. By the sixth day out, after another magnificent day's sail of 164 miles, we were halfway. To confirm that we were well and truly in the tropics, a glorious all-white tropicbird, or bosunbird, its 'marlin-spike' two central tail-feathers as long as its body, sought *Tryste* out, flew for a few minutes at the masthead and then, after a squawk or two, left to return to its fishing. Later a squadron of ethereal flying fish materialized suddenly out of a solid blue wall of wave.

That night on watch I could faintly pick up music from Fiji radio. The air was warm, the stars brilliant and the waves, large and regular, seemed specially designed to speed *Tryste* on her way. It didn't come any better than that. This part of the voyage had been our happiest, least stressful time together since we had reached the Tongas, six months before. Perhaps after all we could get along happily for weeks on end at sea. If Ernest could put up with my ineptitude, absent-mindedness and constant obsessive desire to write, then surely I could put up with his hair-trigger temper and impatience.

Only three fine sailing days later we picked up the first sight of Kandavu Island, 80 miles from Suva, and by six in the evening it was getting dark enough that we could pick up Point Washington's light. The wind backed and fell light and all night we tacked off Mbengga Island, getting nowhere. We finally gave up and stated motoring, but it was not until just after lunch next day that we finally reached Viti Levu and dropped our anchor astern of *Karloo* off Suva Yacht Club. That first evening Geoff and Ruth, last seen in the Tongas, insisted on feeding us good Chinese food and the latest cruising news, before we rowed home to *Tryste* for a deep and dreamless sleep.

We woke to the remembered scent of toasted coconut. In spite of the windless equatorial heat it was a delight to be back in the tropics in Suva's lovely tree ringed anchorage off the Yacht Club. On this second passage to the Fijis *Tryste* had reached Kandavu pass five minutes faster than the first time, six years earlier; her total passage time being eight days and six hours for the 1,131 miles. She certainly was consistent. On that first passage, we still had all four girls aboard and we remembered Anne's delight at the self-steering gear, and her pleasure at lolling around and not always having to take the helm. I had raved about this after I had sailed back from Noumea in New Caledonia with Ernest. He had worked up there (where the wages were so much better than in New Zealand) for three months in 1971.

In Suva we now found other old friends. Harold and Wendy and their two boys aboard *Kiskadee* were over at the Mosquito Island anchorage off the Tradewinds Hotel scrubbing *Kiskadee*'s bottom. As the Christmas card we had received in New Zealand had told us, they would be staying in the Fijis until their third child was born, before continuing on home to Barbados.

Our duty free shopping turned out to be hard work in the hot humid town. Sometimes we do not shop well together, but now we did, successfully buying a new 35 mm camera, a slide projector and a quartz crystal alarm clock for navigation.

That Sunday was the Suva Yacht Club's opening sail past and first race of the season; a spectacle which we expected to enjoy, although the majority of the yachts in the race would be the children's P class dinghies. Unfortunately the race had to be postponed in the morning because of total lack of wind. In the afternoon they all set off with a pleasant light breeze but soon a huge purple-black cloud started to build and settled over the Tradewinds Hotel and Mosquito Island.

Suddenly the storm broke, with thunder, lightning and lashing rain, before the wind came howling in. *Tryste* started to drag but we were ready with the second anchor. Waves built up from nowhere, luckily beating in towards the Yacht Club. Capsized P-class dinghies started washing in towards us in wind and rain, little boys clinging to their upturned craft, longing to be rescued. 'Stay with your boat!' They knew the rules and eventually, one by one, all washed up safely on the Yacht Club steps with good tales to tell. Two bigger boats, one a Thunderbird (26 ft sloop) were dismasted, and another boat was towed in swamped. It was an opening day that would be long remembered in Suva.

Three days later we were ready to leave. Customs said unequivocally that we could not go to Rotuma, or at least not unless we were prepared to sail the 400 miles back to the Fijis to clear in and out again. 'What nonsense!' Ernest snorted.

'Just go,' *Karloo*'s Geoff said, in agreement. So we cleared for the Ellices while in our own minds sailing, still undecided, 'Towards Rotuma.'

After three days of light winds and squally weather, a fresh easterly came in which gave us, for the fourth day, a run of 160 miles. 'Fabulous sailing night' Ernest wrote in the log. I had noted earlier in the day, 'hot and happy'. We were speeding along on a superb reach in the sunshine, with *Tryste*'s tan sails pulling to perfection, when Ernest came down the companionway just in time to see water gush suddenly into the forward cabin. The porthole on the bow of the main hull had blown in: the brass fastenings having quietly aged and turned almost to dust.

Ernest held the porthole back in while he thought what to do, then handed it over to me to hold while he fetched tools, his mitre box and hammer and some odd pieces of wood, all of which he used to wedge the porthole back in. By the time it was ingeniously held in place, Rotuma sat chunkily on the horizon. We no longer had to make a decision. Whether the authorities liked it or not, we *had* to stop to make repairs.

As it turned out, John, the young part-Rotuman District Officer, was very friendly and did not attempt to send us back to Suva to clear again. However, to cover himself, he did have Ernest write a note explaining how it was that he had had to make port without permission.

A strong squall had come through as we approached the reef-girt island from the southeast. Ernest freed the main halyard and started to reef the mainsail, then decided to hand it instead. At that moment we were sailing through a flock of feeding birds and hooked onto a yellow fin tuna. Panic ensued as the main halyard wound itself into a tangle. Before we had that problem sorted out the rain was upon us, but by the time we had the fish boated, the wind from that particular squall had gone on its way.

From then on brief sharp rainsqualls repeatedly swept across, blotting out the coastline, but somehow they cleared each time we really needed to see where we were. The tricky navigation was made easier by the presence of a jagged black rocky island decorated with vivid emerald bush that sat on the extreme eastern limit of the reef that we had to clear.

We anchored at mid-day in Oinafa Bay on the northeastern side of the island, by which time we were both tired out from working the deck at a trot while trying to take photos with two cameras in the unrelenting sun. We soon recovered after a swim, but we did miss our old two-girl crew of Susie and Nic. Life certainly had been easier with them around.

We were anchored in only twelve feet over clear coral sand with a small broken-coral reef ahead. Here in a bight formed by the drying reef and a long rock and concrete mole, we were protected from the southeast trade wind, although there was not a great deal of room to swing. A white sand beach ran across the narrow head of the bay, under thick, healthy palms. To the north other large trees sheltered three houses, one with blue and two with red roofs, the largest, we learned later, belonging to the chief.

Before we had properly got our breath back, five or six motorcyclists roared down onto the wharf and shouted something about taking Ernest to the District Officers' office. As this was before we even had the dinghy down from its strapped-on-deck position, Ernest waved them away. We did notice though that they all wore crash helmets. Later we learned that the compulsory helmet law came in 1969. Failure to comply brings a summons and a staggering fine...of two dollars.

By the time we had *Tryste* squared around, a battered green school bus had disgorged a chattering group of schoolchildren who hurried down onto the wharf near our anchorage to inspect us. We had kept the fat yellow fin that we caught a few miles off the island. I rowed ashore with it.

'Who should I give it to?' I asked the children.

'The Chief! The Chief!' They chorused gleefully.

As this was still before we had been cleared, I persuaded two of the larger high school girls to take it to the Chief for us. Carrying it between them they set off down the crushed coral road like a pair of Pied Pipers with all the other children running, jumping, laughing and chattering behind them.

Clearance was fairly informal with two Indian-Fijians dealing with health and quarantine, and D.O. John and a Rotuman policeman checking our papers. They all seemed quite happy to while away a few hours aboard with chat and Scotch whisky.

Next day we started on *Tryste's* repairs. As well as the porthole there was a patch of delaminating plywood (a continuing problem) under the port wing to fibreglass, and most serious marine disaster of all, there was the head, which had stopped working once again. When *Tryste's* repairs were finished we were free to go ashore and explore Rotuma, landing on a white crescent beach where pink convolvulus sprawled over coral sand. The smell was pure Polynesia: the smoke of fires, rotting bananas, copra and flowers; unlike Fiji where the scents tended to be mixed with interesting Indian spices from the half-Indian /half-Fijian population.

We went first to pay our respects to the Chief. As we approached the house, his wife, a large woman in a faded cotton dress, her face wreathed in smiles, intercepted us. She introduced us to 'Auntie', old and thin and worn out looking, and before long we were seated in the shade of a newly built corrugated iron lean-to, outside the red-roofed house with its one-foot thick rock and plaster walls and opening wooden window holes. Peeking in these open windows we glimpsed Victorian-looking knickknacks and artificial flowers, including frangipani, mixed with the usual bright Polynesian cotton prints and decorative shells. With a flick of a villainously sharp machete Mrs. Chief opened a drinking coconut for each of us and before we had managed to down this cool but filling liquid, her youngest daughter (of seven children) had come out of the house shyly proffering plates of *dalo* (taro) pudding. Struggling to dispose of this sickly, sticky concoction of starch and sugar, and to make conversation, we asked after the Chief, who had not put in an appearance.

'He in there,' Mrs. Chief said casually, gesturing to the house interior, then tapping her vast bosom she added proudly, 'He my wife!'

It was extremely hot and the flies were troublesome. As usual, as soon as we were off the boat, I was red in the face and dripping with sweat. The Chief's wife had been vigorously fanning me with a pandanus fan ever since we arrived, and soon found one for Ernest to fan himself too. Before we left she gave me the leaf shaped fan, '*You* take fan,' she said making it obvious that Ernest was not allowed to take his home. I often appreciated mine over the next 1,200 hot and humid miles across the equator. We never did meet the Chief.

Rotuma Island, over eight hundred ft. high, was lush and verdant, with exceptionally friendly inhabitants who were indeed almost all

Polynesian. As we strolled through some of the fourteen villages under flower and fruit trees where children played, chickens scratched for food and tethered goats browsed, women waved and called greetings while men would often turn aside from whatever they were doing to talk and walk a way with us. In this way we learnt how in the past, before the convenience of modern imported cement, the houses were mortared with a lime tediously made from burning coral for day after day after day.

Early that night we were woken by the arrival of a coaster, the *Komaiwai*. There was much excitement of lights and voices and coming and going on the wharf, but once she was anchored, there did not seem to be much happening and we went back to sleep. Next morning early there were excited voices again on the wharf. Like us, the inhabitants seemed to be expecting the coaster to come alongside, since she was making what was supposed to be her inaugural run of a new regular service from Suva. Instead, after we had breakfasted, we watched a grey haired man, whom we took to be the Captain, measuring the depths alongside the wharf with what looked like a plumb bob on the end of a tape measure. He obviously did not like the depth he found, although it was spring tides and would never be any deeper.

Soon lighters from the anchored ship started to go ashore with loads of gas barrels, stores, boxes, and furniture. The centre of activity then became an area under the big *dilo* tree ashore where trucks from the two island co-operatives, the churches and the police happily loaded up while the poor supercargo sorted through a big blue sheaf of bills of lading and scratched his head. I was happy watching all this entertainment, but Ernest, who had done all his jobs, finished the book he was reading and was not yet ready to start a new one, was beginning to become bored.

'Shall we get our photographing done and go?' He asked.

'Today, Ernest?' I said, 'Oh no! Let's photograph today and go tomorrow...if we must.' It was true that D.O. John had begun to ask if we had done all our repairs, and we knew we would soon have to leave, but still! We had only been there a couple of days. The showery weather of the morning seemed to be clearing up so we decided to do the same walk through the villages that we had done the day before, this time taking our cameras.

We had not gone far when an old orange Datsun pick-up we had seen under the *dilo* tree caught us up. The driver, Father Peter, the island's Catholic priest who was a New Zealander, offered us a ride. He apologized because he would not be able to take us back again, but assured us that there would be plenty of traffic on the road and we would easily get a ride, because of the coaster being in town with supplies for all the different villages. He soon stopped again to pick up two island girls who joined us in the back of the truck.

Just outside Sumi, his Catholic village on the south side of the island, with its big elaborate church and huge old mission house, he stopped again to speak to a man who was walking and who was a little way up an incline in the road. Father Peter braked, but we noticed that we slid gently back down the slope to the bottom, with the handbrake on and Peter pumping the footbrake hopefully.

'There's nothing there,' he said sadly, and added, 'It was a good car until one of the boys rolled it at the farm.' Then as the pick-up coughed mufflerlessly up the last hill, he grinned. 'I bet you thought we weren't going to make it.'

Missionaries had arrived early in Rotuma and there had even been a short religious war in 1878. The island had been at peace ever since, but split into two factions, Methodist and Catholic.

Savaii, one of the Sumi Catholics, was the man Peter had stopped to speak to. 'This man has offered to take you to his house,' said the Father, as he drove away. We went with Savaii. After imbibing the ritual drink of coconut milk, meeting his wife and two smallest children and admiring his cool house and the myriad photos on the walls, we were taken to see a large vault where the remains of the ten 'heroes' who had died in the 1878 war were interred. Savaii explained how the Catholics came to live on the south side of the island. When the first Catholic priest arrived originally, 'No one wanted him. (*Not in our back yard!*) 'So they told him to go round the island and find a place and stay there, and he chose this place (Sumi) and all the other Catholics came and stayed here too.'

Then he told us the legend of Constantine. 'The most strong man, Constantine, was the Chief chosen as leader by the men from the other side of the island (Methodists?) to come and fight the Catholics.' (We never found out why.) 'Constantine and some other chiefs brought this band of armed men and he only had a single shot pistol and lots of people had bows and arrows But the man who shot Constantine hit him six times and he stayed on his feet. But then the seventh stone went through here,' Savaii gestured just below the breast bone, 'and he fell down, but he got up again and asked one of the chiefs to finish him off and the eighth stone went bang in the centre of his forehead.' That was the legend, 'And when his bones were moved from his original grave into the vault, there were the stones in all these places.'

Then he explained, 'It wasn't like wars nowadays, they could still speak one to the other, and all those man who came have a brother, a son, among the Catholics, and so they say, "Let's not fight any more", but these men (in the vault) have been killed already and this is why they build this vault so everyone remember.'

Father Peter did not *want* them to remember. While wryly accepting his flock of eight hundred's continuing un-Christian attitude towards the Methodists, he was working with the other religion's Rotuman-born minister to try to make them change it. He hoped to persuade them to celebrate their 1978 centennial year by permanently putting aside their religious intolerance.

Tearing ourselves away from Savaii's hospitality we set off home down the road, but were soon overtaken by Father Peter again, who was driving some nuns to the next village where they were taking mass. He insisted that we sit in the front with him, even though the load in the back included these two white-garbed, elderly (and seemingly rather cross) Sisters of Mercy. We tried to get out when we reached the next village but were not allowed to. Peter insisted on driving us all the way back to the wharf. I think he was enjoying having someone new to talk to.

When John asked us once again if we had not finished all our repairs, we took the hint and left this delightful Polynesian outpost. We headed back out to sea towards Funafuti, the main atoll and the more southerly of the only two Ellice Islands to have navigable passes into their lagoons. We were bidding farewell to both Polynesia and Melanesian Fiji, from now on it would be hullo to Micronesia.

Once we left the Ellices our course for the Carolines would be northwest, and after we had left that group of islands we would be sailing east against both wind and current until such time, probably not before 35°N, that we began to pick up the westerlies and could finally steer for the West Coast and home to Saltspring.

Ernest takes a noon sight.

Val takes a good look around the horizon on her watch in the North Pacific.

Tryste's saloon, looking forward, photos of the family on the bulkhead.

Tryste and *Kiskadee* anchored together in Fanning atoll anchorage.

Mike at *Tryste's* helm while Claude searches for *Wishbone*.

Tryste lies at anchor outside Swallow's Cave, Vava'u group, Tongas.

The entrance to Tom Neale's shack, Anchorage island, Suvarov atoll.

Susie and Greg stand by Val at *Tryste's* helm, on the way to New Zealand.

Tryste sails up the narrowing Awanui River, North Island, New Zealand.

Ernest at our picnic site in the Te Kaeo channel, Parengarenga.

Susie at the kauri dam on Great Barrier Island, New Zealand (in 1978).

Nicky packs to go home to work, from Whangarei.

CHAPTER EIGHT:

A CLUSTER OF EIGHT

Three days after leaving Rotuma we had made good only 250 of the 290-odd miles to Funafuti, and lay disconsolately 40 miles from the atoll with slatting sails, waiting for wind. What little sailable wind that we had been able to use that day had been from the northwest, which the roses on the wind charts did not even suggest as a possibility.

The arrival of a cat's-paw of a breath from the northeast together with a barely audible gurgle, gurgle, gurgle, had us hopefully setting sail, and as we did so we saw the white upper works of a steamer appear on the eastern horizon. She would cross our course at right angles, but since visibility was limitless we merely wondered vaguely how close she would come. As the distance closed between us we began to wonder if anyone was on watch. She ploughed inexorably on; aiming, it seemed, to graze our bows. We had no thought of standing on our 'steam gives way to sail' rights, we would never be so foolish, but surely with so much sea room she would give way.

'I don't think she's going to turn,' Ernest said disbelievingly, as the big ship with her dark-green hull loomed larger and larger.

'No, I don't think she is,' I anxiously agreed. At the last minute Ernest put the helm over and bore away, and at what seemed like the same instant the Greek, for such she was, at last began slowly turning off to starboard to pass ahead of us. Then as we slid under her stern and leapt about in her violent wake, she gave two cheerful toots of greeting while all her crew and officers lined the rails and waved in the *friendliest* fashion. We waved back, rather tremulously. Then she was gone, leaving only the churning wake, the acrid smell of diesel and two shaken small-boat sailors.

Noon position found us still about 20 miles from Funafuti with a failing wind which put paid to Ernest's hopes of closing with the atoll by nightfall. Finally he decided that if we were to lie off all night we *must* be sure exactly where Funafuti lay before the early equatorial sun set. Grudgingly we stopped sailing and turned on the hot, noisy engine. Ernest climbed to the top spreaders with the binoculars while I motored as fast as *Tryste* would go (7 knots with black smoke) for the best part of an hour, before he finally shouted, 'Land!' This confirmed my earlier tentative identification, of a green sheen on the bottom of a chubby cumulus cloud dead ahead, as the reflection of Funafuti's lagoon. Although to the Polynesian navigators of old noting such a reflection was routine, it was the first time we had ever seen it.

We lay off all night and next morning set sail at 0330. When dawn broke, heralding a superlative sunrise, Funafuti lay ahead, and over us came wafting the sweet rich smell of copra. Mid-morning we motored happily past some men in dugout canoes fishing with throw nets, and through Te Puapua pass (on the southeast side of the atoll) into a glorious lagoon. We did not know then that we should be grateful to a team of Royal Navy divers, who only a year before had finally located and exploded fifteen mines (left over from the US wartime occupation of the island 35 years before) in Funafuti's lagoon passes. Funafuti has an unusual number of possible passes, three or four that a shallow-draft yacht like *Tryste* could transit.

Fongafale village on Funafuti was, at that time, the administrative centre of the British Colony of the Ellice Islands, soon to become independent Tuvalu. Tuvalu means 'a cluster of eight', a disconcerting name for a group of nine islands, all of which were said, by our 1969 Pilot Book, to be inhabited. Perhaps the small outlying island Niulakita, to the south, did not consider itself to be 'clustered' with the other eight.

With *Tryste* anchored in crystal-clear aquamarine water on the southeast side of the eight-mile long lagoon, we were close to the handsome white British administration buildings and houses on shore. We soon came to know some of the expatriate administrators and to see a little of the administration—and its headaches—as these mostly young, hardworking representatives of the Queen gradually phased themselves out over the last remaining months before Tuvalu's independence in October.

We had anchored near the coaster *Komaiwai* and a smaller Funafuti-registered coaster *Nirvanga*, and were soon boarded by four polite and charming Customs and Immigration Ellice islanders, in spotless white shorts and shirts, who cleared us in without any fuss. With independence looming they seemed to know all the right questions to ask but did not always know what to do with the answers, as in:

'Do you have any spirits aboard?'

'Yes, two and a half dozen bottles.'

'Oh.' And that was that.

We went ashore looking for mail at the Post Office and found being on land extremely hot. As we were pulling up the dinghy a chubby young woman accosted us and offered us a cold drink in her house.

'Yes please!' We said gratefully. We expected lemonade or juice, but it was the luxury of cold beer. Sheila, our hostess, was the wife of Jim, head of the Department of Works, whom we met later, along with a dazzling array of other department heads like the Financial Advisor, the Secretary of the Resident Commissioner, and the Attorney General.

The mail plane came in next day but there was no mail for us. Perhaps it was a bit soon. However the *Komaiwai* was still unloading. We thought that they might be bringing mail, but they were not. At the post office we had been told there would be no more mail until next week's plane, but suddenly an unscheduled plane came in from Tarawa in the Gilberts, and our mail was on that, with letters from Janet, Anne, Susie and Greg, and Nicky, and others from friends, but Carol's letter seemed to have gone astray. Mail from the family meant so much to us that it was always a major disaster for us when a letter was mislaid. After we had collected our mail we met the friendly Secretary of the Commissioner, Brian, who had returned on the Tarawa plane. He took us home to meet his wife, Shirley, and have a cold beer, obviously the done thing on Funafuti.

Our plan was to hunker down aboard next day and read all our lovely mail, but we had not realized that as it was the weekend, the ex-pats were into socializing. Later at the pub we met more of them including Frank, the manager of the Philatelic Bureau. We invited them aboard *Tryste* and they invited us back to their cool comfortable houses. On the Sunday we planned a *Scrabble* tournament at Frank's house in the evening, as we had discovered that he was another *Scrabble* addict. Unfortunately the weather blew up with heavy squalls, so that we did not really want to leave *Tryste*. As well, I was not feeling 100% so Ernest rowed ashore and made our apologies. Too bad, we could have put that with our collection of pastimes played in unusual places like bridge in the Galapagos and euchre in Knysna, South Africa.

Each evening after that was calm, and as we sat on deck sipping our evening rum and limes, a 360° sunset extravaganza exploded around us and we used rolls and rolls of film trying to capture the colours. Some evenings we did manage to tear ourselves away from the sunsets and joined the local people in strolling on Funafuti's most popular promenade, the splendid long, grass airfield, another relic of the war; now used for football, parades, drying pandanus—and even the weekly mail plane. Sadly this was almost the only contact we had with the local people, since most of our socializing turned out to be with the British ex-pats.

On the far side of the airfield lay the ocean and we tried to imagine the power of hurricane Bebe's tidal wave which in 1972 dragged the coral beach 100 feet offshore to make a separate ridge, which now formed a small lagoon, down the east side of the atoll. The immense wall of water that swept across the atoll buried the village of Fongafale to a depth of over six feet and destroyed all but two or three of the buildings. "Little boxes" made out of imported materials had since replaced the original native-style housing. But even houses made of concrete could look attractive in Melanesia, smothered in flowers and tropical greenery, with fairy terns and frigate birds circling over them and with black-haired beauties in short cotton dresses riding past barefoot on Hondas.

After hurricane Bebe, there were very few palm trees left on Funafuti and in 1978 the coconut crop was still negligible, but the Philatelic Bureau, which employed thirty-five local people, was a good money-maker. Frank showed us around and told us that last year they had cleared 150,000 pounds sterling, the local stamps being sold all over the world. Apart from working for the administration the only other export in the Ellices was manpower. The young men often went to work mining phosphate on Nauru Island, or signed on as merchant seamen after training in Fiji or the Gilberts. German shipping lines were glad to employ them although they apparently had a reputation for being too ready to pull a knife.

We wanted to visit Nukufetau, as it was the only other atoll in Tuvalu, with a navigable pass. It lay only a day's sail away to the north, but as we were to discover, half a century away in lifestyle, with the people still living in traditional housing at a subsistence level, fishing and harvesting their few crops. Since the distance pass to pass was 60 miles, the passage had to be negotiated at the right time for good visibility in both passes. We planned to anchor inside the northern Funafuti pass overnight and make an early start.

After a week in Funafuti we went ashore to say goodbye to Jim and Shiela and Frank. That afternoon we left our anchorage off Fongafale and crossed the lagoon to the northwest corner to anchor. It looked a reasonable anchorage on the chart, but when we arrived we found that the wind had veered and the lee we had expected was not there. We were a little dubious about what we were putting our hook down in, but passed a quiet, restful night.

First thing next morning we crept carefully out through the pass while the light was good and we could see the coral heads. As so often seemed to be the case in the Pacific that year, the wind blew a brisk easterly, and we had a fast choppy sail. We approached the Teafua pass on the east side of Nukufetau atoll about 1600 that afternoon. Since the wind was deadheading us, we handed all sail, disengaged the self-steering gear and motored in towards the pass. The wind was pouring out, kicking up a nasty short chop against the water flooding into the lagoon over the shallow water.

As Ernest conned *Tryste* through, again with me at the helm, I found the wheel harder and harder to control. It was not until we were through the pass and back into calmer water that Ernest said, 'That reminded me of the wind-against-tide slop in the Hatea River.'

'*Of course!*' I said, 'I wish you'd said that sooner!' All the leaping about in the chop had re-engaged the self-steering, as it had done back in New Zealand, so that the main rudder and the self-steering rudder were in conflict. No wonder I was fighting the helm.

We sailed about three miles right across the lagoon in search of a lee for the night, avoiding a large danger area of coral by taking a bearing on a tall white beacon on the far shore, mentioned in the Pilot Book. The 'beacon' we were aiming for turned out to be a gap in the trees, and we were both relieved and grateful for our shallow draft, when we located the spreading coral patch still to the south of us. We anchored south of Vasamotu Island, on the east side of the atoll, in fifteen feet.

We had hoped that (like the beacon) the Pilot Book's warning of *'flies abound"* was out of date, but we found that it still held good. We rowed ashore next morning intending to cross a narrow strip of land to where we could hear the surf roaring in on the outer ocean beach. All remained quiet fly-wise as we struggled through the totally green, creeper-strangled jungle of an old coconut plantation. Vines swarmed over the ground, over tiles of coral, climbed across bushes and up palm trees. But on the way back from the ocean beach, the flies descended on us in hordes. They crawled all over us, trying to climb into our eyes, our ears and our mouths. Maddened, we hurried back to the dinghy, which was itself covered with a solid black skin of flies. Ernest tried unsuccessfully to drown them by sinking the dinghy, before we rowed hastily aboard, hauled up *Tryste's* anchor and sailed across the lagoon to a coral head-dotted but less fly-ridden anchorage off the village of Savave in the southwest corner of the lagoon. Then we put in the fly screens and committed much murder below.

Ernest dived to check the anchor before we rowed ashore, anchoring our dinghy with the small grapnel anchor at the edge of a quarter-mile of drying sand that lay in front of the village. Here the black dugout canoes with their claw-shaped cotton sails were anchored at low tide when the island men sailed home from fishing or from collecting coconuts, papaya, breadfruit, bananas or taro from smaller motus on the lagoon's rim. They took the perishables such as fish, lobster, coconut crab and turtle meat ashore at once and at high tide they waded out to the canoes and brought the rest of the loads in, then lined up the canoes on the sandy shore, often covering them with mats to prevent the hot sun checking the wood.

The canoes, one to each family, had single outriggers and were beautifully made of a single trunk of *puka* wood chopped and scooped. They were high sided, with extra freeboard provided by the addition of 'sheer planks'—exquisitely shaped and fitted boards—sewn on with sennet, the whole finally coated with tar.

We walked through the long, well laid out village on either side of a six-foot-wide coral roadway, edged with upright pieces of coral tile. The village lay on a wide strip of land between the lagoon and the reef, under magnificent shading breadfruit trees. These huge trees and the tall coconut palms suggested that Nukufetau had avoided the worst of hurricane Bebe.

The traditional houses looked comfortable and airy, built of poles with thatched roofs and open sides with drop-down woven pandanus panels for bad weather. They were built on raised six- or ten-inch platforms of coral with a sand floor, or occasionally concrete.

The women we met smiled at us but seemed very shy as they went about their business of sweeping around their houses, collecting firewood or drawing water. This last was done with a can on the end of a long pole from a large central well and tipped into bigger cans, which they carried home on fore-and-aft type yokes. The well was lined with coral blocks and plaster with a square tub-like insert in the bottom. One young woman asked us for paper and pencils, which we were happy to be able to give her.

Several of the men visited *Tryste* that evening. After a while one of them, who was a merchant seaman on leave, said something odd about seeing our flag in Mauritius.

'You saw our flag?' Ernest asked doubtfully.

'Yes.'

'In Port Louis?'

'Yes.' We had been in Port Louis, Mauritius, for one day only, five years earlier in 1973. Although it seemed a bit unlikely, we fetched out the relevant photo album, and there was *Tryste*, with *our* Canadian flag, tied up alongside *Nanook*, with our friends Katie and Mo Cloughley and *theirs*. A triumphant brown finger stubbed at one of the freighters in the photo of the port,

'That my ship!' Proof positive! We all beamed.

Later the Nukufetau radio operator came out and reported that he had had a conversation with Funafuti about *Tryste*:

'They ask me, "Is this boat here?"' and I tell them, "Yes, it is in this port."' To our relief he told us that he had a telegram for us in his radio hut ashore. Although we had been waiting for it anxiously, we had not expected it in Nukufetau. Before we left New Zealand in April, we had applied to Saipan for permission to enter the US-administered Trust Territories of the Pacific, at Kusaie Island in the Eastern Carolines, but had received no reply. In Funafuti we had sent an anguished repeat telegram (for an even more anguished *ten US dollars*) but had still not heard back when we sailed for Nukufetau.

Next morning we went ashore to look for the 'radio hut' and eventually tracked it down. It was a tiny white box of a shack, not much bigger than an outhouse, under a palm tree near the police station. We had walked past it once without even registering it. There was our friend of the evening before and there was our telegram, a little garbled, but confirmation at last.

440/11/5.78

67   saipan   ck65/64 10th   1254 pm slt redirected ernest heigh yacht trayste 112 funafuti gilber and ellice island(gstx)nukufetau

T.entry permit no.2290 and yacht permit no.y-56 were issued and sent to you At New Zealand of zapquuz gukii the permits are valid until august 8 1978
Proceed with your cruise plan thru micronisia you must possess a copy of this msg up on entry into the trust territory

Hicott Saipan

There was nothing now to stop us from moving on, except my recalcitrance, which was largely due to the fact that I had gone ashore that day with only the slide camera, and *without a spare film.* I had seen a hundred pictures that screamed at me to be taken. I wanted one more day ashore.

The night that followed removed any argument I would have given Ernest about leaving so soon without going ashore again. He had wanted to move out of the exposed anchorage off Savave Islet for the night, back over to the other side of the lagoon to fly land. I dissuaded him. Later an onshore wind got up. With difficulty, in the dark, we changed to the heavier Danforth anchor, in our coral-head-filled anchorage. Once the Danforth was down Ernest slept trustingly, but I lay awake most of the night listening to the wind, and to the chain grinding on coral, feeling guilty.

Early next morning we lifted the Danforth, noting the shiny chain where the rubbing up and down on coral had removed much of its galvanizing, and sailed peacefully out of the lagoon. Ernest found he had no argument from me about leaving such an anchorage. Besides, at last, we were heading for Kusaie in the Eastern Carolines, my long anticipated, chosen destination.

CHAPTER NINE:

A VERY IMPORTANT MAN

'No one knows,' Ted Sigrah said, his brown eyes intense, 'who built them'. He was referring to the 900-year-old ruins of Pot Falat on Kusaie Island in the Eastern Carolines. Though less famous than those of Nan Madol on Ponape about 350 miles to the NW, they were believed to have been built by the same invading force, perhaps from Indonesia.

Ted was aboard *Tryste* at the time, the day that we made our landfall at the end of May 1978. He was the grandson of the last king of Kusaie who had died in 1967. Before the king died he had elected to do away with the monarchy, so Ted lived as a lowly commoner. After we had anchored and the officials had cleared us, Ted came aboard, bringing bananas, to welcome us. We remembered Noel Barrott telling us about him, in Whangarei. He worked for the Education Department and, as I had scribbled on my notes about Kusaie, 'Ted likes rum'.

Leaving Nukufetau, we had had to endure two slow days of sailing, before we could enjoy six or seven of delightful northeast trades. On our fifth day out we made good 185 miles and crossed the equator. 'We're back in our home hemisphere,' Ernest cheered. 'Our homosphere.' I made a special apple pie, ambitiously decorated as a world globe, with *Tryste* crossing the equator and with the sun and moon and stars overhead. We ate the tinned ham that Sheila and Jim insisted on giving us in Funafuti, on our last visit before we left when we took them a few potatoes and onions. Now we toasted them as we celebrated with our last bottle of New Zealand wine.

On one of our fast sailing days we hooked onto a monstrous fish. The heavy black rubber strop holding our fishing hand-line stretched thinly out to about ten feet, hardly thicker than monofilament, before Ernest grabbed the line and wound it round the sheet winch, and started winching it in. By the way it behaved we thought it might be a shark. It kept sounding like a whale, going down deep and then making a sideways run out abeam of *Tryste*. After five full minutes Ernest was still steadily winching it in, no longer expecting to boat the fish but hoping to save as much line as possible. In the end he retrieved most of it before the fish broke the 100 lb wire leader and swam away with the lure. We both had a good look at it and could see that it was not a shark, but a huge yellow fin tuna, probably 200 lbs of solidly muscled fighting fish.

After that excitement the wind eased and we were finally becalmed 60 miles from Kusaie as night was falling. A little light wind and an hour's motoring in the night found us only 30 miles off by morning. We could see Kusaie ahead: a long island with a backbone of rugged black mountains, the lower slopes covered in lush green vegetation. We would anchor after a reasonable nine day run of 1,231 miles. Feeling securely legal with our telegram of permission to enter the Trust Territories in hand, we entered through a pass in the barrier reef, well marked by brilliant fluorescent American entrance markers. The sea creamed in over the coral either side in a smother of pale green and white. This led us into Lele Harbour, a comfortable anchorage lying between Lele Island and the 'mainland' of Kusaie, the two joined by a long causeway.

Lele Island anchorage, with its village on the shore and long Congregationalist church with rusty tin roof and masonry bell tower, is what we visualise when we think back to Kusaie. We arrived on a Sunday when the church was well attended by worshippers, all in their colourful Sunday best. We had been surprised not to meet anyone out fishing, but learnt later that Sunday was a Day of Rest on this staunchly religious island, converted by Congregational missionary efforts way back in the mid 19th century.

We knew next to nothing of the island's history, and first became aware of the Japanese influence as we approached the island and picked up the local radio station. Music with an obvious oriental influence was followed by an announcement that this was 'Radio KUSI' (Pronounced Koo-shy), and then by a girl singing to a ukulele in a light and melodious voice which reminded us of the once popular song

'Rose, Rose, I Love You.' Later we learned that the Islands of Micronesia had been under formal occupation by the Japanese, under a League of Nations mandate, from 1920 to World War II. To us, taking our information from Noel Barrott and from the Pilot Book, (which like all our Pilot Books was British Admiralty, this one being The Pacific Islands Pilot Volume I) the island's name had always been Kusaie. Now with American administration and with the advent of tourism (expected to be, at first, mostly from Japan) someone in administration had apparently discovered that Kusaie in Japanese had some vulgar or undesirable meaning. The island's official name (as seen on the car license plates) had therefore been changed to the American sounding Kosrae.

Shortly after we left Nukufetau, Ernest had frightened us both by plunging a rusty marlinspike into the web of his hand, while pounding sinking-holes in cans. (Bang, bang, 'Ouch!') The wound became badly infected. As with 'the foot' in Great Barrier Island, I soaked it in hot Epsom salts, which was all the First Aid that he would consent to at the time. Two days later he was feeling ill enough that he finally started a course of penicillin. Perhaps I would *not* have to '*Core it out*' as the First Aid book so luridly suggested.

That same day he also made me take and work a sight, to prove that I remembered how to do celestial navigation (I didn't). I really began to worry when he started giving me helpful nautical singlehander tips, in case I had to work the boat by myself. I was relieved that he did not go so far as to specify whether he wanted 'the body' wrapped in the Union Jack or the Maple Leaf ready for burial at sea. He really believed that I could not possibly manage on my own. Although a bit offended, I encouraged that opinion, hoping that it would persuade him to finish his full course of antibiotics and, more generally, make him super-careful not to fall overboard. It would have to be a hurricane before he would ever consider wearing a safety harness.

Before we reached Kusaie Ernest was back to his normal rude health, while I on the other hand was a mess, with a sore throat, blocked up, inflamed and infected ears, almost totally deaf, and hoping desperately to find a doctor on the island. The first few days on Kusaie were to be times of extreme distress for me.

We soon appreciated the fact that we had anchored well out from the shore, rather than accept Ted's invitation to tie up to the rusting wreck of an old WWII landing craft, which was grounded near his original old house and labelled KUSAIE YACHT CLUB. Not only was it cooler out at anchor, it was out of reach of cockroaches and also further from the many tide-operated privies that graced the shoreline among the trees.

Ted Sigrah's old-style house was close by the water, but he had built another temporary house behind it, in which he and his family were living. As well he had built a more modern house across the road from it, which he had rented out to Baptist missionaries from the States: Lin and Arlene Randall, who had only recently arrived in Kusaie to wrestle for the souls of the local people. Missionaries are not generally on our visiting list and those who attempt to visit us on Saltspring are seldom made welcome, but in spite of our lack of empathy, Baptists Arlene and Lin were extremely kind and hospitable to us. Arlene allowed me to use her washing machine and Lin, ignoring the fact that Kusaie was experiencing a gas shortage, offered to lend us his jeep to tour the island.

Once aware of my troubles, Arlene took me firmly in hand and drove me across the causeway and along a wonderful straight American road of ground coral to the hospital. Here, to my embarrassment, she pushed me to the front of a much-more-deserving line-up of smiling local patients; waited with me while the doctor examined me; and took me back home to *Tryste*. Doctor Rudi Yucheongo (from the Philippines) told me to soak my ears with hydrogen peroxide and come back three days later (it was taken for granted Arlene would bring me) and gave me prescriptions for antibiotics and eardrops which were filled at the hospital dispensary.

Kusaie was such a fascinating place that I nearly went mad with frustration over the next three days. There was so much almost inaudible conversation going on around me. I could ask questions, but not hear the answers, and only hoped that Ernest was absorbing it all for me. It reminded me of being in Mexico where we knew enough Spanish to ask directions but not enough to understand the replies; but gradually, over the next few days, I began to hear part of what was being said to me.

Before long we met Ted's wife Satako, and also Yutaka, who was introduced as Ted's cousin and bodyguard. Did Ted really, as a commoner descendent of the king, need a bodyguard? Or was it a perk that went with the bloodline? He certainly made use of Yutaka. Over the next few days Ted dispatched him to fulfill all his own ideas of hospitable ways of giving us pleasure, like climbing palm trees to bring us cooling drinks of coconut milk, and picking green limes and tangerines for us. These citrus fruits were delivered in an enormous battered metal bowl big enough to bathe a toddler.

Ted was working at his job with the Education Department one morning when Yutaka met us on the road and offered to take us to see the ruins of Pot Falat. Ted later was not at all pleased to hear this. He had wanted to show us them himself.

The ruins, a fortified centre of a civilization that began around AD 500 and lasted a thousand years, were also known as In-Sa-Re and referred to locally as 'the castle'. They lay within the confines of the village on Lele Island and were not at first sight impressive, seeming to consist of a few tumbledown walls of large black rocks. Closer examination revealed a well laid out enclosure about 200 by 400 ft. with dried up choked canals, huge gateways, two sacrificial wells and walls carefully crafted of gigantic basalt boulders and shafts, topped by criss-crossed blocks of basalt prisms. These rocks and blocks, some as long as 14 feet, had been collected from areas like Ponape Island's harbour entrance headland, Jokaz (Sokehs) Head, 300 miles to the north northeast. Some of the blocks were square, many triangular or random shape, still others pentagonal, all split apart originally by volcanic action.

Mystery still seems to surround the builders of these walls, although they were almost certainly part of the same race that built structures on both natural and man-made islands at Nan Madol in Metalnim Harbour on Ponape. I looked forward to finding out more when we got there. We did learn a bit when Ted lent us his treasured book written by archaeologist F.W. Christian, who visited Lele Island at the end of the 19th century. At that time the walls of Pot Falat were still 25 ft. high in places. We copied a lovely photo of him in a white suit and looking about six feet tall, standing in front of a massive black rock wall, way up above his head. Bomb blasts in WWII had since accelerated the effects of time and gravity. They also accelerated the filling up of the sacrificial wells that Yukata claimed were, 'For dropping bad people in', although in a folder we had about the Nan Madol site, similar rocky holes were described as prisons.

Later Ted told us some of the local legends. He assured us that Pot Falat was sacred ground and that: 'Ghosts will haunt the villagers of any other village who go there', and, 'They say they used magic to get the stones to the top of the walls.' Archaeologists have suggested as a more prosaic alternative, that at a time when the life and labour of the Micronesians was cheap, the blocks might have been rolled or dragged up ramps, perhaps made of coral. They believe that the invaders enslaved thousands of the original inhabitants.

We were soon glad we had been warned to have a good supply of rum aboard for Ted's visits. Some more of Yutaka's job skills and responsibilities then came to light. One evening we were all sitting aboard having a tot, when Baptist Pastor Lin came back from fishing outside the pass in his speedboat and gave us a rainbow runner, a delectable fish we had never met before. Ernest invited him aboard *Tryste* to join us for a drink, but he refused politely. It was not quite the way Lin liked to socialize. He told us that on his previous posting on Ponape, he had used his boat to visit the various coastal villages of his ministry. Here, on Kusaie, he seemed to use it mostly for fishing.

'I know what you're after,' he said to Ted, wagging a reproving finger, and went sadly on his way. We had been impressed to discover that he spent so much time off the coast, looking for schools of tuna. Then he would load up his boat and, as he had earlier told Ernest, there would be 30 or 40 people waiting on the dock for him. 'Talk about taking the ministry to the people', we remarked to one another admiringly, 'Feeding the five thousand and all that.' Later we discovered that he charged them 40c a lb. Oh well, he did give *us* the rainbow runner as a gift.

After Lin left, Ted handed Yutaka our fish to clean on deck and then sent him ashore to fetch breadfruit chips to go with the drinks, and then again to collect Satako and a jar of American green relish to go with the meal. While he was away Ted took over, demanding flour, water, lime, onions and lots of salt and pepper for the fish batter. When Yutaka came back with Satako, Ted handed over both fish and batter to him to cook in *Tryste's* galley. I had produced the ingredients as demanded and at first hovered anxiously over Yutaka at *my* kerosene stove, but he was so obviously extremely competent that I soon accepted that I was redundant. I went back under the cool awning on deck, while sweat poured off poor Yutaka below. Although over the evening Yutaka also tucked away rum and orange happily, he luckily did not match Ted drink for drink, and was still sober enough to look after his reluctant cousin when at last we managed to ease Ted off the boat and into the dinghy, without sinking it, himself or Satako.

Next morning Arlene asked Satako, 'Was Ted drunk last night?'

'Yes, he drunk,' Satako answered happily, 'but that alri', he not Baptist…he Congregationalist.'

Although Ted was easily the more handsome of the two, I fell madly in love with Yutaka. He was about four feet high, fairly pot-bellied and about thirty years younger than me. As well he was as strong as an ox, a mass of rippling brown muscles. Being handed across a dried-up canal by him was like being helped by a massive tree branch.

One morning, when we had been there the best part of a week, Ernest came up with his usual restless, 'Time to be moving on!' So often he came up with that while I was still content to stay, but this time I was almost ready to leave, to head for Nan Madol, my appetite thoroughly whetted by Pot Falat.

Word that we were leaving for Ponape soon got around and a local man in a canoe came alongside and asked to speak to the captain.

'Are you going ashore today?' He asked Ernest.

'Oh probably, some time.'

'A Very Important Man wants to see you at the District Administrator's Office.'

'I'd better go and see what's up,' Ernest said, intrigued. In the 'Dist. Ad.'s' office he was introduced to a 39-year-old American Savings Bank president from Guam called Bill Thomasson, who had been looking for a ride to Ponape and wanted to sail with us when we left. Bill had flown in ten days previously, via Ponape, for what he intended to be a 24-hour visit, to consider setting up a branch bank. No one had told him that both local planes were due for an overhaul, one going to Guam for its 400-hour check-up, and the other all the way back to the States to be replaced. Normally that would not have been too serious since he could have gone on the inter-island coaster *Kasahielia,* but at the time she lay at the wharf in Ponape with a damaged shaft.

'We don't usually take passengers,' Ernest told Bill dubiously, adding 'but if we do, it's Val who gets all the extra work. So if you want to come with us you'll have to be prepared to help a lot with the dishes. What's more,' he added, 'we try not to use the motor except for entering and leaving harbour. So if the winds are light it might take as much as 10 days to do the 300 miles.'

Nothing negative Ernest could say seemed to deter Bill (he merely said, 'Don't tell my wife,' about the dishes) and so we agreed to take him. He *claimed* that being stranded on Kusaie was costing him $3,000 a day. We were remarkably unimpressed.

We left two days later loaded down with presents from Bill's hostess ashore, the Hawaiian wife of the Dist. Ad. There were baskets of oranges, loaves of bread and lots of chipped ice, presumably from the hospital. Bill's gear was the usual overnight flight bag, together with something no one had ever brought aboard before—a golf club, probably a #7 iron, to remind him of his younger glory-days as a pro golfer. He must have been a bit harder and leaner then. Now his well-covered body gleamed with good living. He was—he claimed and later suggested that Ernest was also—an 'over-achiever'.

A small crowd saw us off from the landing near Ted and Satako's old house: the Dist. Ad.'s wife; Dr. Rudi and his wife who was also a doctor; the Baptists, Lin and Arlene; Yutaka, and Ted and Satako and their children. Yutaka's last kindness-from-Ted that he performed was being sent into the hills for bananas. He arrived on the wharf on a green motorbike, shirtless but wearing an electric blue crash helmet, with—riding pillion—an enormous stalk of green bananas for us.

CHAPTER TEN:

THE RUINS OF NAN MADOL

As soon as we were through the pass Bill said, 'This is the furthest I've ever been from shore in a boat'—for him the first of many such new experiences. Before we had gone much further we encountered petrels and tropicbirds working over a school of leaping tuna. Bill settled down on the foredeck to watch and soon became mesmerized by the gleaming splashing fish, which kept company with *Tryste* for over an hour.

The wind was light and variable but with enough east in it that we could often set our small homemade chute, although we had to keep an eye out for squalls. These variable winds soon died away and we were totally becalmed. In spite of Ernest's threat to Bill, we did motor from time to time to cool off both the boat and ourselves, and in all over the next three days made good 90 miles under power.

On the second night that we were becalmed, I was on watch when I heard the 'phoo, phoo,' of whales. I woke Ernest, and then Bill, and we watched enthralled as two pygmy sperm whales more than half as long as *Tryste* circled the boat in the starlight, investigating this strange raft that had floated into their domain. They came within ten feet of the boat, exhaling in turn and sounding like slowly shunting goods trains. Bill was captivated. When Ernest shone the spotlight on one of them I cursed him roundly, adding crossly, 'That's the end of that.' I was wrong. Although the whale was spooked, and breached his full length out of the water before sounding, he came up again, and they both circled us some more before leaving. I had found Bill hard to wake. No wonder: we learned later that he was taking both sleeping pills and seasickness pills.

On the morning of the fifth day, in squally conditions, we sighted mountainous Ponape Island from 56 miles off. All day, when it was not disappearing in rain showers, the island grew larger and greener. By the time we were sailing up the west coast a fresh northwester was blowing. It was too late to make port. All night the wind kept up, as we lay off at the north end of the island trying to keep within the arc of a six-mile navigation light, waiting for dawn—for once we would have preferred to be becalmed. Bill, usefully, was able to tell us that the high red light we saw above the harbour area was on a bluff at the edge of the airfield. Between showers we could see the loom of land quite clearly in the starlight as we waited for dawn.

Around lunchtime the day before, Bill, who was alone on deck, had called down, 'Have you seen this ship? At least I guess it's a ship.' We had not, and changed course slightly to avoid it. It was a Korean-type fishing boat. This was a marked improvement in Bill. Earlier he would not have bothered to mention it, counting it our responsibility. He had become amazingly relaxed considering that he had left Guam on May 16th for a two-day trip and that we had now reached June 1st. He had never, outwardly anyway, fretted at all, and (a lot to be said for this) he had eaten all the food I put before him, gratefully and uncritically.

After spending five days at sea aboard *Tryste* it was obvious that Bill would never be quite the same again. He had kept to his bargain and been scrupulously ready to wash every dish and pan used, admitting that it was the first time he had done the dishes in 20 years. He had stripped and gone, a little nervously, overboard for a swim, 100 miles from land, when we were becalmed. He had soaped and scrubbed himself clean in a stinging, whistling rainsquall. He had been woken suddenly from a deep drug-induced sleep and expected instantly to admire enormous whales. He had taken the helm (though, from choice, only under power) and gazed and gazed into those far off introspective ocean distances, and he had talked and talked about his life as a high-pressure bank president, and our lives as low-key cruising sailors. It was bound to have some effect.

We were not too surprised when he began to ask about the mechanics of cruising and wistfully wondered out loud if his wife could ever be persuaded to 'live like this'. Really we all three knew that it was just a passing dream and that in spite of Bill's seeming acceptance of our way of life he still found cruising people like Ernest and me almost as incomprehensible as we found Very Important Men like Bank Presidents.

We lay off all that night and around 0600, with the wind dead on the nose, we *motored* in through the pass, saving me the usual tension of actually sailing into a strange port. We followed a well-buoyed winding channel into Jokaz Harbour, coming to anchor opposite Jokaz Head, a spectacular 900 ft headland topped by a sheer perpendicular bluff of black basalt.

We fed Bill breakfast and then he insisted on doing the dishes for the last time. When Immigration came aboard they took him back with them into the main town of Kolonia in a torrential tropical downpour. Later he came back in a rental car and kindly took me to the Post Office, where there were letters waiting for us from all five daughters. Once we had arrived in Ponape our over-achiever left *Tryste* and literally and figuratively hurried back to his real world again, sending off telexes and hiring cars and making phone calls and booking flights, leaving us breathless and wondering…was his the real world, or was ours?

After Bill left we settled down comfortably to our old selfish, self-centred lives and to the pleasure of talking to some other yachties for the first time since we left the Fijis in May. In seeking out the less trodden paths we had succeeded almost too well; but now there were the crews of four cruising yachts to meet. Three US boats lay tied alongside an old scow at the dock, together with a New Zealand cutter, *Taurewa,* a Taiwan-built CT37.

Ernest and I had reached Ponape in a strange mood. We had sailed 300 miles out of our way to the west to reach these two Eastern Caroline Islands, but no sooner had we arrived in Ponape than we were eager to leave again, for when we left *this* island we would be heading home to Saltspring—the completion of our circular Pacific voyage.

We were missing the family badly by now and there was one more to meet and miss, a cute little dark-haired baby, named Rhiannon, Carol and Gerry's daughter and our second granddaughter, now six-months-old. Although up to now we had theoretically kept open the option of heading further north and visiting Alaska on the way home, in reality we both knew that we were too homesick. We would save Alaska for another voyage.

We were happy to do all the work that had to be done in preparation for the 5,000-mile passage ahead—maintenance, provisioning, laundry, letter-writing, but we had far more trouble when it came to relaxation. There were interesting places to see and people to meet out there, but we had the greatest difficulty in shaking off the future and enjoying ourselves in the enervating present.

After only a week in the heat, humidity, red earth and equatorial showers of Americanized Ponape, where managing to dry the laundry became the day's success story, we had had enough. We had no energy and not much initiative. One day we did hire a car to complete our stores-shopping in Kolonia: an extraordinary small town of red earth streets with an American Wild West feel to the buildings. Here we bought several packets of famous Ponape peppercorns to give away at home and mailed a hasty response to a letter from Carol and Gerry, along with Bon Voyage wishes, to catch them before they headed north in their small sailboat *Nomad* with six-month-old Rhiannon, to cruise the waters of British Columbia.

That evening we went out to dinner at a restaurant recommended by some of our new cruising friends. It was fifteen miles away over roads so incredibly rough that we thought we had misunderstood their directions and must be lost. Only the fact that we had laid out cash on the car rental persuaded us to persist. When we finally found it, the Village Hotel proved to be a big open-style building, like an island 'men's house.' We were pleased that we had persisted, even though the food was, as Ernest said, 'Nowt special', but we had been determined to splurge for once and had enjoyed ourselves.

Together we had walked the hot and humid two-mile trek to and from Kolonia several times. Even after we took the rented car back Ernest went off on his own to do one last shop. He had decided to buy half a dozen beer and anything else that took his fancy. His small shoulder bag, bought in New Zealand, might prove inadequate.

'You should have an extra bag,' I said helpfully. 'I'll take the papaya out of the string bag and give it to you.' When Ernest asked for a six-pack, he was told that he could not buy less than a dozen. He was glad he had the extra bag. When he went to take it out he found that instead of the net sack he expected he had the papaya. Halfway down the hot red road home he scooped most of the now disintegrated fruit out from under the two six-packs and chucked it away. Cars and trucks rattled past in clouds of red dust but no one offered him a ride. The afternoon became hotter and hotter. When he finally clumped back aboard *Tryste*, hot, sticky and thirsty, he thrust the heavy bag at me and exploded, 'You gave me the bloody papaya!' I had indeed, as I said, taken it out of the bag and given it to him.

'I'm so sorry,' I croaked as I washed the remaining pulp off the cans. But the tears running down my cheeks were tears of mirth. It was three days before he forgave me.

We officially cleared out from Ponape on Thursday June 8, but before we started on the long passage home there were the ruins to visit, our main reason for coming to Ponape. We would sail round to Metalnim Bay on the east side of the island and see the waterfall and fabulous Nan Madol, and take off from there.

As *Tryste* cleared the fringing reefs at the end of the long twisting pass out of Jokaz harbour, Ernest turned to me. 'You know, Val,' he said, 'It's a fair wind.'

'Oh no!' I said, for I knew exactly what he meant—that it was a fair wind for heading north, for sailing home to Canada right away and abandoning the side trip into Metalnim Bay. The fact that I shared his longing for home did nothing to diminish my anger at this. Yet it was true that the wind was favourable. It was a good force 5 easterly with only a touch of north in it, the sort of wind we had been hoping to find when we left. Sailing in to Jokaz Harbour we had reached almost 159°E, the furthest west Caroline Island that Ernest had finally accepted.

'Oh no!' I repeated. I understood how he felt, superstitiously afraid of offending the wind gods, believing that if you do not make use of an offered fair wind there's a real chance that you will never have another. We really could not afford to risk that—not with a possible 1,400 miles of contrary trade winds ahead of us. In angry silence we sailed on. After fifteen minutes, as frequently happened, we had exchanged positions.

'Well, if it means that much to you...' he said.

'You're right; of course, we have to take advantage of it...' I said, wiping away the tears of fury and frustration. I wished I were stronger minded, knowing that I would always regret giving in, yet knowing too that Ernest would not let me forget whose fault it was if the wind was against us when we left again. I was not sure I wanted to risk that aggravation. I was so anxious to be on our way, so tired of endless days near 90°F and nights of no relief from the heat and humidity...and after all I had seen Pot Falat. I knew how Nan Madol would be—the same only more so—much, much more so.

We were soon going bomp, bomp, bomp, over the brilliant blue and white waves that were breaking over the foredeck. I was seasick, as I usually was on the first few days of a passage; but Ernest cooked our first night's meal of fresh chicken legs and I managed to eat some by staying out on deck. We were moving along beautifully but found we were horribly out of practice below in beating to windward: there was coffee all over the carpet and a jug of milk spilt; and there were rude words, a few bruised feelings and a lot of bruised bananas. Still, once we had eaten the best of these, we still had Yutaka's stalk of green ones to keep us healthy.

That evening Ernest told me we had a stowaway aboard. 'What!' I said. 'Who is it?'

'A mouse,' Ernest said, 'I just met him up forward.' This, I thought, could be a problem, but at least it wasn't a rat. Rats are notoriously disastrous aboard a yacht, getting into and destroying stores and being wily and hard to trap.

By noon the next day we had made good 157 miles on the wind, the last 12 hours with the mainsail reefed, and Ernest, while genuinely sorry that I had missed out on the ruins, was congratulating himself on having made the right decision. Not only had we knocked off so many miles; we had also made some easting.

'One hundred and fifty-seven miles,' he gloated, 'who says *Tryste* won't go to windward?' Only you, I thought crossly. Next morning at 0815 when Ernest got a sight, we were happier still, for we had made good 308 miles in all and won a total of 30 miles to the east.

Our jubilation was short-lived. By noon we were heading south again, limping back to Ponape with a jagged hole in the plywood under the port wing and our hearts in our boots. Like Pooh Bear counting his jars of honey, Ernest had been counting his bottles of rum, which he kept in the locker that ran across the forward beam at the head of his bunk. As he checked the treasured bottles, each wrapped in a piece of winter clothing, he felt wind on his face and discovered that some of his clothes were wet. Fetching a flashlight, he found water slopping in and out of a crack in the locker, which formed part of *Tryste's* under wing.

This sort of disaster had overtaken us before, but that first occasion had been on the way to the Galapagos in 1970, when *Tryste* had been grossly overloaded with six of us aboard, and a six-month supply of food and water. With just two of us on the boat we really had thought that we had the problem licked. We had obviously been too obsessed with the fear of being swept off to the west towards Japan and those nasty curving red lines denoting typhoons on the Pilot Charts, and had pushed *Tryste* too hard. Really we had brutalized her, crashing and banging close-hauled into big seas, knowing that we should ease sheets a little or shorten sail, or both, but not wanting to.

Because from time to time *Tryste* had buried her bows headlong into a wave, had come to a shuddering stop, shaken off half the ocean and then gone on her way seemingly unmoved: two of our hatches had started leaking. Ernest had tied canvas over the main hatch and "bandaged" the hatch over my bunk with strips of sailcloth. Now no more water sneaked in that way. As always I had been much impressed by his ingenuity. Earlier that day though I had written in my diary, 'Poor old girl, it sure is hard on her. God knows what'll be left under the wings when we get home.'

Nine months earlier the same piece of plywood had started delaminating after only a few days of windward work on the way to Fanning. Ernest had filled and fibreglassed a small patch of it then. Now the sea had torn off the fibreglass patch. We had no option but to turn around. As we sailed sadly back to Ponape Ernest suggested *very seriously* that I should take an airplane home. I considered it *very seriously* and rejected it. How could I leave him to sail this long journey alone? In an attempt to cheer him up I said, 'At least we can buy a mousetrap.' 'Too late,' he said. 'I disposed of it.' I hastened *not* to ask for details.

For a while after we turned back, the wind was astern; but it soon turned southwest, so that we were hard on the wind again. This occasioned much bad language; *Tryste* and I both came in for some pretty nasty remarks. Two days later we made a night entry to Ponape at 0400, grateful to see the high red light above the harbour. It would be dawn in an hour.

By the time we anchored in the Jokaz Head anchorage where we had weighed anchor and left, five days and 614 miles before, it was 0615. We had hoped to lie in the one empty space alongside the scow, but saw that *Taurewa* was now there. Everyone turned out, even at that early hour, to see why we had come back. Elizabeth from *Taurewa* rowed out to talk to us and we passed down to her three-quarters of a yellow fin and a small albacore that we had caught close to the island, to share out.

The crews of the four boats were soon all up and dressed and offering help and advice on availability of supplies for the repair. After breakfast we were able to go alongside the scow where we would be able to use the power tools that some of our friends had offered.

It took us all the first morning to locate two sheets of three-eights-inch fir plywood at the Kolonia Co-op. By now Ernest was almost frantic. He wanted to leave again in two days time, partly because of the nature of the beast, and partly because we hoped to get away without the time-consuming business of clearing in and out again.

We walked rapidly into town, and since the last part was uphill I was beginning to flag a bit by the time we got there. After shopping around for building supplies including sheets of plywood, we were off to the Post Office up another small hill, in the hope of more family mail. Ernest was walking faster and faster and I had to ask him to slow down, which he did but still, we were almost there when I, as they used to say in our native rural England, 'Came over queer,' and had to sit down at the side of the road. I persuaded him to leave me under a frangipani tree beside the church to recover, while he reluctantly went to the Post Office and stood in line, something he hated. His original plan had been for the two of us to carry the plywood back to the boat between us. Luckily it didn't come to that. The Co-op store was happy to deliver.

The following day, we started our agonising repairs. For my part, I was half sitting, half lying, in the stern of the dinghy, keeping it in one place under the wing by holding on with one hand, one leg, one head—whatever worked; while with my other hand I held up a wide strip of plywood overhead. Somehow Ernest, in the other end of the dinghy, managed to hold the other end up and fasten it on as well. The complete first day's repair job had been to cut out all the rotten wood, sand, cut to size, dry fit, glue, nail, screw and finally fill the patch. Next day we doubled up the plywood in this vulnerable area under *both* wings.

Altogether it took us two extremely long days drenched with sweat and tormented by sand flies. We neither of us slept well that night or the next, after such horrible demanding days. On the first night Ernest had a bad time with mosquitoes, and on the second I suffered—from itchy sand fly bites, being kept awake by the dock lights and from palpitations after too much rum. We were both a bit pathetic.

The following day we were ready to sail again, just one week to the day since we had left the first time. We had flown no flags and kept a low profile (not difficult in a trimaran) and the authorities had not come near us. Perhaps they never noticed us.

CHAPTER ELEVEN:

GALES AND FOG, THE LONG PASSAGE HOME

'It'll never happen again, you can be quite sure of that,' Ernest said, as we sailed out of Jokaz harbour for the second time, remembering the beautiful wind we had had a week before. He was wrong. For two full days the wind blew mainly from the southeast, enabling us to gain forty-five miles of easting. I don't think either of us ever considered stopping off at Metalnim Bay.

Around mid-morning on that first day, Ernest suddenly said, 'I'm absolutely knackered. I'm going to lie on my bunk for a bit. Shout if you need me.' I was glad that he had admitted it. I ached all over from the repairs and could hardly place one foot after the other going up the companionway. After lunch it was my turn to rest. It was an exquisite pleasure to lie down, even though my muscles groaned with ache and my back felt bruised and uncomfortable when I lay on it. Two hours sleep made an immense difference. On the second day of these lovely southeasterlies, Ernest had just taken and worked a noon sight (which, as he pointed out later, meant that *he* was officially on watch.) We were both below having lunch with the curtains closed over the starboard porthole to shut out the burning sun, when I suddenly gasped,

'Oh my God!' My view to port, of empty blue sea, had filled completely with a vast white hull. Grabbing clothes and cameras we rushed on deck.

'Ullo,' the smiling crew of a big, high-sided Japanese fishing boat shouted as they all waved. We waved and shouted back, and we all took pictures before the fishermen turned back on course. Although our hearts were still going pit-a-pat at being caught out, we felt grateful that they had taken the trouble to come out of their way to make sure that the crew of this strange small boat, sailing along with no one at the helm, were not in trouble.

The next morning we endured frequent assaults by '*All-hope-abandon, ye-who-enter-here,*' squalls. They were not the short sharp ones that march across the horizon in columns, but ones blotting out half the sky in a purple-black menace and lasting as long as an hour. We frequently entered them uneasily, fearing to find too much wind with the rain.

We were both dancing around washing our hair, in the surprisingly cold God-given fresh water of one of these squalls, when we suddenly saw a spreading light-patch ahead of us. Ernest freed the main sheet to prepare for whatever was to come—a brutal increase in wind? Perhaps even a waterspout? When at last it reached us we found that it was only a harmless shaft of sunlight coming down though a break in the clouds.

After two days of these unpredictable variables, the northeast trade wind finally asserted itself, building gradually to force 5 as we revelled in superb close-hauled sailing. *Tryste* creamed along: the woo-oo-oo of the wind, the swish of the water of her three wakes, the watery crunch of waves breaking to starboard, the rattle of the big twin pole trying to pull out of its bolted-down pad-eye, and the frenetic slapping of the mizzen halyard; all combining to play us a rowdy symphony. As Ernest wrote in the log next morning:

'Gorgeous sailing, even if not in quite the right direction.'

At 23°N, at the end of the first week's run, of 950 miles, we crossed the Tropic of Cancer. We had already clocked off the latitudes of Guam and of Eniwetok Atoll and would soon be passing that of Wake Island; then there were only the Hawaiian Islands to pass, stretching from 20-30°N, and after that all empty ocean. We were delighted to achieve this first 'milestone' of the passage, which found us officially out of the tropics. Only four days later, at 31°N, these fine northeast trades died and we found to our disgust that we had experienced a strong westerly set and were almost back at Ponape's longitude of 158° 12'E. It would be three more weeks before we crossed the international dateline, longitude 180°.

Ernest had not intended to start plotting our great circle course for Victoria for another 300 miles, but since it would now be the shortest and therefore most favourable course, the steady trade wind had made him de;ide to do it, 'Just for fun.' From then on, to our surprise, we were usually able to head for our destination on this course, as it gradually flattened out over the remaining distance—not much more than 3,000 miles.

After less than twenty-four hours of 'teaser' winds, coming in as cat's paws and persuading us to set sail, only to die way again to nothing; a small breeze sprang up from the southeast and began to rise. This was unexpected and meant that we were able to start our sheets and reach off happily northeast. Then Ernest, crunching the numbers some more, declared that we had sailed a quarter of the way home in only 11 days. 'How about that?' My diary asked admiringly.

We had now reached 35°N and 165°E. Delightedly Ernest calculated that we had regained 100 miles of easting over Ponape's longitude. Maybe we could eventually reach Canada's West Coast after all. We had long since abandoned any thought of going to Alaska.

By June 28 we were, according to another of Ernest's log entries, 'Booming along.' All around us was movement and beauty and noise, but it was pretty wild on deck, and since Ernest would never wear a safety harness I often worried that I might come on deck for my watch to find that he was no longer aboard. Since I was sure that he sometimes shared the same worry about me, I hoped that we would not have too many more such nights. That was always the way as we neared the end of a voyage, we both became over-anxious. At the end of our second week, as the wind rose again, we clocked up the best day's run of the whole passage, 179 miles noon to noon, which gave us a second week's run of 940 miles. We were delighted and I exulted in my diary, 'This trip really is exciting and enjoyable; no two days are ever alike.'

But the next day, the last day of June, we reached 37°N, 168°E and found that in spite of our constant struggles to make easting, this noon sight placed us only 950 miles from Japan, almost within reach of out-of-season typhoons, which were recorded by thin red lines marked with their dates on the wind charts of the North Pacific.

On the afternoon of the next day we were visited by several Black-browed albatrosses, who came running along on the surface of the sea like oversized Mother Carey's chickens to gobble up some canned mussels we had rejected, although, like us, they preferred the last of the venison pâté.

At the end of that good bird-sighting day, Ernest wrote in the logbook, 'OVER 2000 GONE, LESS THAN 3000 TO GO!' We were obviously still enjoying being 'out there.' But if we thought all we had to do from now on was to romp home on a glorious broad reach, we were much mistaken. Four days after Ernest worked the great circle course he noted in the log, 'A few wisps—TENDRILS—of fog.' How poetic it sounded. Next day it was, 'Fog passing overhead and on the horizon.' By that evening we were more prosaically, 'Enveloped in dense fog.' This fog was to be our constant companion for the next three weeks. Visibility was often down to 100 yards or less. We sailed in a hole surrounded by thick fog but often with a circle of sunshine immediately around us search-lighting down upon us. As we moved, our circle of sun moved with us. We decided that, unlikely though it seemed, we must be the Chosen of God.

'Another happy day in sunny fog-land,' said the logbook.

Doing celestial navigation in such difficult conditions involved Ernest in taking dubious sights about every two hours in the morning whenever the sun made a brief, watery appearance. This was helped by the occasional miracle of its breaking through at local noon, or of the fog backing off enough to show an almost clear horizon. He was so persistent that only on five days in three weeks did he have to rely totally on a DR (dead reckoning) position.

At first we rather enjoyed our eerie solitude; the fog shrunk our small world and made us feel cosily cocooned. Soon we became disenchanted. 'Same old thing,' said a grumpy log entry, 'Drip, drip, drip.' As we moved eastward the fog travelled with us, until the forecasters at WWVH (the US station, broadcasting the marine weather from Kauai, Hawaii) no longer gave us its location by area but threw up their hands in despair and described it as: 'A band of dense fog 300 miles wide, stretching right across the Pacific from Japan to North America.'

A few days before the fog socked in, on one of the roughest days of this part of the passage, we were both below peacefully reading on our bunks, each with a good view of the restless sea from the sizeable ports alongside us. Suddenly Ernest yelped, 'A fin!' and dived for the companionway with me close on his heels. Four big muscular dolphins almost as white as Beluga whales, but with black-tipped dorsal fins, were surfing through sunlit transparent green combers behind us. They followed us for only two or three minutes before losing interest in *Tryste,* but they stayed long enough for us to identify them as Risso's dolphins, a.k.a. the Grey grampus.

We started the month of July, and our third week out, with a rare day of brilliant blue sea and sky and a more southerly wind. We set the poled-out twin jibs wing and wing, together with the staysail, and *Tryste*, with the wind free, surged on over a big rolling sea. We thought that we were probably as happy as we were ever likely to be, not missing the family so much, now that we were homeward bound on our last passage.

Before dark the fog began to creep in again. On my night watch Ernest handed over to me, 'A small lively dolphin, at least,' he added, 'I think he's still around.' I stood out on deck, waiting, peering into the thickening fog. There was a sudden tremendous splash of phosphorescence, right close inside the starboard float transom. It was like someone saying,

'Here I am, now watch this!' He started doing zoom trails around the float and jumping and showing off generally but I never really saw him. 'I think,' Ernest said later, 'that it must have been a sea lion, although it was doing so many jumps up forward and rushing around so, that I thought at first that there were several.' We were almost a thousand miles off the coast of California.

We were now far enough on our way to be able to change onto the big North Pacific chart, the one to take us all the way home to Canada, with the encouraging line of crosses marking our daily noon positions on it, from our first passage to Victoria from Hilo in 1974. It also included those scary waters west of Japan as well as covering the Aleutians, the Bering Sea and Alaska.

After our problems leaving Ponape the first time we had not pushed *Tryste* hard and were determined not to. We were pleased with the way she was standing up to the windward pounding. There was no major damage, although there were plenty of minor breakages: the genoa sheet had taken a beating and was badly chafed where it led through a deck block; one of the two pad eyes, where we stowed the twin running poles, had pulled out of the foredeck, the end had broken off the other pole and the motor too had its problems. I thanked heaven for a handyman skipper. 'Poor old *Tryste*,' we said, 'she's falling apart.' But we said it only to propitiate the gods, not because we really believed it.

I remembered one of the dockside questions we were commonly asked: 'Whatever do you find to *do* at sea?' This same day that Ernest had been so busy being a handyman, I had cleaned out under the bunk in the forward cabin and wiped mould off the bulkheads, and then made bread and some croissants. I also filled the jars of white flour, oats (soon to be porridge time), tea bags, brown and white sugars, and treacle. Somehow I never had time to do any writing.

The barometer was dropping fast and I hoped in my diary that it did not portend anything nasty, but my next day's diary said, 'Well it portended a gale, which we now have.' That was the same day that I dropped the wrong sail and got sworn at—which I thought totally deserved. For some reason Ernest very quickly forgave me, which was lucky, as at the next sail change he let fly the staysail halyard, the only one remaining that was not attached to the mast cleat at its tail. It went to the top of the mast, and so did Ernest—enduring *Tryste's* swoopy motion to do a quick efficient re-reeving without getting *too* bruised.

Now at last, when we had sailed twenty days out from Ponape, we finally crossed the long awaited meridian. One day we were almost 178°*E*, the next we were 179°*W*. We enjoyed a double celebration, as we were also halfway home—2,564 miles under our keel—2,475 still to cover. We had Chinese canned duck for dinner with saffron rice, followed by Christmas pudding and custard. We also opened a bottle of Ponape-bought wine, which helped to settle our nerves, still frazzled from the night before.

We had been running gently through thick fog, under mizzen staysail set with lightweight chute sodden with moisture. With the end of my watch coming up I checked the course and read the Walker log before going to wake Ernest, gradually becoming aware of a muffled thrum, thrum, thrum, from astern. At sea we normally ran without lights, but now I switched on both masthead and running lights and shouted down the companionway, 'Ernest! There's a freighter!'

The trauma-filled hour that followed, as we sweated and shivered, stretched forever, as the ship we heard seemed to be overtaking us very cautiously. Had she picked us up on her radar? Was she coming up to port or to starboard? The fog distorted sound and made it impossible to tell which way to take evasive action. Ernest hung the bright white Tilley lantern in the rigging while I blew an occasional forlorn blast on our feeble foghorn. At last we were sure she was coming up to port; then fairly positive that she was abeam of us; then at last that she was drawing ahead. We bore away to starboard until we could definitely hear the throb of her engines dying away.

In the relief of the moment we were both suddenly aware that tiny fork-tailed petrels had been fluttering around the boat for some time, attracted by the light of the Tilley. We took the lamp down and went below together to have hot and strengthening drinks and eat some of the chocolates that Ernest had produced earlier in the day, to celebrate halfway home. These had been such a well-kept secret, such a lovely surprise. He was rather dismayed because they showed a faint spectral-green bloom. 'Very superficial,' I said, gave one a passing rub, and ate it happily.

After Ernest turned in, the birds were still around making gentle night noises. Next time I went on deck I picked up a scent like a drying reef. Was it the birds, something turned over by the sea, or the exhaled breath of a passing whale?

Three weeks out and after a week's run of only 801 miles, we had reached latitude 42°N. It became surprisingly cold. At only 46°F we dug our warmest clothes out of the backs of lockers where they had been for almost a year, brought out extra bedding, and suddenly needed nightclothes to keep us warm in our bunks. I was depressed by the fog and cold. 'We need to see the sun,' Ernest said, 'we're always so affected by the weather.' We had not yet heard of Seasonal Affective Disorder. I cheered up, a few days later, when on July 12th, after another modest run of 799 miles for our fourth week, we could say, 'Less than 1,500 miles to go!' There seemed to be just an outside chance that we might be home by July 24th, Nicky's birthday, and a year to the day that we left Saltspring.

After a few days of moderate northwest winds we reached 47°N, and moved into an area of low pressure that gave us rain and changeable winds, with two days of near gale conditions. Now the barometer swooped down spectacularly from 30.01 to 29.48 mb in 24 hours, and a strong wind sprang up from the south, making little or no impression on our all-embracing fog. By the end of the day it was blowing sou'southeast force 6-7, and we were speeding over steep cresting seas with only two small sail set. From time to time *Tryste* put on a spurt and vibrated like a sound box all along her main hull. We took turns perched in the companionway, watching the sea's splendour all around us.

'We'll soon be on the latitude of Victoria,' Ernest said. 'Then we continue to head north on the Great Circle course, up over 49°, and come down on our landfall.' More and more our thoughts were turning to food, with the oven frequently in use and its heat welcome. Food always is important at sea, but now it became an obsession. How else could we keep warm in those plummeting temperatures? 'Yes!' We said. 'Fat people are happy people!' While disposing of one meal we would dwell lovingly on the next. Unfortunately fresh fish was not on the menu. We had had no luck fishing on this passage, although we had trailed a line all the way from the Carolines and lost several lures to unseen monsters. Now we were down to less attractive home made lures.

We had long since started to play our daily teatime game of *Scrabble* below instead of on deck and had declared daily *Scrabble* to be a Tournament with a capital T, to be concluded at the end of the voyage. Ernest had scored 507 including his seven letter word ARCHIVES, that first afternoon below, beating my previous record solo score of 477 set only the previous day, when I had been so chuffed to get QUANDARY on a double.

I knew he would almost certainly win the tournament, because he was so persistent; in spite of the rare occasion a week earlier when I had both blanks (jokers) and the four top-scoring letters Q, X, Z, and J. As well I had all the S's (very useful) and both 4-point W's and Y's. There was little left for Ernest. No wonder he called the game 'lousy.' He was generally very good about losing, while I used to get quite upset when it was his turn to win. Only three days later he hit a winning streak and I was miserable. Like an addicted gambler though, I always came back for more.

Albatross and petrels were by now our regular companions. One afternoon we found ourselves surrounded by a flock of about thirty white-bellied petrels, wheeling, swooping and diving on our fishing lure, in company with half a dozen Black-footed albatrosses. We were laughing again at the ludicrous albatrosses chasing the lure by galumphing along on the surface of the water, when suddenly, to our distress, one of the petrels caught the hook of the lure in its beak and was dragged along behind *Tryste* at six knots. Ernest hurriedly hauled in the line, trying to save the bird from drowning, but before it reached the boat it broke free and lay upside down in the water with it wings spread, like a white water lily. As we drew away we saw the other birds settle around it on the rolling swells, sobered by the tragedy.

By mid-July we had done almost 4,000 miles. It had been a passage to remember for the rest of our lives—for me, the best part of the year's trip and a great experience. In Ponape we had both been exhausted, over-heated, and disenchanted with cruising, but this passage, in spite of all its ups and downs and irritations, had rejuvenated our love of being out at sea. Once again we were hooked on offshore sailing and felt very close to one another.

We reached our furthest north four days later, at 49° 13'. 'Very, very bumpy,' I put in the log at 0500. The day's excitement was seeing an eastbound freighter appear out of the distant-behind-us fogbank at suppertime. We were thankful that it passed in the daylight

This good fifth week's run, of 957 miles, had left us with only 604 to go. We thought we were almost home, but another gale started building, this time from the northwest. We were soon shortened right down again and still doing seven knots with the wind screeching fiendishly and *Tryste* 'shipping it green' with water crashing over the deck. That night the fog cleared for a few hours and we saw the moon for the first time since Ernest wrote that poetic, 'A few wisps—TENDRILS—of fog,' three weeks before.

The next morning the sun came out, but we were not feeling sunny. Our shared relaxed, accepting mood had changed entirely. 'What a rotten lousy piece of water.' Ernest exploded. 'The only good thing about these last two days of gale is that it has persuaded me never to go sailing again, especially in the North Pacific.' I too had moaned (but only to my diary the day before), 'Oh I am so tired. Too bad, I don't get to sleep so well off watch any more. Still this is probably more natural at the end of a long ocean voyage.'

We had been at sea now for five weeks, had had three weeks of almost continuous fog, had weathered our fair share of blows and had felt we were almost home, yet here we were tearing along with a fresh gale on the beam again and with that demon fog still crouching on the horizon. We were damp, salty, tired and above all grubby, a grubbiness that extended almost to the soul. Lying in my bunk I thought that what I wanted most out of life from now on was a world containing a flush toilet and a hot shower.

All that day we waited for the gale to lessen, but the waves, which had seemed so large at first, grew and widened and crested and toppled and finally the wind began to blow spume across their heaving tops. Once more we went out on deck to shorten sail. When we had fought the yankee jib down we looked at the sea again and shook our heads. What were we doing with any sail up? It must have been at least force 8 and a fresh gale.

'Let's heave to for a while,' Ernest suggested, 'that'll give *Tryste* a rest, and us, too.' For the next couple of hours we lay with only the reefed mizzen set and the helm tied hard over to weather. Towering masses of water curled menacingly over us, waves building until their slopes became concave, but *Tryste* would always sidestep daintily at the last moment, and the whole monstrous mass would smash down either beside us or behind us.

At noon on the third day of this northwest gale we were only 160 miles from Victoria and the wind was still blowing force 7. At last, that evening, the wind eased enough for us to set our two small headsails with the reefed mizzen and in a surprisingly short time the sea began to calm down and look less threatening. I felt supremely grateful; those last two nights of gale had bruised me physically and mentally. As we sailed on, the water suddenly turned from green to brown; land could not be far away. Twelve hours later we were running gently over a small sea in the moonlight surrounded by the strobe lights of about a hundred boats fishing the offshore La Perouse Bank.

At sunrise, after a clear night, we could see the tip of the Vancouver Island mountains peering at us over our faithful fogbank. It seemed the fog could not bear to let us go. It followed us closely as we motored up the familiar rocky north side of the Strait of Juan de Fuca; a thick rolling cloud that obscured the landmarks of Pachena and Carmanah Points with their red and white lighthouses, only moments after we had passed them. Well-remembered fir and arbutus trees loomed out at us through the mist and small patches of murres sprinkled the water around us. Not only the fog but the wind also hated to say goodbye. Although there had been so little breeze in the mouth of the Juan de

Fuca that we had motored for seven hours, into and at the start of the strait, a westerly gale was forecast. As the wind gradually rose again behind us we were pleased, because it meant we should make Becher Bay that night, an anchorage only 12 miles from Victoria., and the day before Nicky's birthday.

As we roared up the strait, we changed down from genoa to jib with difficulty, the westerly wind gusting strongly behind us. At 12 knots we raced through the tide rips guarding Becher Bay. As we tore into the bay we expected to gain a little protection from the headland, enough to drop the jib, but instead one last tremendous gust caught us and we gasped as the head-stay bowed out in a curve.

Nothing gave way but we were almost into the head of the bay before I finally managed to wrestle the sail down. The anchor rattled out and grabbed. We looked at one another in breathless astonishment at such a climactic end to a long passage, before we turned and hugged. We were *home* and what was more, in spite of the vicissitudes of the *Scrabble* tournament (Ernest won of course), and against all the odds—after 5,000 miles and 39 days alone together, we were still good friends. This time I would be ready, in a year or two or three, to sail with him offshore once more, to answer again that enchanting irresistible call, back to the open sea.

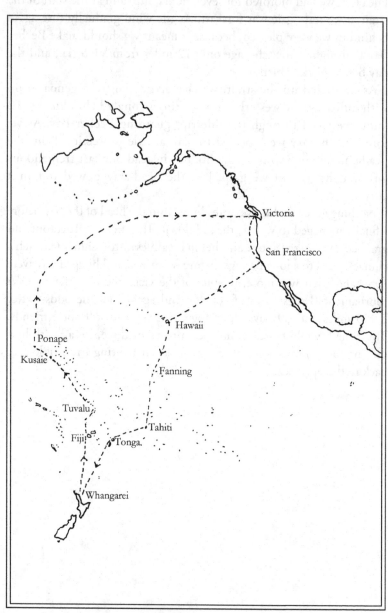

Pacific Ocean. Tryste's *1977/78 route to New Zealand and back,*

BEAUFORT SCALE OF WIND FORCE in KNOTS

There are several versions of Admiral Sir Francis Beaufort's wind force scale, including a U.S. one, but the one we have always used is the old British one, with the reaction of fishing smacks, that helped us to respond sensibly to conditions.

Beaufort number	Speed	Description	Ht of sea in ft	Deep sea criteria	Action of Fishing Smack
0	less than 1	calm	-	Sea mirror smooth	Makes no headway.
1	1-3	light air	¼	Small wavelets like scales (no crests)	Just has headway.
2	4-6	light breeze	½	Pronounced small wavelets crests glassy	Wind fills sails makes up to 2 knots.
3	7-10	gentle breeze	2	Large wavelets, crests begin to break, foam glassy	Heels slightly under full canvas.
4	11-16	moderate	3½	Small waves longer, small breeze frequent white horses.	Wind fills sails, makes up to 2 knots.

5	17-21	fresh breeze	6	Mod. Waves and longer, many white horses	Shortens sail.
6	22-27	strong breeze	9½	L. waves begin to form more white crests	Double-reefs mainsail.
7	28-33	near gale	13 ½	Sea heaps up, white foam blown in streaks	Remains in harbour or if at sea, lies to.
8	34-40	gale	18	Mod. high waves of greater length, crests begin forming spindrift, foam blown in well marked streaks.	Takes shelter if possible.
9	41-47	strong gale	23	High waves, dense foam streaks,crests start to roll over.	
10	48-55	storm	29	V. high waves with long overhanging crests. Surface of the sea white with great patches of foam. Visibility affected.	

| 11 | 56-63 | violent storm | 37 | Exceptionally high waves. Sea completely covered with foam. |
| | 64+ | hurricane | | Air is filled with spray and visibility seriously affected. |

Chapter Twelve:

A TASTE OF THE ROARING FORTIES

'This isn't really a gale,' Ernest said. We were over 1,000 miles out from New Zealand, only 400 miles from Tasmania, assessing this third depression to sweep across *Tryste* in five days. It was *Tryste's* fourth crossing of the Tasman Sea, but her first venture down into the Roaring Forties.

'Oh, *isn't* it?' I asked crossly. As far as I am concerned any time you are shortened down to an 80 sq. ft. storm jib and are still wondering if you are over-canvassed it *is* a gale, no matter what Admiral Sir Francis Beaufort wrote in his helpful Wind Force Scale. Ernest had entered 'force 6-7' in the log; which was Sir Francis's 'Near gale', of around 30 knots, 'Sea heaps up, white foam blown in streaks,' which seemed about right for what we had.

Our passage had started out so pleasantly that I suppose we should have expected to have to pay for it later. Sailing up the north coast of New Zealand's north island on a fast reach had been superb, especially as it was followed by an exciting dash close-hauled across the top of New Zealand with an escort of rollicking dolphins, and then four days when the wind backed slowly from south through west to northwest while we lazed on deck in the sunshine and *Tryste*, on an easy beam reach, steered herself a supremely pleasant 130 miles a day. It was January 1982: year two of our second circumnavigation. We would not reach home again for another year and a half.

In 1979 Anne and Russ Hohmann had been married on Saltspring in a warm civil ceremony in which Russ and Anne exchanged rings and then Russ gave a ring to four-year-old Dana. In the previous year Anne had completed her Early Childhood Education course at Camosun while at the same time, Russ attended the University of Victoria. The three of them, Anne and Russ and Dana, had been living in the Barn before that. When they left Saltspring, we moved off *Tryste* and back into the Barn.

Although we were back to living on land, we were not very good at settling down. We had started our jobs with real commitment, Ernest's as a builder and cabinetmaker and mine back at the Elementary School as a secretary/resource centre person, but the commitment only lasted three years. It probably unsettled us that first year home, when Eric and Susan Hiscock visited B.C., and *Wanderer* and *Tryste* rafted up in a Prevost I. anchorage.

When we sailed away again in 1981 Carol, Gerry and Rhiannon (now four years old) moved into the barn while we circumnavigated. Janet had left the island permanently and she and Jerry soon moved into the new house they had built near Victoria.

Our first year had taken us to New Zealand by way of Hawaii, Tahiti and the Australs. In Whangarei that Christmas Susie had visited us, and we had sailed with her to Great Barrier Island before she flew back to her rented cabin on Saltspring where she designed and made wrap-around batik skirts.

By midnight of our seventh day out from New Zealand, our easy start was over. We were reduced to storm jib and reefed main, beating close-hauled into a 30 knot south southeasterly. In 24 hours the temperature dropped seven degrees. Water began splashing over the boat and even though we were snug enough below I was feeling seasick, something I did not expect after a week at sea. It was the beginning of an extremely nasty eight days. Noon sight the next day gave us only 108 miles made good in rough conditions. We had mended about a metre of the mizzen leach, the first of many such repairs. Although this blow lasted only 24 hours it set the pattern for what was to come since it was preceded and followed by periods of zero winds.

Next day found us in the Forties. As if the line of latitude had opened a door, a series of low-pressure areas with attendant southwest and northwest gales swept in to pummel *Tryste* one after the other. We seemed to spend all our time setting, shortening, handing or repairing sail. The first of these Forties gales came blasting in from the northwest to give us magnificent sailing on a close reach for a few hours, but soon it backed to the southwest, deadheading us. We crashed our way unhappily to windward as long as we could, but when it settled into a fresh westerly gale we handed all sail and lay ahull all night. *Tryste* lay fairly comfortably beam-on to the sea but sleep was almost impossible as heavy rain showers thundered through, accompanied by raucous blasts of wind. The wire halyards chattered frantically against the masts in spite of all efforts to stop them, while the tips of the greybeards crashed over the cabin trunk or under the wings, shaking us back from the edge of sleep.

On the morning of the tenth day out the gale was still with us, but the sky cleared and Ernest was able to obtain a good noon sight. In the log book he entered a big 0 for our noon-to-noon run, since all we had done was to drift 10 miles north and two west. At that time, in 1982, we were still dependent on celestial navigation, as SatNav, and later GPS, were still too expensive for us even to consider.

After the noon sight we were able to set the storm jib and the reefed mizzen. 'Strong gusty wind; extremely rough.' Ernest wrote in the log. It was bone-chillingly cold and wet on deck and we were both immensely thankful for the self-steering gear which continued to function well. Over the next three days the barometer dropped steadily and Ernest wrote in the log 'Bottom falling out of the glass.' On two of these three days the wind blew well over 35 knots from the northwest, building up gradually, forcing us to reduce down to the storm jib but allowing us to keep moving in the right direction.

'Why are we doing this?' Ernest asked bitterly, as we stumbled below after changing sail for what felt like the hundredth time, 'For pleasure?' The memory of that first week when we lay sunbathing on deck seemed like a lost dream. But even as we complained, we did have the feeling that, having taken *Tryste* down to the Forties, we were experiencing exceptionally beautiful seas. The air was full of spray; and especially when the sun came out we spent hours standing on the companionway steps, just inside the doghouse, watching the waves.

From around 40 knots the wind dropped in an hour to zero and we were becalmed, surrounded by confused and disgruntled seas, leaping and twisting into the air and falling back again like some gigantic overfall. Irrationally Ernest's mood improved and he came below singing: 'I would love to live in a movie theatre, where the only weather is made by Hollywood!'

The barometer was rising next morning, but it went up suspiciously slowly. After a sinister yellow sunrise, we set off again, on the starboard tack in a light southwesterly, with a touch of Antarctica in it, eying the overcast sky warily. At noon Ernest managed to snatch a fuzzy-round-the-edges sight which put us only ninety-one miles from Cape Pillar on the Tasman Peninsula.

We were almost relieved when the gale the barometer had hinted at finally built up in the afternoon. When we had once more gone through all the motions of shortening sail, Ernest stood on the foredeck with only the tiny storm jib and reefed mizzen set, feeling the whole boat tremble (and he with it, so he said). Together we smothered this last jib, as the rising gale tried to snatch it away from our clutching fingers, while a Wandering albatross, floating chunkily like a fat-beaked duck on the tortured waves by the bow, looked up at us as if to say, 'What's all the fuss about? Lovely weather for ducks.'

We were now only 65 miles from Tasmania, lying hove to under reefed mizzen alone. We hoped that this sail might hold us up into the wind and mountainous seas, but wondered if it was the best we could do for *Tryste,* or if perhaps we should just lie ahull as we usually did, or should we, for the first time, try trailing warps? We asked ourselves what particular idiocy had lulled us into discounting both extreme weather and *Tryste's* poor performance to windward when listening to Lorna and Jon on *Zephyr V* and Eric and Susan on *Wanderer V* in New Zealand. All four had assured us that Tasmania was so wonderful that it was worth enduring a little bad weather. A little? *Tryste* was never meant for such a hostile sea. Why, we asked ourselves, had we not gone straight to Sydney and then worked our way down the coast?

'I'll give it force 9', Ernest said, coming below, but he only put force 8 in the log. It was â part of our coping mechanism for stopping ourselves from being too frightened. We never admitted being at sea in anything more than 50 knots.

Our need for sleep was now so absolute that we found that neither the noise, the motion, nor the dead, damp air below could keep us awake any longer. It was hard to make our minds unwind; overtired as we were, but once we did it was like floating down into an infinitely receptive pit filled with cotton wool.

By noon next day we were only 35 miles from Tasman Island, reaching fast in a wild steep sea with the wind from the north northwest around 25 knots, under yankee, staysail and reefed main. We expected it to rise yet again to gale force but we were wrong. With this same rig and wind strength we finally sighted land to the northwest at sunset: a square, chunky headland, and behind that another sloping bluff that was the Tasman Peninsula. On Tasman Island, in the failing light, we could just make out strange formations of jagged rocks stacked on end, side by side like organ pipes. Ten miles further west we passed Cape Raoul, where the wind died. In glorious, still moonlight with superb visibility we motored the last 20 miles into and across peaceful Storm Bay, crept cautiously into Bull Bay, the most northerly indentation on North Bruny Island's east coast (only 12 miles south of Hobart), and dropped our hook. As we drifted off to sleep we vowed that however good Tasmania turned out to be, we would never sail *Tryste* that particular route across the Tasman again.

Somehow everything seemed to fall into place for us right from the start in Tasmania. We easily located the entrance into Hobart's Constitution Dock next morning and having no VHF to call them up expected to have to jill about on and off until someone noticed us; but as soon as we neared the entrance a young man walked across the lift bridge and shut the gates and the bridge went up. Our notes from *Zephyr V* queried, 'Too wide?' meaning *Tryste*, but she was not too wide, there were a couple of feet to spare either side. As we motored through, an officer leaned out of the small blue and white building overhead and called out,

Tie up over there, next to that white fish boat with the blue stripe, and then come and see me.'

We followed his instructions and once that was done Customs (who also did Immigration) soon came aboard, as well as the doctor for Pratique. We gave them coffee and chatted them up, so that by the time they got around to asking how much duty free alcohol we had aboard, we were all friends. The young Customs Officer explained that we were supposed to have most of our bottles locked up.

'How many do you have?' He asked.

'About a dozen, a dozen and a half.' Ernest said innocently. The young man looked more serious.

'Is there somewhere I could see it?' He asked. We took him into the head where we kept all our bottles in one locker and he pulled one out and broke the seal on it.

'Perhaps you should break the seal on a few more.' He suggested. 'Well, you're not going to take them ashore are you?'

'No, no! Just entertain aboard,' Ernest answered. And so it went: charm, innocence, friendly officials and wonderful Hobart! Everyone was super friendly and everything worked out well, with hot showers nearby, and new friends and the sheer heavenly feeling of being totally safe again.

In the middle of a gale, only a few days earlier, Ernest had said firmly, 'When we get there I want to do land things for a while. We've had enough sea time for now.' So we did, quite a lot of them and in the process, spent about four weeks, on and off, in cosy Constitution Dock.

In Hobart we met old friends Tim and Pauline Carr whom we had last seen in Hilo, Hawaii, some eight years earlier. They had exquisitely repaired their 1898 gaffer, *Curlew,* after she was smashed in by a trawler in Sydney Harbour. In the coming years they would sail *Curlew* to South Georgia and settle there. We also made several new friends, most immediately Chris and Jenny Smith, who had sailed their 10m Crowther trimaran, *Saxon,* from Fremantle to Tasmania and settled there before their two small girls Clare and Holly were born. When we arrived they were all four living aboard *Saxon* in Constitution Dock and getting ready to sail on around Australia and home to Perth. We shared many a meal and good keg of wine.

We soon discovered that Tasmanians like to make fun of their unpredictable weather,

'The four seasons in one day' they say, cheerfully, 'warm, cold, windy, and wet'. But it had been unusually settled when we arrived in Hobart, consistently hot and dry for several weeks. The third day we were there the temperature peaked at almost 100° and a haze of thick dark grey smoke from bush fires lay over Hobart and the harbour, turning the sun into an ominous red balloon. Not only was it frightening, it was altogether too hot for city living.

A few days later we were introduced to the wonderful Salamanca Saturday Market, only a short walk away from Constitution Dock. There we bought huge cabbages and cauliflowers as well as fresh strawberries and many other vegetables and fruit. Then we motored out of the dock and headed south. We hoped to sail round to Port Davey, the wild West Coast wilderness area, accessible only by boat, small plane or rugged hiking trail. Tim and Pauline had suggested that their live aboard friends, Bob and Sue, who kept their boat *Tunis* in Cygnet Bay up the Huon River, might lend us their charts for Port Davey.

Sailing out of Hobart's Derwent River Estuary we were soon puzzling over large areas of trees on the hillsides showing what looked like fall colouring. Sailing closer inshore we discovered that they were forests of gum trees, their foliage singed to copper where fire had flashed through, blackening the ground beneath them but leaving the trees still standing. Apparently some varieties could survive this ordeal by fire and refoliate the following year.

We must have been very careless but we managed to get lost. We had not at that time realised that some Tasmanian charting was very skimpy and the lights and beacons small and hard to see. After missing one beacon on a small headland, we were one out for several of the next navigation marks, and in the end despaired and anchored between two yachts off the hamlet of Waterloo. Cygnet would have to wait. Later with binoculars, we looked at the one we had missed and found that its light was only a household light bulb in a jam jar on a pole.

In the morning we discovered that we were lying off one of Tasmania's famous apple orchards, and that one of the yachts anchored there was crewed by three young men from Western Australia who had come to pick apples. We thought we might do that too, but they were turning people away. 'It wouldn't be fair for us to take the work away from other people who need it more than we do,' Ernest said virtuously, and we happily abandoned all thought of making money, accepted a bucket of apples, picked another small one of blackberries growing on the foreshore among wild geraniums and montbretia, and went back aboard and made blackberry and apple pie. Later we backtracked to the peaceful farming area of Cygnet, attractive with small white houses, open fields, and mudflats among the gums, and borrowed the charts.

A few days later we sailed straight to Recherche Bay, 30 miles south of Cygnet, the jumping off place for the 60 mile run to Port Davey. On the way there we learned about Tasmania's so-called afternoon 'sea breezes.' It was blowing about 15 knots from the northwest as we sailed out from Cygnet and down the D'Entrecasteaux Channel. A few miles on, navigation became trickier with three sets of rocks and reefs to navigate around. We had passed the first of these hazards safely when the light southerly sea breeze came in.

As we wanted to reach Recherche before dark we started motor sailing; but Ernest, suspiciously watching the weather, reefed both main and mizzen—just before the wind gusted up to 35 knots. In moments we went from enjoying a quiet afternoon sail to fighting to keep off a lee shore. Setting the storm jib and small staysail we slowly clawed our way off. The mizzen tore as we ran for shelter into the Pigsties: a shallow, almost landlocked cove, with a rock-strewn entrance, in the northern corner of Recherche Bay.

The following morning we moved to Rocky Bay, in the southern arm of the bay. Blue mountains towered behind us and hills covered in gum trees sloped down to bare rocky shorelines. The weather deteriorated: the temperature plummeted and great howling gusts of wind, rain, sleet and hail coursed across the anchorage. We shivered in our thick winter clothes, lit the oven to keep warm and visited the cray fishermen anchored there. They advised us to stay where were and wait, brought us trumpeter fish and crays (the small local lobsters) for our meals, and helped us drink the good Tasmanian boxed wine we had stocked up with in Hobart.

After we had been there a few days, one of them, Bruce on *Lanena*, invited us to go out with him to help collect his pots. A cheerful, jocular man with a weather-beaten face, he looked a typical fisherman, so we were surprised to learn that he had only taken up commercial fishing three years ago after retiring as a bank manager. We were lucky with the weather but disappointed with the haul of only 16 legal lobsters from 26 pots: but this was February, and nearing the end of the season. Bruce told us that in November, at the beginning, he was setting his pots four times a day and on his best day had taken 290 cray (worth $4 apiece).

While we were anchored in Recherche Bay, we heard that a 21-foot white-tip shark 'the size of a small car' took a man in a wetsuit in South East Bay 10 miles to the south. Shark hunters came from further north to try and capture it but although it took some of the huge tuna offered as bait, it escaped the hook. We were grateful that the cold weather had discouraged us from any thoughts of swimming.

Going to Port Davey was to be the one thing that did not work out for us in Tasmania: Since southwest swells continually sweep round the south end of the island, you need either a large motor or a boat that goes well to windward. As *Tryste* does not qualify for either of these we were hoping for a spell of easterly weather. The wind was still firmly in the southwest when Johanna and Alan Bond sailed in aboard their locally built sloop *Solveig*. They had just spent four days in Port Davey, where it had rained every day except one—when it had snowed. Perhaps we would abandon Port Davey.

Alan was a tall ex-English anaesthetist, Joh an Australian-born nurse with a cheerful open face and bright eyes that sparkled at the thought of sharing a 'barbie' on the beach that evening. We braved a light shower, Alan lit a big fire on the rocks and we had a magnificent broiled steak and lobster—their steak and our cray. Collecting beach-combed wood for the fire in our thick sweaters and jeans in the drizzle reminded us of home on Canada's West Coast. It was hard to believe that we had been sweltering in the heat and smoke of Hobart only a week earlier. Next morning Alan and Joh sailed *Solveig* cheerfully away into a violent squally hailstorm to complete their sailing holiday, while Ernest and I cowered below marvelling at the hardiness of Tasmanians.

One day when the wind seemed to be blowing more from the northwest, we made our one attempt to reach Port Davey, but by the time we reached Matsuyker Island, about halfway, the wind was heading us. We gave up and ran back to Recherche Bay convinced that we had to wait for the easterly. It turned out that we lacked the necessary patience and when the sun shone again we abandoned Port Davey and headed *Tryste* back towards Hobart. As we left Recherche in what was still late summer in Tasmania Ernest looked back.

'You know,' he said, 'that's *snow* on those mountains.' It had not been there a week earlier when we sailed in.

When we got back to Hobart it was time to do some more 'land things.' We rented a small camper, a Nissan Urvan, for a week. We decided that we wanted to see something of the interior of the island, which is only 184 miles north to south and 196 miles east to west. We drove past lakes, rivers and waterfalls, then range after range of rugged mountains, the whole interspersed with an assortment of farming areas, including wineries. There were trees everywhere, mostly gums, with much evidence of fires. Areas reforested with gums or *Pinus radiata* reminded us of Canada, but Tasmania had flocks of red and green parrots and road kills of wallabies, and areas of glowing red and gold button grass meadowland through which acid peat-black or copper-coloured streams meandered.

Waterfalls and mountain lakes surrounded inland campsites where Ernest gave away most of our food to tame wallabies and pademelons (a smaller relation with a thicker coat). From the Hobart Museum we had learned that Tasmania's marsupials also included kangaroos, bettongs and potoroos. We hoped that we might see a wombat, but since they are mostly nocturnal and fairly shy, we were out of luck. I would just as soon have missed out on the Tiger snakes, all four species of which are venomous and said to be shy, but we managed to see, and avoid stepping on, two.

Other campsites were near beaches and our last, and favourite, was at Rocky Cape on the north coast. A series of open campsites lay haphazardly among groves of tea tree, heather and yellow banksias, busy with honeyeaters and scrub wrens, overlooking a bay filled with the teeth of reefs and rocks of red and white granite. We selected the best site, right alongside the beach, and slept with the door of the camper open so that we could lie in bed and watch the waves rolling in in the moonlight. Although we found it hard to leave these lovely wild places, we decided, after six days, to drive the 180 miles straight back to Hobart without another overnight stop. We were both suddenly struck by the same longing to be back home aboard *Tryste*.

We arrived back to find a sheaf of notes in the doghouse. The local newspaper had interviewed us the day before we left: now we were wined and dined and driven around by generous-hearted local residents. We enjoyed being celebrities for a little while, but in the end the late nights started to catch up with us and we began to long for the open ocean.

Making ready to leave slowed down as visitors stumbled across the two empty boats between us and the quay: a couple who had property on Saltspring; an older lady who was born there and left the island 50 years ago; an Estonian gentleman with no teeth who spoke wistfully of his daughter in Vancouver—no, sorry, we did not know her.

We shared innumerable late night sessions with Chris and Jenny, while Alan and Joh gave us an unforgettable gourmet dinner at their small house in Sandy Bay and we invited them back, for boat food, the night before we left, when they marked our charts with some of their favourite east coast anchorages.

Next day the lift bridge went up for *Tryste* for the last time and in a light drizzle we motored past *Saxon* where soft-hearted Chris and Jenny and the children stood waving tearfully, and anchored in a small nearby bay to sort ourselves out. A few days later we sailed out of Storm Bay between Tasman Island and Cape Pillar in a light northerly, then sailed and motored 50 miles up the east coast, past more spectacular rock formations, to a hidden cove that Alan and Joh had recommended. Here, in Reidle Bay, on the east coast of Maria Island, there was just room for us to swing, in company with a small cray boat.

Low rocky slopes covered in sparse young Stringy-bark gums surrounded the little bay and in one corner a small creek ran out between some large flat rocks above the high tide mark: an ideal barbecue site where that evening we lit a fire and cooked a freshly-caught small tuna.

The moon rose, the silver sea soughed in and out over glistening rocks and giant kelp, and later the Aurora Australis glowed green across the wide night sky.

Ten miles further on and almost halfway up the east coast, we anchored in Wineglass Bay, Freycinet National Park: another of Alan and Joh's anchorages. We hurried in, in search of shelter, after hearing a three-day gale warning. Wineglass, a wide sandy bay with crystal-clear sapphire water, was dominated by the Hazards, a handsome trio of bare-shouldered hills of red granite, 1,000 ft. high, to the north. Button grass meadows spread out behind the bay in a golden haze, and in the evenings, on low bush-covered sand hills to the west, Red kangaroos made brief appearances, as well as an occasional Black swan; while heavily laden bush walkers appeared from a gap in the underbrush one end of the long white beach, trudged stolidly down the length of it and disappeared again at the far end, like bit players in some cosmic production.

Our anchorage was in the southern corner in good holding sand where a stream emptied into the bay. The strong steady wind over the bow allowed us to lie securely to two anchors while the weather passed over and while we got to know the crews of the two other yachts and three cray boats anchored there. One evening when we were sharing our wine with the crews of the three fish boats, the subject of preserving meat and fish in glass jars came up and Ernest mentioned that we had experimented with cray while in Recherche Bay. For the next couple of days it was like having a butcher calling at the house for orders.

'How many cray would you like today?' Conservation was not our 'butcher' Grant's strong point. How could we complain when we were being given those undersize crays that they were supposed to throw back? But we did wince a little when unrepentant Grant told us, with a wicked, happy grin, that on his boat they were having 'swan for tea' (dinner). He explained cheerfully how they made the fisheries officer's life hell:

'Poor bloke though, fair go, while he's chasing Phil for taking undersized crays, I'm knocking off a coupla swans, and while he's chasing me and the swans, Des is knocking off undersized crays.' Maybe things have changed for the better in twenty-five years.

The day we sailed out Grant had taken my morning request of 'I could use half a dozen,' as he went out to check his pots, but had not returned. Halfway out of the bay we met him coming in. He gently manoeuvred his boat *Joy* alongside us as we sailed along, and gleefully hurled a sack of cray fish aboard *Tryste*.

Our last Tasmanian anchorage was in Fire Bay behind an off-lying reef of round grey rocks, 10 miles to the south of Eddystone Light, Tasmania's most north-easterly lighthouse. Here we took shelter during yet another strong wind warning.

After twenty-four hours there, the 5 am forecast called for a final strong wind warning of west to southwest wind followed by light variables, which sounded perfect for crossing Bass Strait. By noon on the following day this notorious piece of water had given us one of our best noon-to-noon runs of the voyage, 172 miles. Lovely, never-to-be-forgotten Tasmania, her wild weather and her Roaring Forties, lay indiscernible astern.

CHAPTER THIRTEEN:

OZZIE DAYS

Our first port of call, after crossing Bass Strait, had been Eden, where revolting rainy weather had soon sent us on our way again, off to Ulladulla, 31 miles further up the coast. We sailed into the harbour on Easter Saturday past a breakwater built of massive blocks of rock. Inside there were concrete floats with lots of fish boats and a couple of yachts tied up, but with not much 'room at the inn' for us. We were lucky to be offered a berth alongside a fish boat called *Mark M.* Her skipper told us that there was a gale warning for the next day which, he reminded us, was Easter Sunday; he told us too that because of the religious celebration, the Italian community (about which we knew nothing) was holding a fete, parade and sail past 'Blessing of the Fleet'. He advised us to stay put and enjoy it.

In the morning we joined the crowds watching the parade. Led by embroidered standards and red, white and green Italian flags, the long parade wound down the main street to the harbour and must have included almost the entire Catholic population of Ulladulla. Later the local Father went aboard a small navy patrol boat that was anchored out, off the mole. Taking up a position on the bow, he sprinkled holy water on each dressed-overall fish boat as it passed. The decorated boats then sailed well out to sea before circling back into the harbour to tie up again. Depending on your point of view of this performance, Ernest's or mine, this was 'Bloody daft!' or 'Very moving.'

We did manage to agree, however, that the fete that followed was a lot of fun: ethnic dancers in bright beribboned costumes leapt and spun, chubby competitors fought to consume the most spaghetti (no points for table manners), and—easily our favourite contest—teams of six tried to be the first to reach the top of one of four 22 ft-high greasy poles with flags on top. They had ten minutes to reach the flag, if no one reached the top then the highest would win.

The first teams had the hardest time since their poles were the greasiest. You might have thought that the teams with boiler suits would have the best chance, but no, it seemed that those wearing shorts with belts to grab did best. Sometimes five men would almost get up, then the one at the bottom would begin to sag and all would come whizzing down. Finally one team got to the flag in 1 minute, 45 seconds. They were fairly light and just rushed up the pole. Then one of the first teams made it, and then the team with girls in it had a second turn and made a good showing. The funniest part of the teamwork was the accidental pulling down of underpants by the following climbers, exposing bare white buttocks—much to the joy of the crowd.

At this time, Argentina's invasion of the Falklands and their claim to South Georgia and the Sandwich Islands was often in the news, as it had just happened. Ernest was talking about it to an ex-Brit Ozzie standing next to him in the crowd. 'I'd go, if they'd take me,' said his neighbour, 'so would I!' said Ernest, carried away with patriotism. '*Men!*' I thought disgustedly.

That evening we moved to lie alongside the fish boat *Molotai*, to be nearer the harbour exit so that we could leave early. *Molotai's* skipper told us that they might leave for the fishing grounds at 4 a.m. Being born worriers, we both woke at various times in the night, but *Molotai* was still there when we left at 0530.

It took us just over twenty-four hours of easy sailing to reach Sydney, past 'bold' St George's Headland and into the harbour. We found the famous Sydney Harbour Bridge looking surprisingly small and partly obscured by low cloud, while the Opera House was only a foggy white blur.

Sailing in, looking for Rushcutters Bay, our chart seemed to be distressingly small scale. We really should have bought a better one in Hobart. However a yacht motoring out gave us good instructions and we managed to find our way in, pausing only to go aground once on a patch of soft mud and eelgrass, cutting a corner on a falling tide. Ernest had seen it coming but not soon enough to stop. With me on the wheel, the motor in reverse and him manfully pushing off with the boat pole up forward, we got free, and slightly chastened rounded the corner to anchor astern of several overseas yachts off the Cruising Yacht Club of Australia. The following morning Ernest went row-about and found our old friends Jane and Shelley de Ridder, aboard *Magic Dragon,* tied up at the yacht club.

Next day we walked to Edgecliff's metro station where we found fast, efficient double-decker electric trains. Sydney's metro system surprised us by being large and complex, but then we found Sydney itself surprisingly large. Coming up into the crowds from Martin Place station Ernest had a bad case of demophobia. Although I could handle the mass of people, being below ground had frightened me, even though I had spent my teenage years happily riding London's Underground.

As usual we were getting ahead of the dates we had given the family, and as usual there was little mail for us at the Post Office, while at the bank they did not yet have the money we had requested from the Bank of Montreal on Saltspring. We would only have been surprised if they *had* had it.

The second day that we were in port the Harbour police boat came alongside. We wondered what we had done wrong, but it was only that they had a message for us,

'Celia is aboard *Magic Dragon.'* Our enormously cheerful long-time New Zealand friend from Opua had, typically, sweet-talked the harbour police into carrying a message for her. For as long as we had known her Celia had been single, but had recently married. Now we met her husband, Keith, who seemed to be making her very happy. They had a house further north in Queensland.

By the time we reached Sydney we were trying to decide whether to sail home across the Indian Ocean, round the southern tip of Africa, up the South Atlantic and through the Panama Canal, as we did the first time; or should we join some of our friends in trying to obtain clearance for Bali (which had become more difficult in the last few years) then visit Sri Lanka and sail the 1,500 miles up the Red Sea and through the Suez Canal into the Mediterranean. Never having sailed in England or around Europe at all, we were tempted, but by the end of the week we had finally decided *irrevocably* to abandon the Red Sea route. Unlike others of our irrevocable decisions; we kept to this one. Now we could settle down again and be happy, and Ernest could admit his reservations: about the sometimes extreme weather, about the blistering heat and already in those early days, about the risk of piracy in the Red Sea. 'It's really no place for a rather tired trimaran,' he said.

At last our money arrived in Sydney: a certified cheque for $2,000 Canadian to the ANZ (Australia and New Zealand) Bank. Unbelievably the Sydney branch refused to cash it.

'How are we to know that the money is in Australia and that the cheque has not been stopped?' The young, pale, overweight manager asked rhetorically. Ernest was furious. 'We need our money,' he said, 'surely you can do *something*!' We just sat stolidly in the manager's office and waited him out. Eventually he phoned the Sydney office of the Bank of Montreal which was on the 55th floor of the huge MLC building nearby. We had had no idea that there was one.

We soon found ourselves being whizzed up to the 55th floor, where the manager listened sympathetically to our story and then cabled our branch in Ganges, who guaranteed the money to the Bank of Montreal, Sydney, who in turn eventually guaranteed it to the nervous local branch of the ANZ. At that time it still took twenty-four hours for the requisite telexes and cables to cross the world; but only a day later we were able to collect our desperately needed money.

By the early 1990s, when we sailed to Australia in our new boat *Truce*, the whole world was open to credit cards and even we, so slow to accept new things, could with delightful plasticity, buy our way into anywhere. Back in 1982, two days after we collected our money from the ANZ bank, we sailed under the Sydney Harbour Bridge to Birkenhead, where we tied up to a long yachties' two-hour shopping float and went ashore to an Aladdin's Cave of possibilities called Franklin's. This huge complex of shopping halls contained everything we could possibly want or need for *Tryste*. We stayed there for three hours and spent two hundred of our brand new Aussie dollars. That bought a lot of stores in the 1980s.

On the way back to Rushcutters we anchored just off the dazzling Opera House in what was probably not an anchorage, and went ashore and gazed and gawped at it and enjoyed walking on glitzy Pier One in the hot eternal sunshine. I almost went to a performance of Swan Lake at the Opera House that night, but in the end was too nervous about *Tryste's* anchorage and backed out. I have always regretted it. A few days earlier Ernest had taken the long train trip out to Allowrie to buy a case of canned butter from the factory and had seen and been depressed by beautiful Sydney's grubby industrial backside. In contrast we were both really wowed by the Opera House.

When Ernest went back aboard I walked through the lovely Botanic gardens to the downtown Post Office where I found a great swatch of mail from family and friends, as well as an acceptance letter from SAIL magazine for an article they had requested about lonely anchorages—which meant money in the pipeline.

On another day we sailed under the Spit swing Bridge, which was opened hourly on the hour. We only had about five minutes to wait before a red light came on, warning bells rang for the traffic and a little man came out to the end of the bridge to see us pass. We both waved and he looked surprised, then waved back. Later we sailed into another bay in the harbour where we were soon admiring fabulous waterfront mansions perched above cliff sides where brilliant patches of green, and even palm trees, were dotted among great rocks all the way down to the water. Many of them sported amazing staircases.

For the most part we were happy enough with our anchorage in Rushcutters Bay off the Cruising Yacht Club of Australia, as they gave us an honorary week's membership that allowed us to use the showers and the bar, while each night great panels of window-glass in the high-rises around us reflected the red sunset light as sheets of flame.

We moved on to Pitt Water, about 30 miles up the coast and visited some friends, but spent most of our three days there making *Tryste* 'in all respects ready for sea'. Ernest had suggested and 'we' had decided, to sail out to Lord Howe, a lush mountainous island only about seven miles long, that lay roughly 440 miles due northeast. Our Opua friends, Ted and Molly, had sailed there in their yacht *Kakawai* and said it was well worth a visit.

'It should be easier than bucking the current all the way up the coast.' Ernest said, referring to a reputed four-knot current on the nose. We planned to enjoy a few days on the island and then sail northwest back again to a point further up the coast, probably Mooloolaba.

It was two days before the end of April, Anne's birthday, when we left Pitt Water, and we celebrated it by seeing our first albatross of the passage. By noon we had made good 25 miles with a fresh westerly and both felt that it was, 'Heaven to be well out of sight of land again for the first time since Tasmania.' On the next watch the wind was a force 5 westerly and we set our poled-out running sails. By 1800 the wind was gusting up to force 7 west southwest and we were down to reefed mizzen and one small headsail.

I was making supper when Ernest shouted for me to take the helm. There was something wrong with the self-steering gear: the fore and aft rod holding the turnbuckles had broken. We handed all sail and he took the gear apart; before supper he had repaired the rod, and later he insisted on putting it back together in the early tropical dark while being regularly doused by big unruly waves.

A threatening sunset of tumbled grey cumulus intertwined with pink showed, quite erroneously, mostly in the *eastern* sky. This was followed by five hours of lightning with no audible thunder—hardly the peaceful start we had hoped for, but noon sight next day gave us an encouraging 116 miles made good. The wind was still southwest force 6-7 with big seas causing occasional barely-controlled surfing by *Tryste* of 12 or 13 knots. With only the yankee set we sailed on through a wild night.

Soon after 0600, after we had cautiously shortened down to storm jib and reefed mizzen, I was overriding the self steering because Ernest wanted to take a star sight, when I suddenly saw the Speedo needle touch 18 knots, a most unsuitable speed for *Tryste's* safety. Almost at the same time, Ernest shouted, 'The self-steering's broken again.' No wonder she kept going off course. This time it was much more serious: the self-steering rudder (a separate one from the main rudder) had broken off, twisting the trim-tab all askew in the process. We rescued all the pieces, dropped the storm jib and had breakfast lying ahull.

'Steering from now on,' Ernest said grimly. For a start we would take two hours at a time, watch and watch about. We were not looking forward to it in these conditions of high wind, big seas and frequent rainsqualls. Around 1000 the wind was down enough to set a slightly larger jib on the forestay with the reefed mizzen, and around 1600 we were able to set the reefed mainsail. From then on we took two and a half hour watches, finding that taking the helm all the time was hard work. We hadn't had to do that since the very early days of our sailing life with *Tryste*, when there were six of us to share the steering.

By noon the next day we had made a wild twenty-four hour run of 185 miles, and were only 94 miles from Lord Howe. That evening we handed sail for supper and a rest and then sailed again for two more hours until 2200, when we were about 40 miles from the island. Handing all sail again, we lay ahull. Ernest, who had taken the bulk of the night hours, was exhausted and slept pretty solidly from 2300 to almost 0600.

'So much for always being aware of the weather,' he said, amazed that he had slept so long, 'I guess I was worn out.' I was on deck when he woke. When he came out to join me he said, 'Oh-oh! Bloody great lumps of land!' Lord Howe's mountains Gower and Lidgbird had appeared briefly to the east of us, but I had not seen them. A squall soon went through and socked them in again, but at last the weather seemed to be moderating a bit, although the seas were still huge.

'Sure is rough,' Ernest said, but we set the main and mizzen, both reefed, with yankee jib and small stays'l and were soon doing 6-8 knots. Although the island had disappeared again we had a fair idea of our position, judging by a sun sight, a fuzzy RDF bearing, and our brief sight of the mountains. At 0740 Ernest called me out on deck,

'Mr Ball's pyramid,' he said, pointing. This extraordinary offshore peak of volcanic rock, ten miles south of Lord Howe, is 1,811 ft. tall. Now we knew exactly where we were, but we did not feel our usual delight at making landfall. We were both aware that the entrance to the preferred anchorage in the lagoon must be completely exposed and unusable with the big swells from the southwest probably breaking right across.

The radio told us that this was the end of an enormous depression stretching all the way from Australia to New Zealand. Although the wind seemed to be moderating and turning more southeast, we knew we would have to find another haven. The Pilot Book suggested trying the North East Roadstead, and once we could clearly see the island we steered tiredly on up the west coast towards it. Around this time we shipped an enormous wave, which soaked us both right down inside our oilskins. It also filled the cockpit and made the helm sluggish until it drained away. The gale had not quite finished with us. Soon we could see into the lagoon, which was a mass of spume with aqua breakers cresting across it. The wind seemed to be falling.

'It *might* be possible soon,' Ernest said dubiously. I was glad we were going round to have a look at the other anchorage first. We passed rock cliffs like walls of bricks and others marked like Nazca lines, with cracks where tropic birds were nesting. At last, rounding Soldier's Cape, the most northeasterly point, we saw the mast of a yacht lying inshore. A red sloop, *Concord,* on delivery from Auckland to Sydney, lay peacefully there in Ned's Bay. We anchored fairly close in, in 15 feet of calm water over coral sand. Making up the log we found that we had covered 446 miles in not much more than three wild days, including seven hours of one of those days spent lying ahull.

The four delivery 'jokers' aboard *Concord* were happy to accept part of the fish we had caught on the way in—and to borrow our dinghy to go ashore. With our aching arms and shoulder muscles we did not plan to use it for quite a while; all we wanted to do was sleep. We found that we had met one of the crew before, in New Zealand. They were soon aboard, telling us all their adventures. They had not intended to stop at Lord Howe. They had believed themselves to be passing 40 miles to the south when in the small hours they clearly saw a sail ahead against the night sky, a tall sail but: 'The brute was not showing any lights.' Angered, they shone lanterns on it, blew whistles and shouted. Only as they closed with it did they realise that it was Ball's Pyramid. At that they were lucky. About two miles south and east is a 21 ft. high rock, and five miles to the south the sea breaks dangerously in SW gales.

Ned's Bay had a yellow sand beach with rather scruffy palm trees and some mown grass close to shore and three notices which said: 1. No fishing to the south of this point. 2. Landslide area, keep clear! and 3. Ladies and gents toilets and changing sheds. There were also electrically powered ways holding a speedboat with outboard and a yellow steel whaleboat. A large shed on the beach was for tourists and, it being Saturday, that evening they held a very noisy dance. There were also picnic tables, benches, a large bicycle rack and a 'barbie' area. We found it all highly organized and structured, and looked around for the Butlin's-camp cheerleader.

In the afternoon of the following day the wind started blowing into Ned's Bay and we headed off to enter the lagoon. There was not much wind and we motor-sailed with only the genoa set. Outside the pass we dropped the genoa and motored into the lagoon on a compass bearing, before finally picking up the two tiny white triangles that marked the leads. We headed gingerly in past the moorings and over to a spot off the jetty to anchor. I went ashore to see the Harbour Master and ask where a shallow draft vessel could anchor, but he was off the island visiting Norfolk Island to the north. A friendly young man in the office said,

'Help yourself—but don't quote me.' So we stayed there for the night, going ashore before supper for a walk around the magnificent Norfolk-pines-dominated waterfront. Everywhere there seemed to be white fences, neatly mown grass, oleanders, hibiscus, banyan, palms and bougainvillea. The effect was very neat and pretty, including the fields and what looked like toy cows, as well as the tourists on cycles or in mini tour-buses. In the morning Ernest rowed back the way we came in and found the shallow boat pool we had been told about as a good place for a tri to anchor. We trickled into it gently on a falling tide and anchored carefully and to our satisfaction. That was when we noticed a sport fish boat picking its way carefully through the coral patches between us.

'Some officious bastard coming to see us,' Ernest said, but they got scared about depths and started shouting instead,

'You can't anchor there!' Which was downright silly: we just had.

'You have to pick up one of the yacht moorings!' If someone polite had come out in a rowboat we would not have been so cross—but instead they shouted, 'Get out! Get out!' which of course, made us both furious. Ernest insisted that we motor out *immediately*, with only a foot under our 2 ft. 9in. keel. We crept out and picked up a mooring and went ashore to kill someone, but alas there was no one around to kill.

Lord Howe is a wonderful island for walkers, with mountain trails and lush rain forest and palms. We went for a long walk back to Ned's Beach and also to Middle Beach, another ocean beach where the wind was blowing steadily. It was, 'an obvious sailing wind', or so Ernest said. I was not convinced that he was right. I thought one more night of rest and time to get squared around would be preferable, but let myself be persuaded. I too had hated being shouted at. If they didn't want us we didn't want to stay.

We stayed only three days and never regretted leaving. At least not for the first twelve hours when we had a fair breeze and *Tryste* steered herself well on course even without the self-steering gear. Ernest congratulated himself on being the one to choose to leave *right then;* handing over to me at the end of his watch with some foolish words about how perfect it all was, ending with, 'and not a cloud in the sky.' By the end of my watch it was raining and squalling and thundering and the wind had become so fluky that I could not leave the helm to get my oilskins when the rain started to come down heavily.

Ernest came on watch saying crossly, 'Don't get wet! We don't want wet clothes all over the boat.' So I stomped off to my bunk in a sulk leaving him to wrestle with thunder and lightning and torrential rain and constant 30° wind shifts and being caught aback, as squall after squall went through in quick succession. After his four-hour horror-watch he insisted on keeping the helm for another two, only handing over to me when it was almost daylight.

We handed all sail later to have breakfast but set it again after only two hours. This was the pattern for the rest of the 464-mile, *eleven-day-passage*. Light winds were always in the wrong direction, while our strongest winds, and then only force 4, came from the northwest, the direction we wanted to go. When at last we were finally going well in *almost* the right direction with main, genoa and mizzen and were only 60 miles from Mooloobaba, at one in the morning of the eleventh day, I had regretfully to wake the captain.

'Ernest, the forestay has broken.' This was inaccurate. The forestay itself was not broken; the masthead fitting had broken and come down with the spinnaker block and forestay and the genny which had split across the top. After we cleared up the mess, we lay ahull while Ernest decided on the best way to handle things. Soon we were underway again, with the mainsail reefed and a small jib set on the inner forestay. In time that was changed for the yankee, which was larger and which, with its wire luff line, we decided would help support the mast. We ended up motor sailing after Ernest, taking sights, discovered that the dreaded 4 knot current, which supposedly ran close inshore, already had us in its claws.

Just before landfall I saw one of the best Spotted Dolphin shows in a long time. A mother and young one suddenly jumped clear of the water beside the boat. They had all-over spotted skins, sunrise-pink bellies and big, very fine, hooked dorsal fins. An unusually large single one jumped in an arc on the port bow, then a group of five or six did synchronised jumping. They made a lot of big splashes and I yelled with delight because we so seldom saw those pink bellies display, but sadly, Ernest asleep below, did not stir.

At last we were out of the current and when Ernest woke we set the chute and soon a light southeasterly was wafting us in towards the city towers of Mooloolaba, which to our surprise, consisted of high rises. Sadly there were also factory chimneys and ugly smoke.

'Do you think we have come to the right place?' Ernest joked as he showed me the old black and white sketch in the Pilot Book of three handsome mountains, one just like a thumb and described, as the B.A. publications love to do, as 'conspic.' Now there it was ahead of us.

It was late afternoon when we moored between two pilings at Mooloolaba. Only 24 hours later we left again and entered the Great Sandy Strait inside Fraser Island, on our way to Maryborough on the Mary River.

Our destination was the home of our old Ozzie yachtie friends Ruth and Geoff Goodman who had pretty well swallowed the anchor, and had built themselves a house near Maryborough. Ernest felt sure that he would be able to work on our breakages there with Geoff's help. We had last seen them in the Tongas when we were waiting for Susie and Greg to come aboard. They still had *Karloo* and Geoff would be sure to have a good supply of tools and odds and ends.

Three days later we sailed up the Mary River in miserable rainshowers, to drop our anchor in some lovely sticky mud on the far side of the river from a dilapidated jetty. Here one overseas boat was tied up, while an Australian yacht, *Rachel Margaret,* lay at anchor in the middle of the river.

In the morning it was pouring and we realised that we had neither the Goodman's house address nor their phone number; but Zoe and Graham aboard *Rachel Margaret* were able to help, telling us that Geoff and Ruth lived at the end of Granville road, about a mile away. We suited up in our oilskins and went ashore. A mile later we were in suburbia.

'Can't see them living here!' Ernest said, but then the road turned into a vehicle track, a patch of bush and two more-secluded-looking houses.

'This is it!' Ernest cried, leaping up the steps of the first house and totally ignoring the notice of 'Ring the bell and wait here,' because he saw Geoff through the window. Then it was great reunion time and showers of kindness (and lovely hot water) and being made to stay to dinner and finally returning home about 10.30 with all our wonderful mail that had been sent care of their mailbox.

Over the next ten days we learnt to accept endless kindnesses from Geoff and Ruth; to live at a slower pace, to eat more healthfully, to use little salt and to not bother with alcohol; as Ernest and Geoff re-built *Tryste*'s self-steering rudder. We had a distinct break from the healthy non-alcoholic regime when Celia came north to visit and we had a lazy, fun day eating, drinking, visiting and talking aboard *Tryste*. I'm sure Geoff and Ruth appreciated the break. Then it was back to the (salt-free) salt mine again.

As well as attempting to give us all our meals, which we resisted strenuously, Ruth gave us access to her splendid heavy-duty sewing machine to mend our torn sails, and Geoff (who had been an engineer) opened his well-equipped workshop to Ernest and took him in his van to get metal holes drilled, as well as to the right shops to buy plywood and everything else we needed.

One day I did two massive loads of laundry in Ruth's washing machine, and that same day the genoa was mended. I could claim that I mended it, I'm sure I tried, but it was Ruth really who showed me how best to use her machine...by doing it all herself. A forceful character and generous with her time, as well as with her strong opinions on subjects such as food, health, and unruly children, she had also become anti-sailing-offshore for herself since we had last seen them.

Geoff however still rather hankered after one last voyage in *Karloo* even though their passage making did not sound like much fun. Geoff described it as: 'Rather like a bad dose of influenza. You lie on your bunk with a very bad headache, feeling sick, and hot and cold all over, and it lasts about ten days and you are heartily glad when it's over.' When later they did do some more deep-sea voyaging it was as passengers on a container ship.

On the twelfth of May, 1982, we left the Goodmans and sailed out of the Mary River, leaving sandy Fraser Island astern and heading north to cruise the Great Barrier Reef for *Tryste*'s second and last time.

CHAPTER FOURTEEN:

ΟOP THE REEF

In 1972 we had taken three months to enjoy the Great Barrier Reef Province from Gladstone to Cooktown with the four girls aboard; now we covered almost the same distance in a month. To us six aboard *Tryste* the Great Barrier Reef had been a dream, an abstraction, a congeries of sun and sand and wind, of birds and fish and dolphins, of high green islands and tiny navigation markers in a cerulean sea, of low tides spent shelling on exposed reefs, of crabs and oysters and wild goat for our meals, of mainland inlets invaded by mangroves with freshwater springs, and of strange animals: dugongs grazing on underwater grasses, as well as glimpses of wallabies and wild pigs, sea eagles and lorikeets.

We wanted to re-visit some of the places where we had been with the crew: Michaelmas Cay, a wonderful seabird nesting colony; Fitzroy island, where Nicky had stayed ashore overnight and been woken by two kangaroos beside her bed; and Cooktown where Carol and Anne had left us to live their own lives as adults. As well we wanted to see new places like Lizard Island, further up the reef, which we had heard about from other yachties but had not seen.

We were still hooked in to the BBC news, and in spite of the fact that two other wars raged—Iran and Iraq, and the Israeli invasion of Lebanon—'the war' still meant the Falklands to us. In the second week of June, we were anxiously awaiting the assault on Port Stanley. Can one ever shake off being brought up British?

Fitzroy Island, a small 'high island' 17 miles out from Cairns but still within the outer reef, proved to be a disappointment when we reached it sailing in company with German singlehander Wolf Dietrich on *White*

Dolphin. We had known that it was to become a resort, but somehow were not ready for such well-established trees and flower bushes and inhabited cabins. We found, too, that the resident tourists seemed to think that the anchorage belonged to them—and their innumerable water toys—rather than to us rugged world sailors. What a blow to our self-image!

Leaving populous Fitzroy, we went to the other extreme and spent the night anchored off Sudbury Reef, which, in spite of now being on the daytime tour boat itinerary, still had its own strange fascination. This small patch of yellow-orange sand, only eight miles away from Fitzroy and nearer to the outer reef was, like Michaelmas Cay, a nesting site for terns and noddies. We anchored close in and went ashore in the hot sun, amazed at the view of layered purple mountains back on the mainland beyond Fitzroy Island.

As we stood in the shallows, looking out over some coral heads towards the outer reef, a school of mullet came leaping out of the water towards us, chased by some predator. We thought it must be a shark but when it almost grounded itself Ernest saw it clearly. It was a large game fish, perhaps a marlin.

The wind got up in the night, waking Ernest who then lay awake contentedly listening to the anchor chain complaining. We were well hooked in, as we found when we came to lift the anchor after breakfast. Many coral heads lay in our path to Michaelmas Cay. Although we agreed that as it was high tide we could safely sail over them, we cravenly (or sensibly) took the path outside all of them instead.

At Michaelmas Cay there were plenty of tour boats, but they did not stay long, and when they had all gone home or back to their resorts we went ashore and walked around the island to see the birds. Three different sorts of terns nested there, as well as noddies, and we discovered that the cay had been designated a National Park since our last visit. The notice that told us this contained more writing, but so many birds had sat on it and defaced it that we could not see that it also said *Do Not Go Beyond This Point,* and were able to circumnavigate the island on foot and see all the enchanting little fluffy nestlings. Before we reached Cooktown we discovered that the motor was not charging, and after investigating, Ernest diagnosed, 'alternator shot'—the usual direly terminal diagnosis, so I was not too dismayed, with luck we would be able to get it fixed in Cooktown. We had a beautiful sail there from Michaelmas, with genoa and one twin headsail poled out wing and wing, entering under sail to anchor in front of the Cook memorial.

We found *White Dolphin* already anchored there and Wolf Dietrich told us that he had touched bottom on Cooktown's shallow sandy entrance and had had to winch himself off. That windy night he dragged anchor, as did another yacht nearby, which, on starting its motor, managed to cut *White Dolphin's* anchor line with its propeller. That afternoon Wolf came aboard *Tryste* and helped Ernest take our alternator apart and later Ernest helped Wolf drag for his anchor with our grapple without success. However the day before we left Cooktown, on the theory that it *had* to be somewhere, Ernest snorkelled around the area and eventually discovered it—underneath *Tryste's* Danforth.

The alternator's problem turned out to be the voltage regulator and cost only $25 to replace, but in the process of replacing it air got into the lines and gave Ernest a miserable diesel-bleeding job, with much attendant swearing.

Early one morning we woke aboard *Tryste* to the noise of large animals splashing around in our shallow anchorage. Dugongs! We thought hopefully, but looking out we saw two rough-coated cow-cocky's horses being exercised and scrubbed off in the sea. Later we met Blair, the fat good-humoured farmer who owned them, and his sidekick Sid, who were readying them for the races.

Bill, one of the men from the Coastguard Surveillance Office, had told us about the Cooktown Races, a one-day event that closed down the town for the day. The races took place on a rough and ready racetrack outside the town. He had offered to fetch us and take us there when we met him the day before at the Coastguard Office where we had been supplying *Tryste's* particulars, as well as Ernest's bird's eye sketch of *Tryste*, for the patrolling surveillance planes.

At the races we met Blair again and he marked our cards with 'dead cert' winners. We had fun betting on every race with one, two and five dollar bets. The mounts were pretty rough but the assorted jockeys did sport colours. We lost on all the horses except one but in the end were only ten dollars out. We enjoyed the huge hilarity and enthusiasm of the mostly aboriginal punters, who sat on the old beat-up family-filled cars that were their grandstands for a day out at the races.

It was there that Ernest was approached by one of the older broken-down looking aborigines and asked for a quarter.

'If I give it you, you'll just spend it on drink,' Ernest said jokingly.

'It's none of your business how I spend my money,' said the curly-headed swagman, drawing himself up to his full height.

We came out of Cooktown with gusty east southeast winds, and sailed up past Indian Head to Cape Bedford, named by Captain Cook the day he left the reef. The Cape's handsome crenulated rocky heights looked like man-made fortifications, above deep green velvet folded hills that ran down almost to the sea. Once in Cape Bedford bay, anchored alongside three or four prawners, we were well protected. Here the coastguard surveillance plane found us and did a couple of runs over us, no doubt double-checking our identity, newly confirmed in Cooktown, as they would continue to do all the way to Darwin.

Next day we headed off to Lizard Island, where we anchored in the more northerly of two anchorages with several other yachts, some of which would be, like us, sailing on across the Indian Ocean. Here Ernest was able to borrow and trace a chart of Darwin from Gerry on the US yacht *Sea High*.

The following morning we climbed the 1,179 feet to Cook's Lookout, and gazed seaward over the ochre sand and rock beach and the off-lying reefs and coral patches to the outer barrier reef. Here in 1770 Captain Cook looked eastward over these same hazards, which from this height appeared so harmless, like a scattering of pale blue jewels; and longed for the open sea. He had finally finished careening and repairing the *Endeavour* (or 'heaving down' as he said) in Cooktown and repairing her, after grounding on the 'Endeavour' reef, and almost losing his ship. He had had more than enough of navigating through these dangerous shoals, rocks, reefs and islands, and though visibility was hazy he thought he could see a wide break in the outer reef. Later he sent the master in the pinnace to sound the dark blue depths, then sailed the *Endeavour* safely out into the Coral Sea.

We found it a long, hot climb and were glad to read 'NOT FAR!' painted on a rock almost at the top. At the summit stood a sundial which also had many destinations marked off such as Eagle Reef, Cook's Passage, Hobart (3,140 km) and Montreal (15,000 km.)(O Canada!) Looking back from the summit we could see the mainland with its sand hills, all the way back to Cape Bedford, where we had been two days before; looking forward we saw Cape York, with numerous reefs, sand cays and little islands leading all the way north.

Cook named the island after the four-foot lizards that roamed there. Although we saw some tail tracks in the sand and were told that the lizards were always to be seen at the garbage dump in the evenings, we stayed three days enjoying walking and swimming without making the effort to see them, before sailing north again.

On the last day we were there I woke, like Ruth (one day when we were at Maryborough) saying, in a 'Strine', accent, 'I think I'll *bike*.' So I did, making bread, apple pie and maids of honour.

Two days later, as we neared our Flinders Island anchorage with a strong east southeasterly behind us, we incredulously passed a windsurfer inshore of us, and recognised him as one of the young men from the French yacht *Matavai III,* which had been anchored in the Lizard Island anchorage. As we learned later he had left Cape Bathurst, about 15 miles to the south, in a fairly light wind, but by the time we saw him the breeze was so strong that he was having to tack downwind. At least when we reached Flinders Island we were able to tell his anxious parents, where they stood on a muddy reef looking hopefully out to sea, that he was almost in sight.

Poor *Matavaiis,* they had only eleven more days before having to clear the country, having fallen foul of petty officialdom in Cairns. They left again that afternoon. We would enjoy getting to know them properly on Christmas Island in the Indian Ocean.

Later that day, in the Flinders Island anchorage, six trawlers came in and mated—or so my diary said. I know what I meant—that they tied stern to, one to another in pairs, on only one anchor, so that their crews could easily visit boat to boat.

The following night we anchored at Pelican Island. We were hoping to see some pelican chicks, but were too late in the year, and found only empty nests and a couple of desiccated bodies. From here on northward there was much speculation among the boats about crocodiles in the rivers. Two days later we were anchored in Lockhart River only about 150 miles south of Cape York, where 60 foot mangroves lined the river banks and invisible things went clop and glop and clank and *something took our crab pot overnight!* Could it have been a crocodile? We never saw the crab pot again.

Ernest was thinking of going ashore in search of wild pig next morning when we saw a speedboat enter the river with an aboriginal family aboard. They seemed to be on a fishing trip combined with plenty of exercise room for their nine children, who soon disappeared downriver. The parents fished with lines on the end of which were fairly heavy weights which they twirled around their heads and then let fly, then hooked a loop of line over a stick planted firmly in the muddy sand. They displayed endless patience and fished away all afternoon. 'They look so right,' Ernest said; we were the obvious interlopers.

We sailed on again next morning and caught a 28 lb. Wahoo or barred mackerel, making lots of meals and lots of jars of fish for me to process in the pressure cooker. It was too bad we hadn't caught it the day before in time to share with the local family.

Much tricky navigation around groups of islands as well as many coral patches, lay between Portland Roads and Cape Grenville, and made us wish we had a larger-scale chart, but two days later we were through them all and anchored safely in about 8 ft over good-holding sand, in Margaret Bay to the north of Cape Grenville. Our biggest excitement of the day had been to have a close encounter with a dugong. He was a pale fawny tan with a very shiny skin, and he arched his back and tail and disappeared just like a small tubby whale.

We were very happy to be back in this delightful anchorage that we remembered sharing with Susie and Nic. What we had forgotten though, was that the handsome rocky headlands were defaced by huge painted yacht names.

On shore were miles and miles of beach interspersed with mangrove sloughs forming rivers out to sea. In the distance high sand cliffs with bush looked enticing. Ashore we found big black-lipped oysters for our evening meal, while terns and noddies were busy about the boat, where baitfish continually broke the surface. We stayed two days. We began to see fewer fish boats on this top part of the reef, but were seeing three or four steamers a day and were surprised how well used this inside-passage steamer lane was.

The following day was probably the most spectacularly scenic one of the whole Barrier Reef passage. High sand hills, some white, some yellow, some hundreds of feet high bearded with bush, were interspersed with jutting low red bluffs. As we reached Albany Island, big red anthills began to appear on curved red cliff-sides of sand and rock. A steady force 4 southeast wind had encouraged us to set both big headsails poled out, with the main. As we rounded Albany we had taken the genny pole out and started to get the sail down, but as we turned through the passage between Albany and Pitt Islands to enter Pioneer Bay we still had the full mainsail up.

When Ernest went forward to lower the remaining pole and sail he saw that we had hooked a big fish, and as we raced on he was hauling it in with three sharks after it, all of us hoping for lunch. He pulled in the fish and once it was boated he took out the pole, hauled in the twin, and finished bringing in the genny as I steered us sharply to port to enter Pioneer Bay under main alone. It was all a bit breathless for a minute or two in the flurry of lines, sails, poles and fish, but somehow we had the anchor down and caught our breath before Ernest cleaned and filleted the fish (which had a large bite out of it) while I cleared up the sheets, poles, sails and lines. The fish had a strange deep body and reminded us of the *paiere* we had caught off Fanning in the Line Islands after our abortive search for *Wishbone*.

We had been thinking of bypassing Pioneer Bay, which was rather open, but as the weather seemed set fair and the bottom was sand we had decided to try it, and since it shelved very gradually, we anchored fairly far from shore in only 7½ ft. Going ashore we found a two-mile-long beach of white sand, with crab tracks low down and those of small pigs, wallabies, lizards and birds further up. We looked for oysters but gave up that idea when we found a huge midden of old oyster shells together with a big pile of bottles. Obviously the 'black fellers' made regular stops here.

We wandered uphill in the corner of the beach, and were soon in rough red sandy country with low bush, totally churned up by wild pigs. There were more anthills on the east coast nearby, some as high as six or seven feet, and below them a lovely beach of pale red and yellow sand.

Slightly south of the pig rootings, a big grove of feathery casuarinas grew on heaps and hillocks of golden sand. Small scoria littered flatter areas, interspersed with patches of pockmarked lava in red or black, although most of the east side of the island was made up of an assortment of fine or more granular sand: white, gold, rust and vivid red. Down towards the weather side beach on the east side of the island ran a cut in the cliff full of enormous bleached shells, a long way up above our heads, mute testament to a long ago change of coastline.

We kept our eyes peeled as we went up through bush, as we had been warned of poisonous snakes, which, like so many of Australia's nasties, could be lethal. There were also green ants, which bite viciously, to avoid. We met a small black porker and were alert all the time for the monster razorback boar that might be 'lying piggo' waiting to jump out on us. Where it became more open we soon found ourselves out on the cliff edge with brilliant brick red anthills everywhere. At last we were looking down on a lovely small bay with a whole anthill quarry on its cliff side and waves creaming shallowly in onto a white beach, where a wallaby sat looking up at us.

Leaving Albany two days later, we rounded 275 ft. high Cape York, with its many big handsome off-lying islands, and anchored in Cape York Bay. Later we looked down on *Tryste* lying in a pool of aquamarine water, between two curving sand spits, one from Cape York Island and one from the mainland shore. There was a large gap between them that we would sail through the next morning when we left for Thursday Island, one of the most southerly of the Torres Straits Islands that straggle down south of Papua New Guinea.

People come a long way to visit Cape York, as well they might. Some come for the excellent fishing and some simply to see the extraordinarily beautiful area of large rocky islands, curving bays and beaches, turquoise water and interesting birds, animals and sea creatures. Inland the Cape York Peninsula is one of the last remaining areas of wilderness on earth, with wild rivers, tropical rainforests and savannas. (Although we saw none of this; a common drawback of sailing your own boat, you tend to see only the edges of the countries that you visit.) On the beach we met a family (all male) from Adelaide. Like us they took notice of the warning not to swim because of sharks and crocodiles. They told us that the last part of the road was a horrendous four-wheel-drive track with rivers to cross and a truck winch essential.

We sailed to Thursday Island next day and put on a few expensive necessities and one or two luxuries like a T-bone steak apiece. It was there that we first met *Wasa*; a German yacht from Wilhelmshaven owned by Rolf Webber and his wife, Helga, a tall strong woman like a Wagnerian heroine. *Wasa* was one of the yachts, like *Matavaii III*, that we would meet again in Christmas Island.

It was on the beach at Thursday Island that Ernest, after carrying two heavy five-gallon cans of diesel from too painfully far away, put them down at the head of the beach for a rest; whereupon Helga swooped down out of nowhere, and to Ernest's chagrin, picked up one in each hand and carried them casually down to the dinghy with Ernest trotting behind her saying, 'Let me take one, let me take one!'

The next morning we were off, 'Towards Darwin', on the shore of the Timor Sea, where we had never sailed before. The first time we had sailed this way we had been out of the Arafura Sea after only a few days, and heading north of west straight to Christmas Island. This time, we had decided to have a look at some of Australia's northern coast first, before leaving from Darwin where we should be able to stock up well on stores for the Indian Ocean crossing.

The ten day, 720 mile passage through the Arafura and Timor Seas was slow but unlike any we had made before. The warm shallow waters we sailed through were full of life, from dolphins and huge tuna to evil-looking mustard-coloured sea snakes that swam right on the surface of the sea and lifted their heads to peer at us. Like solid rubber hose, these were about an inch in diameter, and we much preferred the white ones whose thin stripes of brilliant blue or green about an inch apart showed up much better. Once, as a change from snakes, we saw a turtle float sleepily past with a Black-capped tern riding on its shell; while a noise, like rain falling from trees after a shower, told us that a cloud of butterfly–sized flying fish had taken flight nearby.

As with our earlier crossing with Susie and Nicola, the bioluminescence was exceptional, while daytime plankton sometimes produced a brownish 'red tide' that covered the surface of the sea in long thick streaks; two sharks lazily following the boat seemed to swimming in soup. The wind was almost always favourable but of unpredictable strength: our best day's run being 156 miles and our worst only 40. On windless days it was always too hot, the temperature varying from 72° to 88°F, day and night.

Once we had crossed the Gulf of Carpentaria, a huge indentation on the North Coast between the Cape York Peninsula and Arnhem Land (The northeastern part of the Northern Territory) we often had land in sight, but we found that navigation lights were few, while frequent patches of burning on shore made for early darkness and riveting sunset skies with a sun that often set like a big red ball.

After Cape Croker the shallow Arafura Sea gave way to the marginally shallower Timor one. Once we had passed this cape we still had to round the large landmass that was the Cobourg Peninsula to enter Van Diemen Gulf. As we came in to Port Ellison on the Peninsula, around the sixth day out from Thursday Island, we knew there were patches of rocks, as well as patches of off-lying coral to avoid and Ernest admitted, 'Our chart really is a bit inadequate, a bit more local knowledge would have helped', but we managed not to hit anything.

We went ashore at Port Ellison. The Park Ranger who met us on the beach told us that the whole Cobourg Peninsula was a wildlife sanctuary.

'Do you have a permit?' he asked. It reminded us of our first circumnavigation when, in vile weather, we took shelter off Bird Island on South Africa's south coast. It too was a wildlife sanctuary and the welcome exactly the same.

'No,' We said and asked, 'but could we just take a walk along the beach?' and received a grudging, 'Yes, but no fires!' That would never have occurred to us; but perhaps he had been bothered by speedboats coming out from Darwin for an evening picnic. We walked a short way along the shore and soon found tracks of animals and birds, perhaps even an emu. A trail led inland, and we walked down it a little way but soon became swelteringly hot and, having obediently lit no fires, we went back to *Tryste* and decided not to stay overnight, but to move the boat and move the air through it, to cool off both it and us.

While we had the dinghy in the water Ernest rowed over to a big trawler anchored nearby and found out that the range of tides in Darwin was 19 ft at the moment. We anchored that night after dark, but with a sunset lit sky, still on the Cobourg Peninsula; coming in to Alcaro Bay on *Wasa*'s anchor light and dropping the hook astern of her. We left the next morning at 0400, before Rolf and Helga were awake, and were sailing very slowly south down the Van Diemen Gulf when *Wasa* motored up behind us with flapping sails. After a quick conference we all decided to anchor for the night west of Cape Hotham.

The following evening at sunset we anchored off the Darwin Sailing Club in Fanny Bay, along with a group of overseas cruising yachts, including *Wasa* and *White Dolphin*, many of whose crews would become our friends on the long haul across the Indian Ocean.

An island visitor leaves *Tryste* for his outrigger canoe, Nukufetau, Tuvalu.

Yutaka, Ted's bodyguard, climbs a palm to pick coconuts for us in Kusaie, Carolines.

WWII landing craft, now the Kusaie Yacht Club, Lele Harbour, Kusaie

Taurewa and *Tryste* lie at anchor beneath massive Jokaz Head, Ponape Harbour.

With *Wanderer IV* and *Tryste* rafted up, we entertain Eric and Susan Hiscock in Prevost I. B.C.

Scrabble addicts Val and Ernest on the long passage home to B.C. from Ponape.

Early morning anchorage at Bruny Island near Hobart, Tasmania.

Tryste lies alongside a fish boat in Constitution dock in downtown Hobart.

Easter Sunday, handsome Ulladulla fish boats, decorated for Blessing the Fleet sail-past.

Tryste anchored off the Sydney Opera House.

Ernest and a tern examine one another on Michaelmas Cay, Great Barrier Reef.

Val enjoys the terns, Michaelmas Cay, Great Barrier Reef.

CHAPTER FIFTEEN:

THE EMBARRASSMENT OF HMAS PERTH

Our first stop across the Indian Ocean from Darwin was Christmas Island, that rocky phosphate island 500 miles south of Java. It had been an interesting stop in 1973 with Susie and Nic aboard. Although in most ports nowadays, officials insist that you stay aboard until you have been given pratique by the local doctor and cleared to land by customs and immigration, all coming aboard your boat, there are always exceptions. Christmas Island in 1982 was one. You were expected to go ashore yourself and walk up the hill to the police station, as we were told by a couple passing in a dinghy. They were just going up to clear out, since they were leaving next day. The harbourmaster was giving them a ride and we could go with them and avoid a long hot walk.

As we were rowing ashore to do this, we were hailed, in a very British voice, by a portly swimmer near the beach. We took him to be another yachtie, but he introduced himself as Bill Yates, the administrator of the island, and after a chat invited us to come up to the house on the cliff top above the cove for drinks in a day or two. He would get his secretary, he said, to send us an invitation.

Later, blonde smiling Julia Hazel came aboard to say hello, as she was leaving for the Cocos Keeling Islands in the morning. We were amazed to hear that she had learnt welding and then built her 28 ft. steel cutter *Jeshan* herself, which she sailed singlehanded without any kind of an engine. She had also done the joinery, outfitted the boat and made the sails. Julia was then 34 years old, South African by birth, but had emigrated to Australia ten years earlier and built her boat there. We would become firm friends, meeting several times in ports across the Indian Ocean and in South Africa.

'Bon voyage, Julia,' we heard next morning on Christmas Island Radio's delightful local news broadcast. We heard too that another yacht had been sighted to the northeast, bringing the number in the anchorage back up to five.

That evening we again met the Blanchard family aboard the French ketch *Matavaii III*, whom we had met briefly on the Great Barrier Reef. Nanu and Roger, an ex-airplane pilot, were sailing with their adult sons, Loic and Yan. We achieved instant rapport in mangled English and fractured French and were pleased when we were all invited to the Administrator's Residence together for drinks.

Approaching Christmas Island we had seen flocks of hundreds of boobies out at sea feeding, as well as a few frigate birds and some of the apricot coloured tropicbirds that had made such an impression on us in 1973. We had sailed all day with a light following wind, our unique 'chute' pulling us gently along. With so little wind we did not expect to be in before dark, but to our surprise by sunset we were sailing along beside the rocky, undercut north coast of the island, while flocks of homing seabirds flew high overhead and others swooped low over the boat, as we turned south to enter Flying Fish Cove. We had barely dropped the chute and started the motor before a lighter came swooshing alongside us in the dusk, where we had just enough light to pick out and avoid the big mooring buoys dotted in the entrance.

A friendly Scottish voice welcomed us, 'Sorry, it's a bit crowded, there's four yachts already,' and 'Sorry, it's coral,' and then, 'We'll show you the way, only one more small buoy to avoid, follow us.' They led us in among the other yachts and left. Next day we would learn that the Scottish accent belonged to the harbourmaster, Jim McMasters, who would become a good friend to us.

The second day we were in Flying Fish Cove we celebrated our thirty-third wedding anniversary by going to the movies, one of the many forms of entertainment that the Australian Phosphate Company provided free to keep their workers happy. This large open-air area with screen and bench seats was the nearest Christmas Island came to a drive-in movie theatre. We went with a few yachties and a few hundred Chinese and Malay phosphate workers. The film featured the hero's improbable adventures in a hostile wilderness. We were late, missed the title and the first few minutes, and never really grasped the plot. The print copy was old and bad and the sound execrable, while much of the dialogue was drowned out by passing cars, but it was free and we could have left anytime. We shared a cushion and enjoyed the challenge.

The next afternoon, having received our official written invitation to drinks at Government House, we went ashore for showers, then collected on the beach with the *Matavaiis,* sweet-smelling, dressed to the nines, and all of us wearing real shoes instead of thongs. Nanu looked spectacularly Parisian in a silky patterned skirt and matching blouse, while the two gentlemen looked equally splendid in their blazers as we sauntered up to the handsome, two-storey residence.

We had carried Ernest's blazer all the way round the world on our first circumnavigation, believing that some time, some where, we would be invited to meet the Governor of some far-flung outpost of the empire. It had happened to people like the Hiscocks and the Smeetons. Surely it would happen to us? Now at last we were invited to a Governor's Residence, even if under Australian administration the Governor had been downgraded to Administrator.

As we waited on the portico of Government House, Oliver, the administrator's son who was visiting the island, called down to us from a window overhead, then ran down and let us in. Bill Yates poured liberal drinks. 'What would you like?' he asked, 'Gin and tonic all right?' He and his wife Camille were soon chatting away, mostly in French, while Oliver passed round shrimp canapés. Bill Yates, who sported a red cummerbund with his Palm Beach suit, looked like a slightly less tubby Robert Morley, with a stiff leg from an old war wound. We had earlier learned from Jim McMasters that Bill had the distinction of being the only man who had been a Member of Parliament in both British and Australian parliaments.

We had not long had our second gin and tonics before Bill told us of the upcoming 'Show the Flag' visit of the Australian guided-missile destroyer, the HMAS *Perth,* in two days time. It was to be a great day for everyone on the island.

'She'll be here at 8 o'clock in the morning,' he said. 'We shall fire the cannon and send up the flag on the dot of 0800 hours.' We all looked at one another questioningly. 'The cannon?' Someone asked. 'Yes, the cannon. That's why we've cut a hole in the trees. Come, you shall see the cannon.' We all obediently followed him out to a grassy area in front of the residence, where a police sergeant was practicing smartly sending up the ensign. Near the flagstaff stood a rust-encrusted 6-inch gun, dating back to World War One, cast in 1903. The breech, which was chained up with a rusty chain, pointed out through the newly cut gap in the palm trees. No one could possibly fire this cannon, could they?

'You will see. You will see!' Bill Yates chuckled. 'Eight o'clock in the morning, you watch, you'll see!'

At eight o'clock, two mornings later, we all had our eyes glued to the flagstaff. Up fluttered the flag and 'Boom!' went the gun. We could see the muzzle smoking. It was most impressive. Later we learnt that a few sticks of dynamite were placed alongside the gun for the 'boom', while smouldering sawdust poked down the muzzle had made the smoke. The *Perth* had been suitably saluted.

The big grey ship had picked up one of the moorings well off Flying Fish Cove and after the welcome salute her officers came ashore for breakfast at the Residence. That was the start of the all-day celebrations.

Most of the crew came ashore in batches: for guided tours of wildlife and industry; for games of football, volleyball, tennis and golf; as well as for a barbecue lunch at the Boat Club, an attractive open building like a large roofed veranda on the shore. Meanwhile, all morning, the Christmas Island schoolchildren, mostly Chinese and Malay, were ferried, beaming, out to the *Perth* for tours.

One of the powered lighters from the phosphate works was pressed into service, along with the pukka navy pinnace from the *Perth,* to carry the schoolchildren and the liberty men to and fro. Both the coxswain of the pinnace and the navy helmsman of the borrowed lighter were shown how to come safely in to the coral-dotted shore, perhaps resentfully accepting instruction from the Malay seamen who usually worked the lighters. This necessitated running straight in alongside the gantried jetty, (normally used for loading bagged phosphate) and reversing out on the same line, avoiding the coral shelf that lay only a few inches below the surface. Both boats did many trips throughout the day.

In the middle of the day the administrator and his wife, and the company manager and his wife, were taken by launch out to the *Perth* for lunch. No doubt the wardroom hospitality included plenty of liquid refreshment. Just before 2 o'clock, they came ashore again in the *Perth*'s liberty boat. Approaching the jetty, in spite of earlier instruction, the coxswain decided to do a turn around and come alongside the jetty bow out. It was meant to be an impressive flourish; instead there was an impressive CRUNCH as the heavy steel boat came to a jarring stop, landing the Queen's representative high and dry on the coral.

Immediately, half a dozen sailors, ashore in their number one rigs, leapt into the sea and swam out to try and push the liberty boat free, with predictable lack of success. Meanwhile the crew aboard the boat, totally distraught, still had the motor going and the propeller going clonk, clonk, clonk on the coral. It was obvious that they would have to be towed off.

The powered lighter soon arrived and hung off the edge of the coral in deep water, while the swimmers clustered around the navy boat to take a line to it. Before this, some of them had commandeered a dinghy from the boat club and the ladies and the manager were taken off. Bill Yates, however, was obviously prepared to go down with his ship. 'No,' he said firmly, to offers of rescue, 'I shall stay.' By now both Ernest in *Tryste*'s dinghy and Yan in *Matavaii*'s, were hanging off to see if there was anything they could do to help.

The only line aboard the pinnace was a skinny rope only 3/8" diameter. When the swimmers had taken the end of this to the lighter and it had taken the strain, the line immediately broke, whipping back lethally across the heads of the sailors in the water and the people in the navy boat. At this point the administrator decided to abandon ship after all.

Ernest having gone back to *Tryste* for a heavier line, Yan took Bill Yates over to the jetty in *Matavaii*'s inflatable, which was ideal once he was embarked, as he was able to rest his stiff leg up on the side. Once safely on the wharf, he saluted Yan and, unsuccessfully trying to get the ratings there to join in, shouted 'Vive La France!'

By now Ernest had brought our spare 5/8" anchor-line out to the lighter. They fastened it aboard and Ernest took the other end over towards the stranded pinnace. As he got close, one of the tars swam out with the tag end of their 3/8" line to tie it to. In response to such idiocy, Ernest, once a naval rating himself, said something forceful and our heavy line was then properly attached. The lighter again took the strain and this time easily dragged the liberty boat off the coral.

They did not stop to return our line but used it to tow the launch all the way out to the *Perth*. Ernest waited around hopefully for it to be returned by the crew of the lighter, but it had gone up with the pinnace, which had been hastily hoisted aboard the *Perth*. Shortly thereafter, after firing a 15-gun salute, the *Perth* sailed, late already and horribly embarrassed, shaking Christmas Island's apricot-coloured phosphate dust off her feet. We never did get our line returned.

Back on Christmas everyone sympathized with us for the loss of our spare anchor warp, including Bill Yates. 'We must do something about that for you,' he said. But Jim had already done something. He had taken us to the harbourmaster's store which was full of gigantic mooring buoys, vast anchors and enormous shackles and chain, and had replaced our warp with the smallest line they had, a full inch nylon soft-lay rope, beautiful as an artifact, but almost useless to us, since it was too big to fit under most of our cleats. We accepted it gratefully, in the spirit it was offered.

To cheer us up Jim offered to take us to see the Abbott's boobies. We had mentioned our disappointment that we had still, on this second visit, not seen these unique birds that breed only on Christmas Island.

'It's my day off today,' Jim said. 'I know where there are some close to the road. We'll just run out, see an Abbott's, and be right back.' He made it sound as if it would be a ten-minute trip. Fleetingly I thought of my camera left aboard *Tryste*. Should I mention wanting it? Probably no chance of a picture, I thought. We bundled into Jim's car.

We had not gone far before he stopped the car and pointed out three or four of the handsome birds in their leafy nests at the top of tall trees. The Abbots, bigger than most of the other boobies with which we were familiar, had marble-column necks, sharply marked black backs and funny pale faces.

That was the start of a drive that was an ornithologist's delight. Realizing that we were genuinely interested, Jim soon found some other unique Christmas Island species for us and then continued down the exposed east coast, where we soon turned off on a side road to a colony of dozens of Red-footed boobies nesting in bare trees close to the road. Each nest contained a big fluffy white chick with grey beak and big black eyes. One smaller tree held five single-occupancy nests.

The boobies shared some of the trees with frigate birds. This was the closest we had ever been to these big elegant flyers who seem so gawky on land, the closest, that is, until we turned one more corner to find frigate birds squatting all over the dusty road, with their wings spread out like cormorants. One in a bush with his wings hanging out 'to dry' looked so extraordinary that even Jim was marvelling. By now he had tuned in to the fact that I was almost sobbing with camera-less-ness in the back seat. 'There's a good shot,' he said cruelly.

Eventually Ernest and I realized that we could not spend the rest of our lives driving around the island on a bird hunt, and that we would have to let Jim get on with what was left of his day off.

On the evening that we had drinks at the Residence, we and the *Matavaiis* had all been invited to join Camille and Oliver Yates on an outing the Company had organized. This was a train ride in a passenger carriage like a small mustard-coloured bus, on the now mostly disused narrow-gauge railway to the west side of the island, through the jungly interior and down to South Point. The train had once hauled phosphate from South Point, but even when we were there in 1973, the phosphate in that part of the island had been worked out. On the train ride we saw large areas where the phosphate had been taken with grabs, leaving a dead landscape of jagged rocks and hollows. The jungle areas though were lush with acacia, pandanus, wild cherry, trees covered with little yellow flowers, and trees entwined with hoya vine.

The Malay train driver, friendly like all the people we met on the island, was happy to stop along the way for us to pick wild peas and search for papaya, offering round his cigarettes as he took time out for a smoke. On the return journey our long train-ride finished with what by now seemed to be a typical Christmas Island climax, when the driver attempted to take the train into a big open shed up in the old dryer/crusher complex at the top of the cliff. Here the rails, which appeared not to have been used for years, were covered in shell and gravel. As we passed over them, the engine gave a horrible screech as if it had stripped it gears, and quit, apparently for good.

By now *Wasa* had arrived in Flying Fish Cove, and Rolf and Helga joined us when we were invited by the Company Manager's wife, Kaerest Houston, for a drive out to see the silver-backed tropic birds nesting near their home, and also the exposed anchorage at Waterfall on the island's west coast, where hundreds of boobies were diving and feeding just offshore.

Two days before we left, to the delight of all the yacht sailors, as well as the residents, a refrigerated supply ship came in from Australia. The local trade store closed at noon that day to re-stock and when it opened again at 8.30 next morning we were all there waiting: a crowd of chattering good-natured shoppers of all three races—Chinese, Malay and Caucasian.

The aisles were packed with big plastic baskets loaded with both tropical and temperate fruit, vegetables and salad makings, as well as cheese, bread, bacon and meat. The prices were surprisingly low since most goods coming to the island were exempt from import duty because it was the company store. We bought some of almost everything fresh for only $20Australian (under $20 US) I spent most of the afternoon stowing it all aboard, to be used/kept/watched for the next 6,000 miles, to Durban, South Africa.

In this hot and humid climate our icebox's block of ice would last only a week, if that, so that a strategic campaign had to be planned to eat everything in the correct order. Broccoli and salad first, cauliflower, mushrooms and leeks next—in the first ten days—while carrots and potatoes, assuming they had been grown in a cold enough climate, would last a month or more, with luck. It was the same for the fruit. Everything needed daily checking; but sometimes bad weather and the demands of sailing and consequent tiredness might result in my neglecting this chore. The result could be offensive-smelling rot and deliquescent vegetables or fruit.

In 1973 Susie and Nic had been with us on *Tryste* to help us eat everything we could buy at the trade store. Now instead of their presence we had to make do with their letters, as well as ones from the other girls, Janet on Vancouver Island, and Carol on Saltspring, where Susie and Nic were also still living. Anne and Russ had moved to Port Townsend, Washington State, with their daughter Dana, now seven, and their second daughter Caitlin. We worked hard to complete our letters to catch the mailing on the supply ship and also sent off a plaintive letter about our wandering anchor warp to the commanding officer of HMAS *Perth*.

On our last day there, we settled our accounts at the company office—our harbour dues, modest bar bill and two shopping sprees at the company store. We were rather dismayed to find that this left us with only $200 to reach South Africa.

That evening, we used some of our trade store cornucopia to cook a last shared meal for the *Matavaiis*. Much of the day had been used up in jobs like watering the ship and getting our departure clearance at the Police Station. We had to scurry around. We opened a jar of cray from Tasmania to make starters, prepared the cauliflower and potatoes, made two salads, opened a can of peaches as a base for a fresh fruit salad, and both had showers ashore, all before our guests arrived. For the main course we had bought some silverside (salt beef), which we had learned to love in New Zealand.

Our evening with the *Matavaiis* was a delight. Roger recounted his experiences of learning English as part of his international pilot training. He wondered then if it would really help him be a better pilot, knowing how to say, 'Please pass me my dark stockings,' in English, or learning, 'The weather is beautiful,' but nothing negative, so that he might be flying through a thunderstorm blinded by torrential rain when he gave this misleading report.

Despite our laughter, the evening was tinged with mutual sadness. Our brief friendship with the Blanchard family had been one of those bittersweet experiences that are an integral part of cruising. *Matavaii* was headed for Sri Lanka, then through the Suez Canal into the Med and home to the South of France. Helga and Rolf aboard *Wasa* were also on their way home to Europe by way of the Red Sea. They too had been good companions and we would treasure the memory of Helga at a get-together at the boat club, a little unsteady on her legs (after the hospitality of the company manager's wife, on our trip out to see the birds) as she sat her fairly hefty posterior down with a bang on one edge of a big round table, sending a flock of small round pizzas up into the air from the other side. *Tryste*'s destinations of South Africa and Canada made it unlikely that we would ever meet any of them again.

If we should ever return to Christmas, we would find the island much changed. We had heard that the island's remaining A grade phosphate would soon be uneconomic to mine. There was a government enquiry going on looking into both the economics of the mining and other possible futures for the island. Tourism based on bird-watching or a casino was suggested, as well as market gardening, pig or poultry farming, tropical fish export or fish farming.

Later, after we were back in Canada, we learned that the Australian phosphate company closed the mine in 1987. In 1991 it was bought back by the Worker's Union to ship phosphate to Southeast Asia by mining old stockpiles, but it seemed that tourism was gradually taking over.

Early next morning, as our friends waved us farewell, we finally tore ourselves away from Flying Fish Cove. By late afternoon we had sailed westward along the coast for a few hours and were heading out to sea. Around us there were still some boobies feeding, and high overhead there were small black specks that we knew to be hovering frigate birds.

Christmas Island sank into the sea behind us. We were sorry to be leaving, and saddened too when we picked up the local radio news for the last time and heard, 'The trimaran *Tryste* has left Flying Fish Cove and is continuing on her way around the world.'

CHAPTER SIXTEEN:

'MY FAVOURITE OCEAN' NICKY

We might have expected, after over 15,000 miles of our second world voyage, to have learnt that if you go back to a place that you enjoyed several years ago, it will almost certainly be different. Even if it *seems* the same, *you* will not be, or if you are, the place may have altered physically, since weather, anchorages and even depths may have changed.

We would never forget our frightening night landfall at Cocos Keeling Islands that first time across the Indian Ocean aboard *Tryste*, with Susie and Nicky (17 & 15) as crew; trying to dodge hard-to-see unlit beacons under sail. At least this time it was daylight, but the weather was similar, squalls at the end of the passage clearing suddenly to reveal Cocos surprisingly close. We hastened to pick out Direction Island, which we had to round, and then Horsborough Island well to the north. Thanks to Ernest's celestial navigation we were exactly where we wanted to be, although approaching excitingly fast, even with only reefed main and mizzen, yankee jib and small staysail set.

At twelve knots we roared into the anchorage in a squall, hastily sending down the main and getting a few ties on it, handing jib, stays'l and reefed mizzen, until at the last possible moment Ernest started the motor and I readied the anchor. Two large powerful dolphins had joined the ship just off Cocos, now they escorted *Tryste* all the way into the anchorage, apparently revelling in our only-just-controlled burst of speed as we headed up into the wind. 'Look out!' I shouted foolishly as I dropped the hook almost on top of them, but they were not foolish, and with what could well have been a parting smile, they slipped away.

We looked in amazement at Direction Island. In place of the open grassy area of gracious palm trees, between two of which we remembered Susie hanging out the laundered sheets, there appeared a regimented plantation of serried ranks of much smaller, fat-boled trees. Among these trees we thought we glimpsed bright blue and orange canvas. Was this some sort of a holiday camp? Well, almost.

In 1973, Home Island had been the only inhabited Cocos motu. The Malays who lived there were the descendents of those labourers originally imported by the two Clunies-Ross brothers in the late 1800s to work the copra plantations. Now a colony of over 200 Australians lived and worked on West Island as well. This had been established as a cattle quarantine station by the Australian administration. The workers six-month stay at Cocos, or as most of them seemed to see it, their incarceration there, was mainly to be *endured,* and that only because they could spend roughly one weekend in four on Direction Island camping with their families. A scow from West Island seemed to be on call to bring them relief supplies whenever they ran out of beer or ice. But all this we learned later.

In the shelter of Direction Island, we found three friends tucked well in out of the blustery trade wind: *Invictus, Catriona M,* and smiling independent Julia Hazel on her little red *Jeshan.* We anchored inshore of Julia.

Exhausted as we were by the last gusty twenty-four hours, we settled for an easy dinner helped along by *two* celebratory rum-and-oranges—celebratory because we had never expected to sail in before dark. No wonder I kept falling asleep onto the dinner table. We were turned in by eight.

We never managed to make it ashore next day. First we had to be cleared. A small but heavy tug came alongside from administration on West Island. Ernest was ashamed of me because I shouted,

'Go away! You're too big', with the result that Len, the customs and immigration man, had to take a huge flying leap to land on our deck, briefcase in hand. He landed with a thump and a smile for me, much readier to forgive me than Ernest was. Later I felt justified when we learned that the same boat coming to clear Julia had bent a stanchion on *Jeshan,* 'coming alongside' bow on.

Once the officials had finished with us, we were able to visit aboard our friends' boats. There was water to collect too, in a heavy squall. We filled all our tanks, as well as cans and buckets for laundry, so that we did some of that too. It was an extremely busy day. The other boats in the anchorage all decided to leave and later in the afternoon a Tahiti ketch, *Puki,* came in and anchored.

In the morning we had watched a lighter from West Is. bring a load of Malay children over for a day's outing, turning Direction Island into Brighton Beach. In the late afternoon the lighter collected them and then returned in the early evening with a load of male Aussie workers for their turn of weekend camping, together with mountains of supplies in cold-boxes, and several half-45-gallon drums, which we later found were packed with ice, beer and soft drinks. Marsh and Fran on *Invictus,* whom we had last seen briefly in Darwin, had told us that some of the Australian wives and children were already camping on Direction Island. Their activities were unlikely to impinge on us, we thought.

The day ran out but we were content. We were still tired and turned in by nine. Half an hour later our easy sleep was broken. Some 'Aussie blokes' from on shore had come out in an inflatable, looking for a party.

'Ahoy the yacht! The yacht ahoy!' They shouted as their circled *Tryste,* 'Ahoy the yacht!' They tried again, then, meeting no response, they zoomed over to *Puki* and beerily rounded them, perhaps not realizing that Steve Anderson and Mary Pond, the young American couple aboard, had come in just that day.

'Ahoy the yacht!' They shouted, 'Is there anyone awake?' 'Why don't you come ashore?' There was no response. Back they came to circle us again.

'Ahoy the yacht! Can we come aboard?' 'Would you like a beer?' Finally Ernest stuck his sleepy head out and groaned, 'We're trying to sleep. How about tomorrow?' Disappointed, they went away, and we heard them trying *Puki* one last time, their 'Ahoy the yacht!' blending with our dreams.

We did go ashore next day and visited with the campers, but this was not really a success. They obviously had us tagged as party poopers, and hard as they tried to welcome us and press ice-cold beer or rum and coke on us, they had the glazed look of people trying to listen to a football game and be polite at the same time. In their case we soon realized that it was horse racing, the Australian addiction, that they were obsessed by, which was coming in on an enormous radio in one of the larger tents. We stayed for a while and helped to drink their beer, which was perhaps unkind as it was already disappearing fast and was obviously cause for anxiety.

'Get on the blower,' one said. 'Can't leave it too late,' another agreed seriously; 'It'll be dark by six.'

Leaving them to their horse racing, we walked across the island to the outer reef and gazed at the brilliant blue waves creaming in. On our way back to *Tryste* we came across the big old water tank that we remembered, now much decayed, and the old seaman's refuge, a hut for shipwrecked sailors, which would once have provided shelter and food for a few days. It still contained some dubious food cans including one of corned beef.

We had planned to leave next day but Ernest said, 'Let's not leave today.' I was delighted and agreed at once and went ashore to photograph palm trees. I suppose I should not have been surprised when we sailed out soon after lunch, 'towards Chagos'—creatures of impulse do tend to change their minds a lot.

'It's really not the same as it was, with all those people ashore,' Ernest explained; while ashore, one of the camping Aussies had complained, 'So many yachts come in now. There were twenty-two in the anchorage at one time! Hardly room for us!' Maybe Chagos, some 1,500 miles ahead, would be more like cruising as it used to be.

The huge Chagos archipelago stretches in ambush across the Indian Ocean, below the equator and southwest of Sri Lanka, from roughly 5–8° S. It was one of those places which, when I heard about it, had me catching fire.

'It sounds so *interesting*,' I enthused to Ernest as I read it up in the South Indian Ocean Pilot Book. He, meanwhile, had quietly planned an entirely different, non-Chagos, course across the Indian Ocean. This lack of clear communication was not unusual for us. He thought I had agreed; I thought he had.

The Chagos archipelago, the pilot book told me, spreads almost 180 miles north and south and 120 miles east and west. Simply to sail an equivalent distance either way would be an excellent 24-hour day's run. The archipelago consists of an assorted collection of atolls, shoals, coral reefs and islands dotted around the Great Chagos Bank, a still sunken atoll growing towards the light. Almost invisible, this underwater atoll is the largest in the world, 60 miles by 90. The coral ridge around it is steep-to, with at least 24 feet of water over it at the shallowest point. Inside this sunken 'lagoon' the depth is around 48 fathoms, but it is scattered with isolated coral heads. The whole archipelago is dangerous to approach in bad weather—which is exactly what we were doing in September of 1982 aboard *Tryste*.

Our original plan, on this our second crossing of the Indian Ocean, had been to go up to the Chagos Archipelago from Cocos Keeling and then on to the Seychelles; but hearing that the political situation in the Seychelles had become unstable, we decided not to go there. I still wanted to sail to the Chagos but Ernest wanted to scrub the whole idea and go back to the more southerly route by way of Rodrigues Island and Mauritius.

'Just when I thought I had persuaded you,' Ernest groaned.

It was Patrick's fault that I was digging in my heels of course, his fervour was contagious. Patrick was a South African ex-yachtie we met working on Christmas Island, who spoke in glowing terms of the deserted copra settlements of Perhos Banhos, Egmont and the Salamon groups and of the teeming bird-life on The Three Brothers, the isolated islands inside the bank—and also of the ease with which one could cross the bank to them in good weather. The Pilot Book did not agree but cautioned: '*Vessels should not cross Great Chagos bank when there is much swell on, and [then] only in case of necessity*'.

Our first five days on passage from Cocos to the Chagos were happy, with *Tryste* averaging 160 miles a day under twin poled-out running sails in the glorious Indian Ocean trade winds that we all four—especially Nicky—remembered from our first circumnavigation. By noon of the fifth day, the last happy day of the passage, we were halfway, getting out of the trades and into the doldrum belt. For the last seven days we endured black squalls, rain showers, fickle breezes that suddenly shifted 90 degrees, endless gybing and sail changes, and periods of lying ahull for hours at a time in strong gusty headwinds. Our mercurial spirits plummeted and Ernest became morose and hard to get along with.

On the eleventh day out from Cocos, a miraculous clearing just before noon allowed us our first reliable position fix for seven days and we found that we were only 80 miles off our destination, the east side of Salamon atoll, which lay 20 miles to the northeast of the Chagos Bank. That night we faintly picked up the radio beacon on Diego Garcia, to the south of the Salamons (at that time a top-secret shared British and American military base and a forbidden destination to yachts) which gave us a cross bearing. When our dead reckoning position was 20 miles off the Salamons we pulled down all the sails and lay ahull, closing with the atoll as soon as it was near light next morning. We had hoped the weather would clear, but rainsqualls became heavier and heavier while visibility dropped to less than 50 ft. We crept on, through our thick grey world, with one of us on deck all the time. In my usual craven fashion I begged to abandon the whole idea, but Ernest was made of sterner stuff.

'I like to finish anything I start,' he said grimly. When we believed we still had 5 miles to go, and we were both briefly below, I glanced up from washing dishes to give a yell,

'Land, Ernest! Land!' I had suddenly seen a tiny patch of brush-like grey fuzz centred in the overcast picture in the galley porthole. A moment later it was gone. Without that momentary vision we might have missed the Salamon islands altogether and found ourselves crossing the Great Chagos Bank.

Close hauled we started beating our way north. Rain poured down and we were soon drenched inside and out, our oilskins useless against such torrents. Before long, more wind forced us to reef both main and mizzen. We were still doing about ten knots, closing fast with a big grey island Ernest identified as Boddam, on the southwest corner of Salamon atoll. Suddenly the wind boxed the compass, rain poured down with mind-numbing force, and we were completely disoriented. We had never seen such rain. We scurried to hand all sail, and then let *Tryste* lie-to until the worst of it passed through.

Under way again, Ernest demanded rum in our mid-morning coffee. As I shakily handed him a well-laced mug I looked at the time. Although it *felt* like mid-morning with so much extreme living going on it was not yet even 0900. To me it now seemed so frighteningly dangerous that I again suggested abandoning Chagos, but Ernest, at his most comforting, said he thought we could safely find our way in. The entrance passage to the Salamon lagoon was north and east of a long island, Isle Anglaise, on its western reef. We set sail again and, hard on the wind, sailed up the coast until, just as another super-squall came blindingly in, we hastily dropped all sail, turned on the motor, and anchored in a small patch of poor-holding sand, just inside the pass into the lagoon.

At noon, when the overcast thinned, and the coral heads showed up well enough, we crossed the lagoon to a spot between two islands on the eastern reef, Takamara and Fouquet, and anchored in a small patch of coral sand which Patrick had marked on our chart.

Once arrived, after such a dramatic landfall, my inclination is always to lie down, preferably for several hours. Ernest, once fed, is eager to explore. Patrick had given us a rough plan of the atoll, and on Takamara had marked huts and fruit trees, but his visit had been several years ago. When Ernest went ashore, leaving me comatose, he found only 'thick jungle-like palm tree rainforest.' He came back declaring the island (and by inference the whole Chagos archipelago) 'A dead loss.' We were both so depressed that we even considered turning round and leaving immediately. We were neither of us in a fit condition to realize that we were simply exhausted by the difficult passage.

The next day the sun came out and Salamon atoll was a wonderful place to be, an Indian Ocean extravaganza of svelte palm trees reaching for the sky, of aqua lagoon waters sparkling over huge coral heads and of tiny desert islands of brilliant green and white. Walking on the beach of Takamara was a joy, with friendly fairy terns and noddies flying overhead wondering who we were, even though, as Ernest had claimed, the amazing tropical growth of volunteer coconut palms and vines made the island impenetrable without a machete.

Like all the islands in the groups of the archipelago, Takamara was an overgrown copra plantation, abandoned between 1965 and 1971. All the indigenous inhabitants had been removed and resettled in Mauritius, when Diego Garcia was leased to the US as a top secret, combined American and British base.

With the clearer weather we were able to sail the length of the coral-floored lagoon to Boddam Island. A large US ketch, *Don Quixote*, was anchored in the coral well offshore, but with our shallow draft we were able to anchor in a patch of sand closer in, near the remains of a small concrete jetty. We soon met the captain of the ketch, Don Stewart, who told us of their welcome at Diego Garcia. They had entered there in search of a new alternator. In spite of being a U.S. boat, they were boarded and told bluntly,

'Neither the British nor the Americans want you here. You may stay 24 hours and then please GO. You may not go ashore.' They pleaded a marine emergency and did get their alternator, but after working on the motor for four days they were shouted at by an irate Royal Navy Commander.

'OUT!' He yelled, and out they went. Whatever was going on at Diego Garcia was obviously clandestine. Surveillance ships circled the island groups. From time to time patrol boats appeared in the atolls and the yachts were forcefully told to sail on.

Boddam settlement was a perfect deserted village. Close by the jetty we found the dilapidated shell of the manager's two-storey house, with touches of past elegance still showing in the remains of its curving staircase and gilt paneled doors. Other houses were scattered around, together with a church with stained glass windows but no roof, a bakery, a four-room jail, a store and one long building, dated 1897, where a cupboard full of outdated drugs marked it as the hospital.

Not far away we found a path leading to a large area of old copra-drying sheds, and stumbled over the rusty remains of small stubby rail cars and half-buried narrow-gauge rails leading into and through a large open shed. This contained a strange miscellany ready for a vagabond's garage sale: bamboo poles, a bath of engine oil and a dead outboard; as well as an oar and a piece of sail, obviously connected to earlier yachties. Odder items were: a baby's bottle and a high chair, an old desk and some painted kitchen chairs, as well as a mandala, a pair of handsome pews from the church, a pile of faded fabric, a book on meditation and some hippie beads and sticks of incense. Inside several of the houses there was evidence that notwithstanding the naval patrols; some yachties had spent months there.

We could understand the attraction of this back-to-the-land solitude, although for us the climate was too hot and humid. There were fish and crabs to be had as well as coconuts and breadfruit, and in one of the houses there were big wallboard charts, marking the position of wells and fruit trees, in both English and French, not only in the Salamon atoll but also on Perhos Banhos to the west. Following the paths between the Boddam houses we soon found and picked both oranges and lemons.

Don and his crew, Phil and Dori, came over from *Don Quixote* for a drink of rum and orange, and we planned to share a barbecue the next day; but when the time came we all backed down. We had none of us caught enough fish; the wind was blowing into the anchorage; and *Don Quixote* had decided to leave the following day and wanted to make an early start. Dori was disappointed as she had already started cooking a big pot of rice for the meal, but she cheered up when I gave her some sugar that they needed and our good bread recipe, which she had asked for.

Abandoning Boddam to its past, we threaded our way through the coral heads, with Ernest on lookout on the spreaders, back to Fouquet and Takamara motus. Here, off Fouquet, we snorkelled together in a sea-garden of delight over a wide variety of corals: chunky brain and mushroom, interspersed with finer corals like seaweed, flowers and branches. Fish of every colour of the spectrum, totally unafraid of us, darted in and out of their myriad homes and hiding places. A small school of mauve-green parrot fish with over-made-up lips kept us company as we swam along the edge of the fringing reef and clouds of tiny creamy-lemon ones floated over big mustard-brown boulders stuffed with reef clams. Small damselfish in electric blue hovered curiously in front of our faces while butterfly fish, their fins ending in long trailing filaments, hung head-down, nibbling and chewing coral polyps, like so many tethered balloons.

We tore ourselves away from this most indolently pleasurable swimming, where the water temperature varied from blood heat to almost-too-hot, because we wanted to see more of the archipelago. We decided to move on while the weather was fine, choosing Egmont atoll to the southwest for our next stop, rather than nearer Perhos Banhos, which was larger, deeper and more exposed.

This fitted in with my longing to see the Three Brothers Islands and all the birds Patrick had told us about, that I had set my heart on. Ernest thought this a foolish yearning, 'We probably won't be able to land, you know,' he said, but I just wanted to *see* them. It was our old problem of the romantic dreamer versus the pragmatic realist navigator. In spite of this he was prepared to try to get there for me; consistent with *Tryste's* safety. He planned to cut across the northwest edge of the Chagos Bank to the Egmonts, by way of the Three Brothers.

Fairy terns circled our sails in farewell as we sailed out of the pass. Outside we found a fresh south southeasterly. We were soon hard on the wind and quite unable to fetch the Egmont islands without beating our way almost due south into the Chagos Bank. With no wish to do this, we both accepted defeat. No Three Brothers, no bird colonies, but the course that the wind was forcing on us was almost perfect for

Mauritius, 1,200 miles ahead, which had the added lure that there perhaps we might find mail from the family.

Sadly we accepted the fact that Chagos, that large and remarkable Indian Ocean experience, would in our minds forever mean only Salamon atoll and its memory-haunted settlement of Boddam, together with some of the dirtiest, nastiest, most continuously squally weather that we had ever met.

CHAPTER SEVENTEEN:

CLOAK AND DAGGER DAYS

We had abandoned Chagos for Mauritius, 1,200 miles away, shortly after breakfast and had soon picked up the southeast trades. By noon we had covered 30 miles, with our first noon-to-noon position the following day of another 180. This surely was the 'dynamite weather' that we remembered from 1973: 180 miles with the main reefed all night! We were both well content as *Tryste* rolled over the waves, close-hauled but comfortable enough. The wind had increased gradually so that the seas never became extreme; few broke over the cabin trunk even though *Tryste* had begun to speed up to 9 and 10 knots. We made landfall almost before we could get our breath, arriving in just under eight days with a daily average of 156 miles.

In the dark early morning we sailed past Grand Bay on Mauritius' north coast where we would anchor later. By the time it was my watch, dawn was breaking and Port Louis with its fantastic skyline of old volcanic mountains lay ahead, with all the lights of the port still showing and 3 or 4 large vessels lying off. We sailed in towards the leading lights but just as we approached, lost the back one when they turned all the lights out. We decided to hand our sails and wait until it became light enough to pick out the now-unlit leads. Heading in, we left big black and white mooring buoys to starboard all down the entrance channel right into the boat pool.

The officials cleared us quickly and courteously, although Customs kept us waiting so long that finally Ernest stomped off to the bank. This was no problem when Customs finally appeared. I filled in the forms and everyone was happy, at least Customs and I were; Ernest at the bank was not. He had gone off confidently with his MasterCard, but found that they did not accept it. They suggested that he could use a cheque form from his Canadian bank. He rowed back aboard for the chequebook but then discovered that they would give him only $50. Perhaps, we thought, we might be luckier in Grand Bay, for we intended to sail out again as soon as we had cleared and been to the Post Office, and visited Port Louis' crowded Indian market for cheap fruit and vegetables.

At the P.O. we found letters from four out of five daughters. Only Nicky's was missing. Carol and Gerry were back on Saltspring, living in the Barn with four-year-old Rhiannon, and expecting our fourth grandchild any day. We planned to phone home before we left Mauritius. Anne and Russ and Dana and their new baby Caitlin, who had been born in England in 1980, were living in La Conner, Washington State. They had bought a thirty-six-foot classic motor launch called *Glory Be,* built in 1914, and were living aboard her.

Before leaving the bank Ernest asked them to send a telex to our Ganges bank. We were asking for only another $100, a pathetic amount but enough, we hoped, to get us to South Africa. The Mauritian bank teller assured him it would take only four working days.

The fourteen miles back up the coast to Grand Bay was a blustery sail, a hard beat in fresh southeast winds with williwaws whistling down the valleys between the spiky mountain peaks. Halfway along we met *Jeshan* running back to Port Louis reefed right down, with nothing much of Julia showing but her sun visor and foul weather gear.

A squall hit us as we entered Grand Bay, splitting the top seam of the mizzen. We handed both it and the genoa, turned the engine on and at full throttle, motoring into the teeth of the wind and making little more than 2 knots, we entered the bay, carefully avoiding the drying reefs to either side.

Roughly 15 overseas yachts, many of whom we already knew, including *Invictus* and *Puki,* lay in the bay off the yacht club, and we anchored to seaward of them all, grateful for the good holding when squalls and heavy showers hammered at us overnight. The Grand Bay Yacht Club made us welcome with hot showers, cold drinks and a pleasant lounge area, while water and diesel were available at a concrete jetty. Inexpensive buses ran from a few minutes walk away into Port Louis, but most stores were available locally and there was delicious French bread baked daily.

After a few days we began making enquiries about our telex and received a sympathetic hearing from the kindly bank manager in Grand Bay who allowed us $50 each on the strength of our MasterCards.

Soon after our arrival in Grand Bay we were invited to a pineapple party on board *Invictus*. We had, probably mistakenly after a short acquaintance, pegged Americans Marsh and Fran as non-drinkers. Marsh with his white hair and beard and his open cheerful character and tendency to nod off, was both a Rotarian and a super-keen ham (amateur) radio operator. He took their yacht's name from the W.E.Henley poem of the same name, *Invictus*, but whether Marsh really believed himself to be the master of his fate and captain of his soul, as the poem said, we never found out.

Fran too was respectable and well-dressed, so we were not in the least surprised when the party turned out to be a non-alcohol pineapple-eating treat with much-nicer-than-us people like Steve and Mary off *Puki*, Julia from *Jeshan* and the two Austrians Ossie and Linda aboard *Windward*, whom we had met only briefly in the Cocos anchorage. The party centred on fresh pineapple, cored and cut in slices, which we dipped in thick whipped cream and then demerara sugar. When the slices were well coated we cooked them over spirit lamps until a delicious crust formed rather like toasted marshmallows.

Julia had sailed back in, the day after we arrived in Grand Bay, and she and I soon decided to use the cheap buses to see more of Mauritius and, we hoped, get some good pictures. Ernest was feeling out of sorts (another way of saying anti-social) and decided not to join us. We set off to cross the island by bus, hoping to reach the resort area of Mahebourg on the east coast.

On the outskirts of Port Louis bougainvillea and flamboyant trees grew lushly. Small houses lined the road, often with Buddhist shrines with red prayer flags fluttering in front of them. Behind these small houses stood even smaller shacks made of beaten tin or corrugated iron and these too were houses, with opening board windows and red mud floors, the red volcanic soil having made a wash in the rainy season a couple of feet up the outside walls. Miraculously, out of this primitive housing emerged women in spotless saris, children in crisp cottons and men in neat slacks and starched white shirts. Laundry hung drying on every available bush and wall. We wondered how on earth the women managed it when all water had to be carried from a communal tap.

We passed a large mosque like a pink and white iced cake, even to the blobs of pink icing on the gateposts, with the message, 'There is no conqueror but Allah', in the glass over the doorway; and further on a tall Hindu temple, intricately decorated and painted.

As we drove up into the mountains towards the inland town of Flacq we were mentally marking out places where good pictures could be taken if we left the bus to photograph on the return journey. As we climbed up and up, the brilliant green of sugarcane predominated in the fields, sometimes with lines of enormous black volcanic boulders collected between the rows of cane. We passed areas growing tea, as well as others of coffee and tobacco; Indian women in cotton saris doing laundry in a wide boulder strewn stream backed by grey-green mountains; tiny boys herding flocks of innumerable goats or Brahma cattle ten times their size; and oxcarts carrying sugar cane, people, or loads of rubbish, which sometimes calmly blocked the bus's way.

In Flacq the bus stopped in a crowded market and everyone else disembarked, but Julia and I were firmly restrained by the driver then courteously driven to a cleaner, drier section of the market to alight. To judge by the interest we excited, not many tourists achieved the heights of Flacq. No doubt Julia's long blonde hair contributed largely to the stares.

We bought huge buns and a hand of bananas for our lunch and soon boarded another bus, this one to Curepipe to the southwest, right across the middle of the island. In Curepipe we hoped to catch a third bus and head southeast to Mahebourg. But in Curepipe it started to rain, gently at first but then in big round drops, which soon became sheets. We could not explore the town in such pouring rain, let alone take pictures, and there seemed no point in going on. Rather sadly we climbed aboard a bus that would complete our clockwise circle back to Port Louis.

Sitting in the front seat, the only empty one, we were soon almost asphyxiated by exhaust fumes coming up through open floorboards while Julia was also attacked by drips coming down through the roof. Luckily the ancient noisy engine started coughing and backfiring and in a cloud of smoke the driver drew off the road and turned off the motor. A brand new bus soon arrived and we all boarded it and reached Port Louis safely. Since we never managed to take any photos in the pouring rain our pictures had to be committed to memory, but at least we saw some of inland Mauritius.

We spent two weeks in Grand Bay in all, waiting for news of our money and Carol's baby. We found that we could not call Canada collect. Perhaps we would be luckier in Réunion, which was only 145 miles further on. A few days before we left, Ernest swam to scrub *Tryste's* bottom. I swam to help for a few hours each day but lacked Ernest's stamina. Poor *Tryste*! She had virtually no copper paint left and was growing gardens of weed, especially near the waterline where it would not come clean. Ernest managed to finish it himself on the third day, leaving us both with earache.

We celebrated his 56th birthday by going out to dinner, which partly made up for the disaster of a special teatime treat that I had made him, a yearned-after memory of yeasty Yorkshire teacakes. Unfortunately I made them with salt instead of sugar.

Before we left Grand Bay we had dinner with *four* singlehanders. We had first met Wolf Dietrich, who provided the venue on *White Dolphin*, in New Zealand, but we had not met Bernie Marshall before, a short stocky Kiwi with sandy beard and hair, although we had seen his small yacht *Cautelle* in Darwin. Julia on *Jeshan* was the third and the fourth was Jeannique Le Nénaon on the French yacht *Jonathon*. She had caught a dorado on the way up to Grand Bay and we were all invited to dinner to share the *poisson cru* that she had made. Ernest and I combined with Julia to produce a large fresh fruit salad; Bernie brought some duty-free Bailey's Irish Cream, while Wolf Dietrich, not noted for his extreme generosity, surprised us by producing a bottle of good local wine.

We aboard *Tryste*, as well as *Jeshan* and *Invictus*, were all soon leaving for Réunion. Our sixteen days in Mauritius had been frustrating time, since the hoped for baby telegram never arrived, neither did our telexed-for-money. We were not really surprised that there were still glitches in the Indian Ocean. Mauritius was now a parliamentary republic, albeit still within the Commonwealth, while Réunion was a little piece of France. Perhaps we should have more luck there.

We sailed back to Port Louis to clear, leaving next day at 0700 and covering the 145 miles to Réunion comfortably in less than 24 hours, arriving at dawn and entering as the pink sky of sunrise outlined Réunion's peaks. These were even more spectacular than those of

Mauritius, since Réunion boasts the highest point of the Indian Ocean, *Piton des Neiges*. At 3,000 metres this mountain is half as high as Mount Kilimanjaro and is tipped with snow each winter. As we sweltered on Réunion we found this hard to believe.

The island is so steep-to that there are no natural harbours at all, but there are two man-made ports, *Port des Galets* on the northwest coast and the one at St Pierre in the south. The entry to *Port des Galets* (known as '*Le Port*') was straightforward, but led into a horribly grimy, concrete-lined commercial harbour. Visiting yachts had to lie alongside large black hard-rubber cyclone fenders chained to high walls. Further inshore there *was* an inner yacht basin, but this was crammed with local boats and just a few overseas ones with no room for us. We lay in *Le Port*, with conditions horribly unsuitable for a thin-skinned vulnerable trimaran, along with Julia and several other across-the-Indian-Ocean friends.

Passers-by on the dock immediately warned us to lock our boat, which we did each time we left but not overnight when we were aboard. 'Watch out for teefs', someone suggested helpfully. A passing French matelot advised, 'You'd be better off in St Pierre.' Failing that, he suggested, why not tie alongside the *Kli Kli*, a Yugoslav yacht with no one aboard, advice that Ernest thought made most sense and acted on. Here we would also be further from the noisy nightclubs and fish boat generators along the wharf.

I thought we would be better off in St Pierre, although, as always, my reasons were more those of a dreamer than of a realist. I remembered what Patrick had told us on Christmas Island about Réunion: about the unique *cirques*, the amphitheatres high in the mountains that were long-extinct volcanic cones whose craters had collapsed, leaving almost vertical cliffs. Here whole villages were reputed to live out their lives with no contact with the outside world.

I knew that if we were anchored in St. Pierre, nearer to the *cirques*, Julia would be game to go looking for them with me. But, 'Patrick again!' Ernest snorted and being practical, took more heed of stories of the famous blind rollers which could suddenly appear out of nowhere and could close either port for several days or exceptionally in St Pierre, for as long as three weeks. This was most unlikely now since these rollers were most prevalent in the cyclone season, but it was a risk Ernest would not consider.

Yet would it really have mattered if we had been weather-bound for as much as four or five days? Not as far as I was concerned, although on the other hand, knowing that Ernest *time-to-be-moving-on* Haigh would become impatient and frustrated under such conditions it was, realistically, probably all for the best. An impatient and frustrated Ernest was, 'Not an 'appy one.' It was also a consideration that at *Port des Galets* we were considerably nearer to St. Denis, the capital of Réunion, where we had to go for our South African visas.

However we were all eager to see the small walled harbour of St Pierre to the southeast, and took a bus trip, en famille, on the Sunday that we spent in Réunion. 'The family' then consisted of Marsh and Fran from *Invictus*; Julia and a girl crew, Joey, whom she had signed on rather doubtfully in Mauritius to crew aboard *Jeshan* to South Africa; Steve and Mary from *Puki*; and us from *Tryste*.

On the bus trip up into the highlands, 'Les hauts', and down again to St. Pierre, the flame trees seemed further out than those in Mauritius and hibiscus, frangipani, bougainvillea and jacaranda trees bloomed vividly. In the small neat villages in the highlands the gardens were bright with roses, phlox and geraniums, the last of which are grown commercially on the island for perfume oil. We saw no sign of the extreme poverty that seemed to exist in Mauritius—after all Réunion had become a full overseas *département* and administrative Region of France in 1972, with all the benefits that such a status implied.

On the winding twisty roads the big modern coach-type bus demanded right of way on the corners, some of which were so sharp that the bus was right across the road. Sadly the higher mountains were shrouded in mist. As in Mauritius, the huge gullies, where rivers of water thundered down torrentially in the wet season, were now spectacular dry gulches, while down at sea level they were great empty dry beds of gravel-like boulders.

After we alighted from the bus in the sunshine of St. Pierre, we soon found the harbour and its entrance from the sea that we had all wanted to see. The harbour basin itself was like a small English south coast port, walled and crowded, with old cannons for decoration on the seawall. The entrance was narrow but looked unremarkable in the calm sunny morning. Nearby we found a sandy beach full of topless sunbathers, just like France. As well there were little children making sand-castles, just like Brighton. Fran wanted to find the yacht club and someone to change her dollars to francs. Soon some yacht club members were found, happy to exchange money for Fran and Julia, and they kindly opened up the tiny Yacht Club building so that we could as they put it delicately, '*Lave les mains.*'

Back in *Port des Galets* we had our first experience of cloak and dagger involvement. When we left the Chagos archipelago for Mauritius, we had not intended to go to Réunion, but sitting aboard *Invictus* talking to Marsh in Mauritius' Grand Bay we first learned that it might be advisable to go there for a visa for South Africa.

We had never in our cruising lives needed such a thing before, anywhere we had been, and at first Ernest was frankly sceptical, but we well knew that life had been simpler back in the early 1970s. Bearing in mind that when we reached Durban we wanted to go inland to a game park and did not want to have to put down a bond, as South African friends had kindly done for us in 1973, it might be wise.

It sounded simple enough. 'It only takes an hour', or so Marsh's friend Chuck on *Albatross* had assured him on the local ham network. He had also given Marsh an address in Réunion to go to. Innocently we imagined this to be the street address of the SA Consulate and had not bothered to ask Marsh for it. There would be time enough to do that in Réunion, we thought.

The day after our jaunt to St. Pierre, we all agreed that we would catch the bus to St. Denis, Réunion's capital on the northwest coast, first thing on Monday morning. Ernest and I anticipated a great day. We would catch the early bus, do a little shopping, go to the bank, phone the family back in Canada, and then go to the SA Consulate and get our visas.

The bus left at seven a.m. but the bus stop was farther away than we had thought and we left hardly enough time to get there. It was an out of breath collection of nice white Caucasians with good manners who assembled at the bus stop along with a collection of local people heading for the market or to work in St Denis. The seven o'clock bus, when it came, had already picked up passengers from St Pierre and along the way. We had not expected that, nor had we expected to have to push and shove our way on. None of us got on the first two buses but we all took note, and when the next one came along at seven-thirty we fought our way onto it vigorously. We may have looked relatively pale and effete but our survival skills had been well honed across the Indian Ocean.

St. Denis, when we disembarked, seemed a handsome, surprisingly large city with trees and flowers and open green spaces. Situated on the St. Denis River it was coastal but had no harbour, only an open roadstead. Most of us wanted to go to a bank before hitting the Consulate and, this being France, the banks were already open. We split up and went our own ways. We would meet later at the SA Consulate. We still had not bothered to ask for the address; perhaps we were already too hot to think straight.

Once we had bought some groceries, Ernest and I asked our way to *'Le Bureau de Poste'* where we found the right wicket and tried to book a collect call to Canada. Our French was barely adequate but we did know the French for 'call collect' and there was no doubt about the unequivocal *'Non.'* We then managed to elicit that we could call for three minutes for 79 francs. We had only 50 left with us, although we had another 100 francs back on *Tryste*. Ernest was furious and I was horribly disappointed. But we were sure we would be able to get another $50 each on our MasterCards. We asked where the nearest bank was and managed to understand the answer. Aha! But at the bank, having been passed on from a helpful but inexperienced girl teller to an unhelpful but more knowledgeable male, the answer was another, *'Non'*. There is something doubly negative about the French, *'Non.'* All was not lost though: he suggested we try the *Banque Populaire*.

At the *Banque Populaire* a charming blonde girl regretted, but she would ask her superior. Her superior regretted, but would ask his superior, all in French, finally the soft gentle girl was *'désolé'*, and told us, 'No,' and in broken English sent us to another bank. She was so sorry but almost certainly the other bank would be able to help us.

At the other (third) bank they were surprised. Not us, said the teller (in French), but try the BNP, round the corner. All banks tend to look the same from the outside—up to the counter, oh no! We were back with the unhelpful male #1. The buck had been passed full circle.

Hot and frustrated we decided to go back to the Post Office and look up the address of the RSA Consulate and hope to catch up with our friends there. There was only one public phone directory in this main post office of the capital city of a region of France with a population at that time of around 200,000.

Stressed by other people lining up behind us to use it, we started looking. We searched for SA Consulate, RSA Consulate, *Ambassade,* Consul, *Consueil,* and finally Agent. Perhaps we should be looking in the yellow pages? We tried, but that particular yellow page was missing.

Ernest, already upset, was now getting impatient with me as well, the inevitable tension between us mounting. The sweat poured off us both. Taking pity on us, the girl behind the counter lent us her brand new telephone directory complete with all its yellow pages. But wait! The yellow pages offered NO embassies. In despair we wrote down what we were looking for and appealed to the same girl behind the counter. Like us she couldn't find it. She tried the phone operator who would find out for us in *'cinq minutes.'*

How could we find the others if we could not find the address? It still had not occurred to us that we could not find the address because Apartheid was still rife in South Africa and any South African was persona non grata in Réunion. Later we were to find out that the Consulate had an unlisted phone number and an unmarked, hidden away office.

As we turned away from the counter, Marsh and Fran and Julia walked in. Mafeking was relieved! We poured out our troubles and Marsh immediately offered us their phone credit card, but on second thoughts realised that it would probably not be accepted, so offered to lend us the money instead. Julia also offered to lend us the money, but Ernest suddenly developed scruples—he just did not want to borrow—on principle. I thought he was mad! After all we had those 100 francs back on *Tryste*. In the end he weakened and borrowed the huge sum of 29 francs we needed to make our 3-minute phone call. We disappeared into number two wooden phone booth to wait for our overseas connection and in less than a minute our phone rang and there was a Canadian operator; and then Carol's partner Gerry,

'Oh Gerry,' I said, 'have you got a baby yet?'

'No!'

'Have you got any of the girls there?'

I handed the phone over to Ernest who spoke to a sleepy Carol and bombarded her with words off the crib card we had brought with us. He established that everyone was well and told her how we had no money, and then passed the phone back to me. She sounded wonderful, but by now the whole stressful business had gone on too long, and I just wept with frustration and distress,

'We love you,' I sobbed, and she handed me over to Nicky. She too sounded great: warm and loving,

'We love you.'

'You *must* stop,' Ernest said. Our time was up! So that was our phone call. Well, it was done and we had made contact and we could relax about the baby, as Ernest had told them to send a cable to Durban. If we could just get our visas we could leave next day.

With Marsh's inside knowledge from Chuck, and after a few false starts, we found the Insurance Building where, he told us, they would show us to the Consulate. This seemed very strange, but the woman there took it for granted and calmly led the way through some back streets to the back of what looked like a block of apartments. There was no sign at all to show that this was the Consulate. There were no nameplates anywhere. She spoke into a small entry-phone on the wall above the door, the door opened and a small smiling black man took us in charge. He led the way upstairs turning on a timed light on the way up and then pressing a three-tone buzzer above which was another intercom.

Once he had announced us the door opened into an outer office where we found the rest of 'the family'. This office was totally lined with mirrors, apart from one wall, which boasted a large, presumably bullet-proof, glass wall. Behind this sat a black secretary-receptionist. In the wall was set a double-round sort of ventilator to speak into, and at desk height there was a sealed well where you put your papers and passport which then moved through to the other side. Our naïve amazement at all this would not exist nowadays when banks and airports are often similarly equipped. But we were more than a year out from home and, looking back, as innocent as babes.

Eventually the receptionist pressed a button under the desk and we were admitted to the inner secretarial office and waiting room, where we could lounge on comfortable chairs and sofas to fill out the application forms that a bilingual white woman gave us. We found that we needed our passports, extra passport photos and our ship's papers. Although Marsh and Fran had everything they needed they wanted to keep their passports to clear immigration, so all of us had to come back next day. Outside Ernest pressured me to say whether I could find our two spare passport photos back aboard *Tryste*. I could only say that I was 99% sure that I could, and that we *did not need* to get new ones, so we went off to catch the bus back to *Le Port* and *Tryste*, disappointed that we could not leave next day. Julia and *Puki's* Steve and Mary went off to get photos, while Marsh and Fran went shopping.

Later we heard that not only was Julia's girl crew Joey being difficult, other friends were having troubles too. Ann and Dan Roberts on *Shoestring*, another of the Indian Ocean crossers, had also found an extra crew, Pierre, to sail with them to Durban, and the tricky passage round the Cape of Good Hope to Cape Town; but Pierre, like Joey, either could not or would not purchase an air ticket to his homeland, an essential to acquiring a visa; while still expecting to sail as crew.

That afternoon Ernest went off to try and sweet-talk the Port Captain about port dues, explaining that it had been our intention to leave at 8 am next day, but we couldn't, because we had to go back into St Denis then to collect our visas, but that we would leave as soon as were back aboard *Tryste*.

'Oh no, you won't,' the Port Captain told him in French. 'You *cannot* leave later.' He went on to explain that the port was closed daily because of dredging operations, from 8 am until 4.30 in the afternoon. In the end we had to pay for only two days (at 79 francs, about $12 US) since everyone had the first day free. Perhaps it helped that Ernest had started his parley by reporting that we had had a thief aboard the night before and asking, 'Is that what we are paying for?'

It had been just before midnight that I woke because I thought I heard Ernest go on deck. At the same moment Ernest heard the grating at the bottom of the companionway creak, woke fuzzily and saw a figure 'frozen', backlit by the dock lights, near the galley cook-stove. The man, medium height, dark skin, small moustache, said something which Ernest took to be a request for cigarettes. 'You want a cigarette?' Ernest asked courteously. The man spoke again; it sounded to me as if it ended up with, 'Galets'. By this time I was a bit less confused, and annoyed with what I saw as Ernest's idiotic courtesy. Naked under only a sheet, I propped myself up on my elbow and shouted:

'What the hell are you doing here?' The response was gratifying. The cat burglar, 'teef', or whatever he was, sprang out of the companionway and in a couple of bounds was across *Kli-Kli* and off and running down the quay with Ernest leaping out of the companionway to see where he had gone. It was only then that I saw Ernest's untouched wallet on the saloon table. Perhaps we were a little *too* casual. We lay down again and tried to settle but then Ernest decided that he should wake everyone else up and warn them. He found that most of them were locked up tight although the schooner *St Michel* was wide open like us; but her skipper, Joachim, was awake and casually unconcerned. Later he did find a local man asleep on *St. Michel's* deck, but assuming him to be sleeping off a drunk, just let him stay till morning.

We knew that Steve and Mary were having Immigration come aboard *Puki* at 8.30 next morning, so we decided to stay aboard and have *Tryste* cleared too before going on to the Consulate. Ernest had given Julia our completed application forms and asked her to hand them in for us, in hopes of speeding things up as she was going there first thing, but when we finally found our way there, the forms were missing.

We had all planned to meet there at 2 pm to see the Consul, so once again we found ourselves wandering round St Denis hot and frustrated and without enough spare cash to buy a decent lunch; waiting for it to be 2 o'clock. As I was complaining about being hungry we bought a chocolate bar and some expensive milk from Paris to keep us going. Then, searching for a pleasant place to eat, wandered down to a boulder-strewn, hot, dirty beach, found a large rock to sit on and had our lunch. We sulked about how badly life was treating us and squabbled about nothing, and made up and tried harder, but there was no shade and it was much too hot in the full sun and we were miserable. We walked back to a small park we had noticed earlier where there was a little cool shade. We tried to be friends but were obviously not doing too well as an old grizzled black man approached us, and in sign language offered us some of his lunch. Too kind, we thought, but we declined and moved on.

About 1.30 we tried the Consulate again and there was Fran, and there was Julia, very apologetic, with our papers! We were all allowed into the inner sanctum where we could sit in comfort until the Consul could deal with us. He made a brief appearance and apologised for keeping us all waiting. Madame had provided a big heap of a Johannesburg newspaper and the South African yearbook to mollify us. We learned that Tuesday was always a bad day, since all Mauritian applications came in on that day and by arrangement had to be dealt with first. The Consul asked to see Pierre and had a long interview with him, then

Dan asked to speak to him and then he interviewed Julia about Joey. By this time both *Shoestring* and *Jeshan* had had second thoughts and made this plain, and so it worked out. Neither would-be-crew member could fulfil the requirements, neither one obtained a visa.

Back in *Port des Galets* we shopped for 1 bottle of wine, 1 loaf of bread and 1 packet of biscuits with our last scraped up 18 francs. Then back aboard *Tryste* to some oh-so-much-appreciated cups of tea, an easy supper, and too much rum and wine to celebrate tomorrow's freedom. When we reached South Africa we found that we did not need a visa. We were not too surprised.

While there was still daylight we walked along the harbour mole to the thatched watchtower and saw breakers rolling in over the shallow water to starboard of the harbour entrance—finally, the famous blind rollers. We hurried back to *Tryste* for cameras. There was not much light by the time we returned, but there was enough for one recorded image each.

That last night in Réunion, *Shoestring's* Ann and Dan had been invited out to dinner and had asked us to keep an eye, or rather an ear, on their boat, as they had rigged a bell as a burglar-alarm. They had heard that Pierre was in the bar and threatening vengeance about being dumped.

We both slept fitfully at first but then fell into a deep sleep. When our clock sounded four bells, I leapt out of bed shouting, 'The bell, Ernest! The bell!' Unlike me, Ernest wakes well and in complete control of his faculties, but I was fully awake by now too and realised what I had heard. I fell back into my bunk laughing helplessly, but Ernest, like Queen Victoria, was definitely not amused.

CHAPTER EIGHTEEN:

RIDING THE AGULHAS

The passage to Durban from Réunion was 1,650 miles of big seas and dirty weather: the most dangerous stretch of our chosen route across the Indian Ocean from Australia. We soon found that we had left behind the strong, steady trade winds. From now on it would be 'anything goes' for both wind strength and direction.

The second day out seemed almost picture perfect at first. Small white horses covered the sea, and a gentle steady east southeasterly blew out of a clear blue sky. It seemed like a good start to a passage to me, a chance to get everything squared around before we met any real weather. Ernest, however, decided to be disappointed with our slow progress. He was annoyed with himself; since at noon sight he discovered that the day before he had marked off the wrong course. I wondered why it mattered so much at this stage of the passage, but realised that this man of mine who claimed to be 'not in the least competitive,' was, incredibly, on only the second day of the passage, worrying about arriving in Durban the last of our Réunion group.

We were soon reminded that the Western Indian Ocean was a wild place with unpredictable wind, sea, and currents, which nearing South Africa could include the north/south wind switch, of our old friend, the southerly buster. This strong and changeable wind had provided us with one of our most frightening landfalls ever, back in 1973. But first we had to round the south end of Madagascar, the fifth largest island in the world.

On our fifth day out, as we approached the island's southeast coast, we found that we could not hold our course. We had planned to sail south of the 274 fathom shoaling area reputed to create dangerously unpredictable rollers, that lay southwest of Madagascar, but with the southwesterly blowing dead on the nose, and big ground swells coming up from the south, we soon found we were being pushed much closer to Madagascar.

Ernest discovered, after more anguished attention to the Pilot Book, that to sail closer to the coast of Madagascar should at least give us the benefit of the south and west-running Madagascar current. It looked on the chart as if where we were now—heading 40 to 60 miles south of Madagascar—we should pass well north of the danger area. We knew that once we had cleared *Cap Sainte Marie*, Madagascar's most southerly point, we should be able to steer roughly 270° for Durban across the Mozambique Channel. We would hope to be well on the way across before the next wind switch came along.

By evening the wind had backed into the southeast, creating enormous cresting seas. That night and all next morning we overrode the self-steering where necessary to help *Tryste* cope with these awe-inspiring seas that we had found, as they heaped up into extraordinary pinnacles and broke from every confused direction and rolled into *Tryste* broadside while the main body of water broke behind her. At noon next day, when Ernest took his sun sight, we found that we had been carried 30 miles further south than we had expected. No wonder he had called the seas obscene: we must have passed over or very near that 274-fathom patch. By a late lunchtime the rollers were beginning to become rather more regular and lengthen out and we managed, just about, to have lunch together; we had had to take turns at breakfast while *Tryste* needed to have her hand held.

Now that we were running almost straight downwind in heavy seas, we tried to set one of the twin running sails, but the wind was too much up the tail to keep it filled, while handing it and setting the storm jib did not provide enough drive. Having to spend more than usual time on deck had its plus side, it gave us the joy of seeing a wonderful assortment of wildlife. First I saw a shark, and then Ernest saw a large yellowfin following the boat, amongst a constant carpet of terns and storm petrels floating and feeding. We saw other birds too, the smart black and white outfit of a single cape pigeon, as well as a black browed albatross and four very dark fat-beaked shearwaters, one of which Ernest saw take and swallow a writhing wriggling squid.

Around us constantly soared petrels like their distant relations the albatrosses.

As the sea eased we at last had time to wonder where all the other boats were.

'Well, they'll all be clear of Madagascar by now,' Ernest said. I strongly disagreed. I suspected that some of them were still a couple of hundred miles behind us—at least. We would see who was right when we reached Durban only 600 miles ahead.

'Maybe only one more blow,' I said hopefully. 'Yes,' Ernest agreed, and added, remembering 1973, 'It would be nice to have our southerly buster well out at sea, not as we approach the coast.'

On the morning of the eighth day our wild weather had calmed enough for me to cut Ernest's hair on deck in the sunshine and to type a story for *SAIL* magazine below, while Ernest took my easy watch, keeping an eye on *Tryste* while reading on deck, payment exacted for his haircut. By midnight the wind blew force 6 again from the south and it was impossible for *Tryste* to keep on course herself with the wind changing each time a shower whistled through, while at noon on the ninth day out, with Durban only 340 miles away, the weather was still so unpredictable that we no longer assumed that we could get away without more gales.

The southerly blew strongly all that day and Ernest's noon sight, taken after a morning of heavy overcast and no sights, told us that we had been pushed over 50 miles north of our desired course for Durban. We had to attempt to beat back to windward. After a short try with the reefed main set we had to hand it again as the seas were too large and we were, or so I suggested, 'beating our brains out.' Still smarting from what he saw as his careless navigation that had lost us 50 miles, Ernest remarked crossly, 'You might be perhaps, I don't have any to beat.' Later that day we were at last able to set the reefed main and start trying to claw back to our course.

By noon on the tenth day we had regained much of our lost ground but I had lost my credibility as crew. Ernest had woken me at 0500 to take the time for his star sights, kindly leaving me to sleep until he was absolutely ready, which was unfortunate as the result was that I was still half asleep as I peered at the clock—and took the wrong minute, easily done the first few minutes of the hour on that particular clock.

Although I knew that I had done it consistently, (after checking the clock with his watch) the damage was done as far as my veracity and accuracy were concerned. He gave me the benefit of *his* doubt and allowed for this wrong minute, but the sights *still* did not work out. He was all set to throw them (and me) overboard but luckily instead re-checked his figures and found two mistakes. Still we were both happier next day when he had taken a sun sight around breakfast time and found that everything then worked out. Poor Ernest had a lot to put up with from his crew. Although I could be relied on in an emergency to be staunch and true and quiveringly brave, I could never be relied on as a quick-thinking born sailor or a stand-in celestial navigator.

By midnight the wind had changed to east northeast force 4. By early next morning it was up to force 8 and we were lying ahull once again. After breakfast we set the storm jib to try and keep *Tryste* on course. Soon after noon we passed over Marling Bank, not far off the still invisible coast of Africa and the sea turned green. A band of cloud formed and then cleared as the wind blew and blew. Ahead as we approached the coast, something looking like a weather front warned us of worse perhaps to come. Was this the southerly buster coming to blow us north? When would we feel the grip of the south and west flowing Agulhas current? It was a guessing game. We pressed on; over seas such as *Tryste* had seldom sailed before, both *Tryste* and the storm jib performing magnificently.

Noon position left us with only 54 miles to go. By mid-afternoon, when we sighted land, the wind was down enough to set the reefed main and a small staysail, wing and wing. Not much more than an hour later the wind boxed the compass and after a short lull the southerly buster whammed in, force 5 then 6, dead on the nose—the end, we thought, of all hopes of reaching Durban that day. We were so tired now; we longed so much to make port. The storm jib came into play again and we prepared for another full gale but by 2200 the wind had lessened and turned northwest. Motor sailing in the cold rain (so infinitely preferable to a southerly buster on the nose) we gratefully picked up the light on Umhlanga Rocks, confirming our position, as the traditional thunderstorm flashed and crashed and hammered at our brains.

The red and green flashing harbour lights were easy to pick out ahead, as were the leading lights, but they took an eternity to reach. However, we were happy enough in the rain, which even slackened from time to time. I brought out a glass of Grand Marnier which we shared; and at last we were passing through the harbour entrance, now all peaceful and flattened out in the rain and looking quite different from the first time, then into the large night-quiet harbour, which again did not look too familiar. Where was the dear little tug, which we had confidently expected to meet us again and to tell us where to anchor? Suddenly we saw the red and green lights of a small boat heading straight for us, then a searchlight lit us briefly.

'Follow me,' said a voice in that inimitable South African accent. 'I will lead you to the Yacht Club. First I will give you a form to fill out. I will collect it when we get to the Yacht Club. Welcome to Durban.' Off went the little boat and we followed slowly to the International dock where we tied up alongside an Australian boat, *Coquitlam* from Fremantle. Here Tod Phillips, the captain, and another yachtie helped us tie up. It was half past one in the morning but they seemed wide-awake. Tod, very friendly and loquacious, asked for news of *Shoestring*, and told us that we had lots of mail at the Yacht Club.

'Have we got a telegram?' Ernest asked.

'Yes,' said Tod. That was the first of three questions which hovered in our brains when we reached Durban. So finally we were able to write up the log, turn in and go to sleep, very glad to be safe in port where later that night the weather turned foul again. We soon learned that we were the first of our Réunion group to reach Durban, which was the answer to the second question.

Waking next morning we were in heaven. At last we had *the* telegram, telling us that the baby had arrived safely. We had our first grandson, called Christopher. As well we collected our mountains of mostly-family mail and not only that, on our first foray into the town we discovered that at last, every shop, including the supermarkets, willingly took our MasterCard.

Amongst the letters there were various demands for money from customs for duty on a parcel and from the airport freight office for storage of it. This was all the result of the bread we had cast upon the waters back on Christmas Island and was the answer to our third question, namely, 'Have we got our anchor warp back?'

Ernest had optimistically fired off his letter about our warp from Christmas Island to: 'The Commanding Officer HMAS *Perth*,' trying simply 'Perth, Australia,' as address. It was a good guess and the letter had arrived safely.

His letter had said quite moderately, 'We would be grateful if our line could be returned, because we need it.' Off we went to South Africa and behold! When we arrived there were a whole bunch of communications awaiting us, and the line was at the airport. It had been there for some considerable time—there was money owing for storage. There were several messages from customs, please notify, please consult—there was customs duty to pay. We felt very welcome. Ernest went off to find it at the airport, which was a fair way away, by bus. There were three lots of people involved, the customs, the airfreight and the airport storage, and there were charges in all of more than a hundred Rand. Ernest went off to do battle muttering.

'It's the principle of the thing.' He said semi-seriously, 'Why should we pay to have our line returned when we had done this good deed?' He tried this argument on the typical Afrikaner Customs officer, whose rigid approach to rules about paying duty was,

'It's in the book. This is what the book says; the duty on rope is such and such.'

'Ah,' Ernest countered, 'but that is for new rope, this parcel I am expecting is our old anchor line being returned to us from Australia.'

He then told the story of the Administrator of Christmas Island being wrecked on the coral, and of the rescue, and of our number-two anchor line going out to the *Perth* by accident; which he gradually dressed up almost to a heroic rescue at sea—but it didn't do any good at all, since he was talking to a totally unimpressionable man.

Before the Customs officer was prepared to get down to even discussing the charge, he pushed Ernest off to talk to the air freight people to whom we owed about 40 Rand for storage. Here he was lucky. When he told his tear-jerking story to them they said, 'Oh Mr. Haigh, that's fine, fine, fine, of course we will waive the charges, but we can't do anything about the Customs.'

So back he went to the Customs Department. Here after endless arguments, he became more and more irritated at getting absolutely nowhere, until it was time for: 'Take me to your leader!'

'I want to see your supervisor,' he said. He was taken to a very large office, where behind a very large desk sat a chunky dark-haired Afrikaner man whom Ernest will remember to his dying day.

'His eyes were piercing black gimlets like the most evil sort of Gestapo interrogator,' he told me later. It was immediately absolutely apparent that no amount of argument was going to have the slightest effect, but nevertheless Ernest felt impelled to give him a chance and told his tale again, with embellishments; but it was useless.

'It's in the book. Look, you can see it yourself; the duty is at least one hundred Rand.' At this time Ernest was still out at the airport. Very soon he said,

'Well, I want to see the Controller of Customs, I want to see the Boss man, the very top man.' 'He's in Durban.' Said the man with the eyes. 'Okay,' Ernest said. So 'That were decided upon,' and he was told where to go. The Customs building was in the dock area. When he got there the Controller of Customs, the boss man, was out of town, but the second man down saw him and Ernest went through the whole story again and met exactly the same attitude. This is the customs duty (It's in the book) Ernest (again):

'Yes, but this is my line being returned after I've done this good deed, etc.' By this time the Customs department had done their best to save face and get rid of this irritating persistent Canadian by reducing the duty to something miniscule like six Rand. Even in our ever-straitened circumstances, that was quite affordable; but by now it really had become a matter of principle. Ernest had the bit between his teeth and was not prepared to pay anything.

It was now late afternoon on the second day of this filibuster, which had gone on for hours and involved not only the Vice-Controller, but also three or four other Customs officers who had been consulted about this insoluble problem. By now it was after four o'clock and by the way they all kept looking up at the clock Ernest realized that quitting time must be 4.30. With ill grace the Vice-Controller finally gave in,

'All right! All right!' He said, 'There will be no charge. You can go out to the airport and collect it tomorrow.' If I had been there (I was so grateful that I was not) I should then have thought that at last honour was satisfied, and I would have said, 'Thank you, I'll do that.' Ernest however was made of sterner stuff.

'No!' He said. 'I've been all the way out to the airport once; I'm not going out there again. I want to collect it here.' It as all too much for the Vice-Controller, he had never had to put up with anything like Ernest before. With ill grace he said,

'Okay, you can come and collect it from this building tomorrow at 9 o'clock.' Next morning at 9 o'clock Ernest was there. 'Well,' they said when he walked in, 'You can't just *take* it. It's got to be delivered by a Customs Officer, to see it's actually delivered to your ship.' So Ernest got into the Custom's Officer's motorcar and they solemnly drove down to the yacht club and together they put the parcel containing the line aboard 'the ship.'

After the Customs Officer had gone and we opened the duty-free parcel, which had been delivered to our yacht, we laughed and laughed. The line was a hundred and fifty feet of the best, brand-new nylon warp that we had ever possessed, with perfect splices in it, together with a last laugh letter from the Commander of the *Perth*:

> 'So sorry for your inconvenience. You must understand that it was an embarrassing situation and we were rather anxious to get away, and we have taken the liberty of substituting new line for yours, which was in poor condition.'

Space lying alongside at the Yacht Club international dock was very limited, and one risked being sent off into the boondocks to anchor, a long way away where there were absolutely no facilities. Instead, a few days after we arrived, we moved quietly, at three in the morning, to a space Ernest had previously tracked down, behind the yacht club.

It was while we were lying there that we decided to rent a car with three of our friends, Tod and Elsie, and Bernie from *Cautelle*, to see a couple of the less expensive game parks. Canadian Tod Phillips and his partner, Elsie Grieve, sailed the dark-blue-hulled *Coquitlam*. Elsie was a cheerful, easygoing Scottish girl whose only ambition was to marry Tod, while Tod, coming from an unhappy foster-home background, thought he was better off the way he was. Bernie, singlehanding, was yearning after female crew and companionship.

We decided to go for about three days and to visit two game parks: Umfolozi, which Ernest and I had visited in 1973 with Susie and Nicola, and Hluhlue, which we could not even pronounce. When the day to depart arrived, I woke with the realization that I was coming down with flu. In vain I begged to be left at home with *Tryste* (to die in peace is what I felt, though I did not say this), but Ernest would not go if I did not, and claimed, rather unfairly, that he would just worry about me all the time he was away if I did not come with him. Luckily (since my brain had by now packed up with fever) I had written my lists and done most of my packing the night before. We left in good order with the surreptitious addition, on my part, of thermometer, antibiotics from the ship's medical stores, and lots of aspirin.

By the time we made our first and only stop on the way, at a small hotel in Gingindlova for beer and coffee, I was light-headed with cold shakes. By the time we reached our delightful Umfolozi rondavels, I was ready for bed, and with the exception of only a few of the animal-watching outings, that is where I stayed.

Elsie and I had shopped together at a supermarket in Durban, and for the meat course had decided on three braii packs. The South African braii, or barbecue, is put up in the shops as a three-part meal, with lots of meat for the big South African carnivores—one or two chops, a piece of steak and one or two huge sausages visibly packed with meat. I'm not sure whether we discussed this, but my idea was to dismantle the packs and have sausages one evening, chops one evening etc. However that was not what happened and Ernest complained that they had the same meal each night that we were away. I was not too sympathetic. I too had the same meal, of tea and biscuits, every night.

The animals came up to everyone's expectations. None of the party ever saw elephant, but we all saw giraffe, an extraordinary experience, which I was lucky enough to share. Driving along in the crowded car, whoever was driving suddenly stopped and said,

'Look! Giraffes!' I looked over towards the spreading umbrella-like thorn trees, looking underneath them, but then had to look up (way up) to find that the thorn trees only came about half way up the animals. We spotted nine that time, and watched how they drank, having to spread their legs wide apart to reach the surface of a shallow pool. We could not get over how big they were—the trees came up to their shoulders—and how elegant, with such beautiful markings, gentle eyes and long, surely-mascara-ed, eye lashes.

Bernie quickly became our number one game spotter, quick to see movement and, with Ernest, to identify the animals. We soon moved on to Hluhlue where we had learned that there were elephants as well as giraffe. Although we never saw elephants we saw many rhino including one with a baby. This, however, was not Bernie's favourite. His favourite rhino was a male. We all had read how the males sometimes turned their backs and sprayed urine out between their back legs as a deterrent and this was exactly what this rhino did for us.

'Well,' said Bernie, 'I reckon we've seen some good stuff today, but that was the best!'

The third morning I forced myself to get up and get out with the others at dawn to drive around the roads and see the animals again, and was rewarded with warthogs, zebra, and many different sorts of buck, and then the mother rhino with the baby that the others had seen before, this time apparently spooked by something, taking off fast down the valley bottom. Later we saw a cheetah and her cubs traveling fairly fast in the direction the rhinos had gone. After that it was Tod's turn with the binoculars and he picked out a lioness in the distance. There was no way we could get nearer to it and we settled for baboons and vervet monkeys with plenty of enchanting babies, as well as crocodiles, dung beetles and flocks of guinea fowl. Then it was time to go back to the rondavels for breakfast, load up the car and head back to Durban and our cozy boats.

By this time I'm afraid Elsie was not feeling too well, and a few hours later both Ernest and Bernie were beginning to turn bright red. Tod, I think, was the only one who escaped. Somehow they must have forgiven me. A week later they all came over to *Tryste* with Julia, bringing a cake for my birthday tea.

When we were ready to clear out of Durban Ernest found that he had to write a letter to the Immigration Department to say that he wanted to take me on again as crew, having signed us both off and turned us into tourists to go to the game parks. He was not permitted to take this letter back for me. I had to take it myself, together with my passport, to prove to them that I really was *me*.

We had hoped to spend Christmas in Cape Town but a small notice on the tack board of Durban's Point Yacht Club requested overseas cruising boats *not* to arrive in Cape Town until after Boxing Day as there would be no room for them, all available spaces being taken by race boats from the first BOC Challenge solo Round-the-World. We decided to try and reach Knysna, a harbour the other side of Port Elizabeth, 500 miles south and west of Durban, in spite of the fact that conditions at the bar entrance might make entry impossible. Durban's rigid port authorities frowned on this idea as there were no customs and immigrations officials at Knysna, but they did not actively forbid it.

We had long since done everything we wanted in the way of loading stores and preparing ourselves for the frightening trip around the Cape of Good Hope, but this time we had an acquaintance with a Weather Fax. Many other yachts were planning to leave around the same time and we found that the more people were leaving, the more nervous we all became, feeding off one another's insecurity.

After hearing some of the horror stories of the west-going Agulhas current, which can run at 5 knots near the 100 fathom line to the south of South Africa, Bernie had taken Gary Moss on as crew for the passage to Cape Town. Gary, a young fair-haired, open faced Australian, had come into Durban aboard the ferro-cement yacht *Hard Rock*. Marsh and Fran, aboard *Invictus*, also became apprehensive. Fran decided that she just did not want to sail around the Cape of Good Hope, and Marsh, deciding that he did not want to tackle the passage on his own, took on Steve from *Puki* as his crew.

Last time aboard *Tryste*, we took refuge in one bad gale anchored in the lee of Bird Island, 25 miles short of Port Elizabeth. It had taken us fourteen days in all to cover the 860 miles to Cape Town, which included several days in both Port Elizabeth and Mossel Bay. This year it would take us that long to reach Knysna. Few yachts made the passage without encountering dirty weather along the way. We thought we knew the rules. You waited in Durban for a good southerly buster then left as soon as it died down, in the lull that usually followed. The light easterly or fresh northeasterly which usually came next should allow you to make the 260 miles to the first haven of East London. After a rest there you watched the weather and then kept going.

We knew what to expect, but this was an extreme El Niño year with freakish weather all around the world. The trades failed in the eastern Pacific; there were floods on the normally dry coasts of the Americas, as well as cold droughts in Australia and abnormal hurricanes in the Central Pacific. No wonder that around the Cape cold front after cold front came barrelling through with hardly a break, terrorizing yachties under way and pinning others in Durban for weeks at a time.

Like many others we became hopelessly infected by the need to know what the weather forecast was. Julia too was a prey to indecision, but when more light southwest depressions were forecast and we decided to stay put, Julia courageously sailed out. Four days later we finally left, as did *Cautelle*. We did not particularly set out to sail the passage in company with Bernie and Gary, but having left at the same time we ended up sailing companionably along the south coast a fair part of the time. We also ended up moored together in the commercial ports of East London and Port Elizabeth.

We spent nine days in all in South African ports, waiting for favourable weather, whiling away the hours playing Euchre and Five Hundred with these pleasant uncomplicated companions, sharing meals and drinking Australian duty-free grog or South African wine. As a bonus Ernest and Bernie as Captains were able to share both the pain of having to spend long hours clearing in and out of each port and visiting the inflexible Afrikaans officials—and the pleasure of poking fun at them later.

Leaving Durban we had only twelve hours of light variables before the next south westerly came bustling in. We still had 200 miles to go to East London, exactly the situation we had hoped not to find ourselves in. We decided to go on, the alternative of turning back and clearing in and clearing out again a few days later being too terrible to contemplate.

As we continued to beat into the sou'westerly 100 miles south of Durban the great irregular seas grew and grew, the wind howled and screamed and we began to think that *Tryste* was not going to survive. Just before midnight we lay ahull for five hours in 21 fathoms off North Bluff light, where the wonderful Volume III Africa Pilot rightly assured us that close inshore we would find the seas considerably calmer. By noon the next day that wind had died, but by mid-afternoon it was back and we were running fast with a rising east nor'easter wondering if this favourable wind would take us all the way to East London.

When darkness fell the freshening wind backed a little and we reduced sail until we had just the genoa set, knowing that we would be at the helm all night with the wind howling and the seas doing their best to swamp us. That wild ride through the dark with genoa only, with the northeaster at our backs and the Agulhas current running strongly with us, will remain in our memories forever. As we hurtled through the jet-black darkness, the waves, rushing through like express trains, broke in sudden flashes of white. The dim lights on shore assured us that we were indeed speeding through the night and we covered an intoxicating 107 miles in the twelve hours between noon and midnight.

With only 15 miles still to go to East London the northeaster dropped, and without any lull the southwester started to blow again. Incredulously we set the main, and motor sailing, banged straight into it and managed to reach East London ahead of the gale, to find *Cautelle* already there safely snugged down.

The day after we arrived, as the wind gusted to 55 knots, Ernest and I stood on a hill in the town above the harbour with Bernie and Gary and watched huge spume-flecked seas kicked up by the westerlies flying past. We were immensely glad that we were not out there, but worried about our friends, particularly Julia, who, we learnt, had left East London earlier that day. Our belief that it was always a windy place was confirmed next day when we again went uphill to see the spreading sea and found a bridge to walk across that was entirely enclosed in wire netting because it was too dangerously exposed. We could barely keep our feet.

We had been in East London two full boisterous sou'westerly days when *Full Moon*, a South African yacht with two couples and two young boys aboard, came limping in. They had left East London five hours after Julia and had been caught by the buster that we had hurried into port to escape. This had been only the second leg of their maiden voyage from Durban and they had been cruelly mauled. Their brand new tan furling jib was ripped to pieces and one of the boys had become dangerously seasick and dehydrated. For much of the time most of them were lying on the cabin sole. It was a cruel year for a maiden voyage. They had spent eleven years building the boat in Durban.

After seeing what the gale had done to them we were more than ever worried about Julia. Later we learned that she beat her way into Port Elizabeth, 150 miles further on, safely in the teeth of another building south westerly. We asked ourselves then why we all spent so much time worrying about someone as competent as Julia (even though she did sail without a motor.)

At the hospitable East London Yacht Club, where we were all invited to a braii, the crews of the local race boats told us that they too were heading for Knysna for Christmas. Being so familiar with their own coastal weather they were a lot more casual about it than we were. When the northeaster came in, they said, they would usually,

'Just set the bag and go, man!'—riding the current where it was strongest, near the 100-fathom line. That was all very well for them, with their young strong crew. We thought we would take their more sober advice of,

'Watch the barometer, man! If it stays down, don't go!' When the weatherman in Port Elizabeth, forecast fresh east-northeast winds and the barometer showed a healthy 30.06mb, we sailed out and had an easy passage there with sunshine, dolphins, albatrosses and petrels, although we were almost too apprehensive to appreciate them all properly. That evening as we played cards and drank rum aboard *Cautelle*, moored to an uncomfortably high concrete wharf in Port Elizabeth, the sou'wester came howling in again, whistling and piping in the rigging. The yachts leapt and groaned, our fenders proved inadequate and we put up with dirty black marks made by some tires we found rather than risk damage to our topsides.

Not being Ham Radio Operators or having a transmitter of any kind, we had never tuned in to the 'skeds' before, but we had a good Yeasu receiver that we had installed before we left home this time, and now, sailing in company with 'ham' Bernie we learned the times and frequencies of the net run by Alistair, and became addicted to the chatter. The airwaves were busy, not only with requests for weather updates but also with reports of yachts in distress. One was being hammered off well-named Mbashee Point; one was towed into East London dismasted; yet another knocked down off Cape Agulhas, and there were yachts with sails ripped and yachts sheltering from gales in every conceivable bay and inlet between Durban and Cape Town.

We thought it would be all too easy to let our lives be ruled by the radio but we could not stop listening. Bernie was delighted to see Ernest so hooked, and when we could not pick up the transmissions on our receiver teased him with, 'Who's that knocking at my door wanting to know what the weather's going to do?'

We had hoped to catch up with Julia in Port Elizabeth but she had already left. Much later, in Cape Town, she told us that she had had enough of the tension caused by trying to sail *Jeshan* into safe harbours and the nail-biting need to decide when to start out again, and had gone far south, avoiding the shipping lanes, almost to the iceberg limit. She had even come across oil rigs and had eventually sailed directly round to Cape Town, where her parents lived, well offshore.

We had spent four days in East London with *Cautelle*, and now we spent another four in Port Elizabeth, watching the weather. It was there that Ernest and I went to the Customs Department together. We were in trouble right away about a missing piece of paper, a 'transire'. We entered the cool, old-fashioned office to find four white-uniformed officials with their caps on. Which one would deal with us? All four! Ernest offered his *five* transires, each with its own enormous sealing wax seal (the wax previously melted on an electric laundry iron hung on the wall). The officer who looked at our papers was horrified.

'You do not have the transire from Durban to East London!' Ernest offered one that looked hopeful. 'No, that is a DA4, you need a DA1. You must have it back at the boat.'

'I think they kept that one in East London,' Ernest said helpfully.

'They should not have done that, how do we know you had one? You must be very careful that you have all the transires that we need.'

'But we don't know what you need!'

'Well you should have a transire from Durban to East London, a DA1.' Then came the rhetorical question: 'What would happen if you got in trouble out at sea and you didn't have your transire?' Well, what would happen? Would the Rescue Craft refuse to take us off? Would we rush round the deck of our sinking craft shouting, 'We haven't got our transire!' Before we could answer that question Bernie turned up in the office and two of the officials started to deal with him. It turned out that *Cautelle's* DA1 transire was missing too. There were mutterings about East London and finally, a grudging admission: 'Well it is not your fault. They made a mistake in East London.' It was a relief to be forgiven such a heinous transgression.

We left Port Elizabeth at 0200 on the fifth morning with the dying gasps of a sou'wester when it was almost calm, and for once there really was a lull—of five hours—before a fresh sou'easter came in and *Tryste* was off and running with only 130 miles still to go to Knysna.

We knew that in certain conditions of wind and seas Knysna's constricted, rock-strewn entrance, between two prominent headlands, only ¾ cable or 456 ft. at its narrowest point, could become impassable, with the sea breaking frequently over the sandbars, always on one side and frequently right across. Also there is a fast current (up to 12 knots) so it was essential to enter at the right state of the tide. This we did, but we were lucky that the weather was kind to us. We entered with the last of the flood, passing handsome red rock headlands with magnificent clefts and arches and small off-lying rocky islets. We anchored about a mile up the Knysna River estuary, off the Yacht Club, where the manager cleared us in without any fuss.

On Christmas Eve Ernest shopped for beer and ice, while Bernie and I shopped for food including two large frozen chickens. Then, in the afternoon, the two boats motored out and anchored in roomy, quiet Featherbed Bay, just inside the Heads, a holiday destination for many local fizz boats, sailboards and cruisers. To our delight the locals all went home at sundown.

We were so quietly and safely anchored and so relaxed in this small tree-lined bay that reminded us of New Zealand's Bay of Islands, that Ernest decided that there was no need to hold back on the toasts in Christmas Eve wine. We were all beaming by the time a third overseas yacht, crewed by a singlehander, sailed into the bay and dropped his hook. We waved him over to join us onshore. By this time we had a good beach fire going and were well into our Xmas Eve celebration meal of steak and borewors (a meaty Afrikaner sausage), baked potatoes and baked gem squash with Bernie's fantastic salad, enhanced by his special salad dressing.

Bernie hastened over in his dinghy to deliver a proper invitation to the newcomer who soon came ashore, a little dazed after his passage, and we were able to learn from him that *Invictus* was still anchored back in Plettenberg Bay, one of the 'safe haven' possibilities on the passage from Durban.

We apologised for the fact that we had eaten all the meat, but he responded by saying rather dismissively that he didn't use it at the moment. We indulgently set him up with everything else we could find and a glass of wine, and went back to enjoying ourselves. Alas it was not to be. Before long in the course of conversation Ernest and our new friend were soon in a non-productive, antagonistic dialogue about life, the centre of the Universe, compassion, honesty, et al, and Ernest (without raising his voice, as Gary pointed out later) told our new companion,

'I just might have to throw you in the sea!' Later Gary made a good-natured joke about the size of his boat and our singlehander responded, 'How would you like a punch in the mouth?' Most cruising people get along well together and marked antipathy is rare, but there must have been some bad chemistry at work that evening. Perhaps we failed to make adequate allowance for the fact that he had just come in from the sea, perhaps we had already drunk too many Christmas toasts. In spite of our well-intentioned invitation sparks flew.

When he left the party, and shortly thereafter the bay, the four of us stayed ashore long enough to enjoy a glorious sunset with pink clouds, a rainbow, and a wash of golden-red light on the hills opposite, before we went aboard *Cautelle* and Bernie brought out his last bottle of duty-free Baileys and we played cards until Ernest fell asleep over them and I took him home.

We spent most of Christmas Day aboard *Tryste*. We had Christmas-decorated her below with tinsel and paper chains, and we had two smorgasbords, noon and nine, based on cold roast stuffed chicken along with many additions from *Cautelle*. The morning had started out wet but by noon it was warm and sunny which brought out the locals.

We sunbathed, swam and dozed while listening to tapes of Christmas carols and eerie whale songs; occasionally beating off wind surfers, speedboats and small local yachts and freeing one Hobie Cat from our anchor warp. We played more card games of Euchre and 500, helped Bernie finish up the Baileys and drank to absent friends and families. There were no watches to stand, no sails to set, no freighters to avoid and no havens to try and reach. It was the perfect antidote to being on passage.

The two congenial captains decided that we should sail out next morning at 0415 weather permitting, so we were not too late to bed. We were all aware that 330 miles of this unpredictable, frustrating and often frightening passage still lay ahead. The sooner we faced up to it the sooner we would be in Cape Town.

At 0415 on Boxing Day morning Ernest and Bernie had a shouted decision not to go, but at 0600 a faint favourable breeze crept into the bay. The barometer was steady and the firm decision of 0415 was changed. The last thing we wanted was to become trapped inside the bar harbour when the next series of gales came along. Soon both boats were motor sailing out between Knysna's rocky Heads.

CHAPTER NINETEEN:

THE FAIREST CAPE

Our fifty mile passage with a light following easterly from Knysna to Mossel Bay (still to the east of Cape Agulhas) was peaceful, rolling gently westward with a light following easterly, with *Cautelle* ahead of us, and *Invictus* astern. Only the barometer, now at 29.58 and dropping steadily, made us wonder what weather was coming up next. While we still had wind, a whale suddenly appeared *between Tryste's* main hull and port float, then sounded and came up again astern of us. It did not stay around to be admired and only blew twice more well behind us. This 30 ft. whale, which we tentatively identified as a humpback, was the only whale that we had seen in the whole Indian Ocean since leaving Darwin.

The wind failed around teatime and we motored the last 10 miles to Mossel Bay, which the three boats had agreed to make the overnight destination; watching the weather suspiciously all the time, as the barometer had bottomed out at 29.44 and was starting to rise, a sure sign that the westerly was on its way.

We motored past the harbour entrance just behind *Invictus*, to where *Cautelle* was already anchored outside the mole that enclosed the harbour. Once the three boats were safely anchored our friends all came back aboard *Tryste* for drinks and nibbles. Somehow it soon became after eleven, and the others went back to their respective boats for a late dinner. Marsh and Steve had drunk an amazing amount of scotch, putting to rest any fears of Marsh being a teetotaller.

We had planned to anchor there overnight, but we spent the next full day there as well, comfortably sheltered from the gusty sou'westerly that had finally come in after midnight. It was the day of the Agulhas yacht race and we saw the first yacht, *Voortrekker II*, a 60-footer with a crew of 10 or 12, sail in through the yachts and back again. We wondered what they were doing, then realised that they were looking for the boat that was supposed to be the mark for the racers to round. They seemed almost frantic, jabbing angrily at their watches and shouting, 'Take the time!'

We thought they were shouting at us, but they were speaking to a small rowboat with an outboard just astern of us. It was only 0920: the previous record time from Cape Town to Mossel Bay had been thirty hours, which would have made it six o'clock in the evening, not nine in the morning; which explained why the mark boat was not there. When it shamefacedly arrived, it anchored too close to the overseas yachts.

Later the Mossel Bay Port Captain came out and gave us a form to fill in, which Ernest speared with the boathook. This probably did it no good, and since officialdom seemed much less strict in these smaller places, and since *Invictus* and *Cautelle* were never were even *given* forms, there seemed no point in taking ours back. Instead we left early next day, longing to have this unpredictable Durban-to-Cape Town leg of the voyage finished. It became colder as forecast, dropping from 79° to 70, while the barometer also started another descent. We had caught a snatch of the forecast and had heard 'SW 10-20 knots', but thought (and hoped) that it was for later in the day. Ernest woke at 0430 and we woke both Bernie and Marsh before *Tryste* left at 0500.

Bernie was soon underway and eventually caught up with us, before the wind came in strongly behind us, but of Marsh there was neither sight, nor sound on the ham net. We thought it strange, especially since Bernie reported, on the afternoon net, that Invictus was getting ready to leave when Cautelle sailed out. Perhaps Fran, who was travelling to Cape Town by bus, turned up, as she had in East London when she had visited us aboard *Tryste*. A glorious day with hot sun and a fair wind for most of the day made *Tryste* happy, with all sail set once the southeasterly increased. By noon we had made good 27 miles, but were experiencing a 1-knot adverse current. Twelve hours later we were motoring into a sloppy sea in the moonlight, grateful for the little auto-pilot. Cautelle had motor sailed up astern and passed us to become our pathfinder.

It took a long time to get round the corner that was Cape Agulhas, to where we were no longer heading south of west. The wind, predictably, changed to northwest so that it was still on the nose.

'Oh for a fair wind!' Ernest wrote in the log. At 0500 next morning we had only 35 miles to go, to the Cape of Good Hope, as the crow flies—but we were no bird—we were soon tacking out to sea and in again towards the rocky coast. One tack took us near the rocks and shoals off a headland called Quoin Point.

'We cut that a bit close,' Ernest admitted as we came about, watching the green breakers roll in to shore and smelling the pungent smell of birds and fish and seashores. As we tacked our way past the Cape of Good Hope—the Cape of Storms—the weather became overcast and showery, and we mourned the poor photography weather, as we looked across at the magnificent rocky headland that Sir Francis Drake called 'The Fairest Cape in all the world.'

Not only the Cape, but also the wildlife extravaganza clamoured at us. Seals bobbed up to look at us; handsome black and white penguins sank at our approach; shags in flocks dipped in the water and a flock of gannets floated up and down on the waves like spindrift. We came close in to a little cove just west of the Cape, in amongst kelp so thick that it slowed our progress, and then finally came about half an hour before noon, to where we could almost point our course to clear the next two headlands.

Ernest's longed-for fair wind, a fine southeasterly came in, and we were soon hastening up the west coast of the Cape Peninsula in the sunshine, exclaiming at the handsome mountains tipped with white wispy clouds. We were round the Cape of Storms! At last, we thought, all our troubles were over!

Cautelle had disappeared; perhaps she had ducked into Hout Bay. It had looked attractive as we crossed its mouth. As the land trended eastward we were almost on a run up past the little Lion's Head, the Twelve Apostles, and the back end of Table Mountain showing up with a thick tablecloth of cloud spilling down its flanks (a warning perhaps of a stronger southeasterly to come) then the back of the Lion's Head with a Cape Town suburb laid out along its lower slopes. We were nearly there! We rounded Green Point around 1700, passing a big group of mightily roaring sea lions and going, as Ernest said, 'Like a bat out of hell.' We confidently expected to be tied up at the Royal Cape Yacht Club around 1830.

We handed the twin, with its pole, and gybed the genoa to head in to the end of the harbour mole, but suddenly there were obstructions ahead, a LAND AND MARINE barge surround by masses of big buoys. We had to clear them all and then there was another group and we were being pushed out into the harbour, away from our target, the green light on a structure at the end of the mole, and the wind was rising against us. We were soon motor sailing at full revs. I was at the helm and finding it hard to hold *Tryste* up into the wind. I handed over to Ernest who then appreciated my problem as the wind gusted up still further.

'Go forward and drop the genoa,' he shouted, 'and for God's sake be careful!' He usually works the foredeck himself. I found it thrilling to be working up there with the sea surging up over my legs as we tore along. We still had the full main set and it seemed ridiculous that we were within a quarter of a mile of the entrance and could not motor sail in. But because the wind kept catching the main and pushing *Tryste* off I had to hand that too. Then I readied the anchor, just in case.

With Ernest very careful to keep *Tryste's* nose straight into the wind, we headed into the outer harbour with the wind gusting strongly against us. It was two yards forward and one back—when the heaviest gusts came through we actually blew backwards—but gradually between gusts we reached a spot just inside the mole where it was safe to slant off towards the entrance of the inner docks.

All through our struggle, a little orange harbour launch had stood by to render assistance if needed, but in the end we made it on our own. Once we were out of the worst of the wind we found our way into Duncan Dock which had the yacht harbour and Yacht Club at the end of it. Although we were partly protected now, the wind gusted against us and we shuddered to think of finding somewhere to tie up with our light, wind-catching trimaran, among the plethora of handsome yachts we could see ahead. Ernest decided we should put *Tryste* alongside what we took to be one of the Round the World race boats, *Spirit of Pentax*, although it was furthest out and therefore more exposed. We had lines, fenders, boat hook, and anchor all at the ready as we came alongside the 'high-wooded' metal yacht. By the time we were safely tied up it was 2015, almost two hours later than we had expected to make harbour.

Ernest took an extra line from the bow ashore, clambering up onto *Spirit of Pentax*, before checking with the Yacht Club secretary that we could lie there overnight, while I tidied up on deck, wrote the log and started supper.

'I was fine until we reached the harbour entrance,' Ernest said, as we reviewed our day. He was really beat and crawled into bunk right after supper, while I stacked the dishes for the morning. The wind howled and screamed all night, and we never heard Bernie and Gary come in at 0300 and tie up to the yacht ahead of us. They had spent the previous night sheltering in a small bay that Alistair had recommended.

'It was a nice place,' Bernie said, but he obviously rather regretted putting in there and letting us get ahead of him. He had not expected to find us tied up in Cape Town.

Next day was both a Friday and New Year's Eve. The Customs and Immigration officers, probably worried about their New Year's Eve celebrations, were at the Yacht Club and sent for Ernest and Bernie. For once the formalities were dealt with speedily. We were told by the Yacht Club secretary to move *Tryste* around past the Club House, to a square metal scow with good tires for fenders in the furthest corner, where *Cautelle* later came to lie alongside. Here Julia found us, and we had a grand reunion and a re-hash of the Durban to Cape Town passage.

We invited Bernie and Gary to dinner before we all went to the New Year's Eve dance at the Yacht Club. It was a great fun party with lots of dancing for us all. Ernest collapsed around 2.30 am on New Year's Day, and I took him home. The fresh air was a bit of a shock and it was rather worrying steering him along a concrete path on the edge of the filthy basin, but we made it safely. Through clouds of lovely sleep, I heard Gary and Bernie come home about 3. I doubt if Ernest heard anything.

It had been a good year for us, with Tasmania, Chagos, new grandson Christopher, and two SAIL articles accepted...we hoped the next year would be as good. It certainly turned out to be every bit as interesting.

In Cape Town we made many new friends, among them John and Sue Allen on the N.Z. ketch *Chianti*, whom we would meet again in St. Helena. Bernie had met a South African girl, Linda, in Durban and had hoped that she would crew with him, but instead she had sailed on the German yacht, *Spirit of Dani*, which we met again briefly at Mossel Bay and later in Fernando de Noronha. Linda was back in Cape Town now, where her mother lived, so she joined Bernie and Ernest in their climb up Table Mountain, which was not for the faint-hearted, so I did not go.

Ernest, as Elder Statesman, was on his mettle, determined not to lag behind his younger companions. Apparently he tended to lead all the way. The climbers left late in the morning, driving up to the cable station in Linda's mother's car and walking or climbing up from there. I was worried about Ernest as he was wearing new boots, but apparently I need not have worried. When three exhausted figures tottered across the barge that we were tied to, around eight in the evening, Ernest looked in better shape than Bernie and Bernie looked in better shape than Linda.

'The boots were marvellous,' Ernest said.

'Yes,' said Bernie, mock-bitterly, 'they've got springs on the bottom.' Ernest was happy to turn in right after supper, but he was none the worse for his efforts next morning. Bernie too was fine and dropped by, in a social whirl, to tell us that he had decided to take Linda as crew from Cape Town on, in spite of the possible problems in the Caribbean of her carrying a South African passport. Gary was off to Johannesburg to fly home to Australia; all fired up to make a lot of money and to buy a boat of his own one day.

Julia was busy organizing *Jeshan* for lifting out and sand blasting in a yard near the Yacht Club, but took time out to take us to meet her hospitable parents. Hans and Jessie had a handsome Cape Dutch house with its own jetty at the bottom of the garden, in a water-based subdivision.

Next day they took us to the winegrowing area of Stellenbosch with a picnic packed by Jessie, which we ate on the grassy slopes surrounding the open-air amphitheatre of *The Theatre in the Winelands*. They had booked us all tickets for a moving performance of Mark Medoff's *Children of a Lesser God*. In the interval the audience were all served Stellenbosch wine, a nice touch we thought. Julia was amused that while we all discussed the performance, she overheard a pair of Boer farmer's wives behind us comparing stew recipes and agreeing, 'You can't make a good stew without potatoes.'

The following day Jessie met us at *Jeshan* and she and Julia drove us on a sightseeing trip of the Cape Province Reserve, identifying for us, bontebok and black gnu (wildebeest), sugarbirds and red-winged starlings. We drove right out to the Cape of Good Hope and Cape Point, and down a sinuous road to Buffles Bay, where we picnicked on a grassy knoll overlooking a sand beach and a spreading bed of giant kelp with huge, high-floating bulbs. The last expedition we made in Cape Town was to go up Table Mountain in the cable car with Bernie and Linda, and Marsh and Fran, now re-united aboard *Invictus*.

We intentionally left it rather late in the afternoon, as we wanted to have time to wander a little on top of the mountain and then enjoy our dinner before it was dark enough to see the lights of Cape Town laid out below us. As the sun set we wandered into the restaurant where we found a table for six and watched the after light in the sky as we waited for our 'adequate' (as Ernest commented later) dinner. Then we strolled out to gaze at the glorious lights of Cape Town and her suburbs below us—a pearl necklace of lights around the Lion's neck and gold and silver chains of light, with rubies and emeralds around the harbour area—before catching the last cable car down.

Three days later we sailed out, with Marsh clanging away on the Yacht Club's ship's bell as we passed the club house. We were ready for an easy passage which we hoped the 1,650 miles up the South Atlantic to St. Helena was going to be. *Chianti* had left two days earlier while several other overseas yachts were either under way or making ready to leave, as well as several South African vessels, some of which did not intend to return to their troubled homeland.

The first three days we averaged 157 mile runs with the wind having a westerly component, but on the third day we cautiously enjoyed a lovely day with the wind going round to southeast and the gradual acceptance that it was indeed the start of the trades. After that first day the wind fell lighter and never again rose above force 4, but it was always behind us from an occasional S to any variant of SE or ESE. The sun shone all day and every day; although nearer St. Helena there were clouds in the afternoon. We saw our first flying fish of the South Atlantic skipping across the waves, but we had to wait another week before one flew aboard and volunteered for breakfast. The sea varied from a silky pale blue coverlet to one covered in tiny white sparkles. On the windiest days white horses no bigger than Shetland ponies galloped across the sea. We wallowed in blissful day after blissful day of trade wind sailing.

Wildlife was in short supply apart from my early sighting of eight Risso's dolphins on our first full day at sea. They were very big, perhaps over nine or ten feet, with big scimitar shaped dorsal fins and grey bodies so scored with lines that they looked as if they had been in the wars, but that was apparently their normal skin pattern. They looked white underwater, and when they breached they looked enormous. That day we also saw a petrel catch a four-inch flying fish and then lose it, not to a frigate bird, but to a marauding albatross; and we were visited by an assortment of other petrels, gannets and cape pigeons—then suddenly we were too far from land, and from then on birds were scarce.

For the first few nights there was no moon visible and the stars shone brilliantly. The Southern Cross lay on its side directly astern, with a milky nebula above, while Orion, the hunter, re-appeared in our lives. A week later he was at the masthead, the mast and spreaders seeming to trace the outline of his belt and dagger against the night sky. Two days later we saw a slice of moon for the first time this passage.

Although it seemed unlikely that we should ever become really addicted, we were still listening to 'the funnies', the ham net, sometimes twice a day, and still hearing Alistair clearly. For the time being, in such benign sailing conditions, it was fun. We were happy to learn that Steve was back in Durban after crewing on *Invictus,* and that he and Mary and *Puki* were on their way to Cape Town. Next day Alistair was complaining that propagation was bad ('Whatever that means,' we said to one another.) But we were glad to have *Chianti's* position, when Alistair repeated it via Jeff (another ham net operator?) in Salisbury, Zimbabwe. We learnt that they were 230 miles north of us, well on their way to St. Helena.

A week later, and suddenly Alistair was coming through loud and clear again, and so was Marsh, still in Durban, claiming to have scrubbed *Invictus's* bottom and cleaned her topsides. More realistically, we thought, at least for the scrubbing, a small army of black men had done it. *Chianti,* we heard, was out of wind less than 200 miles from St. Helena. We, a little more than a hundred miles behind them now, were still making between 4 and 5 knots.

After dark on this passage the BBC radio reception was excellent. We heard some fascinating programs on our headphones: programmes so good that they made the solitary night watches fly by. I heard an extraordinary one on *Aida* in a prison camp in the Urals in the

1940s. We were prepared to listen to almost anything—news, music, comment, sport, finance, arts, humour—Ernest drew the line at 'religious reflections', although I even enjoyed one of those.

The day before we reached St. Helena I was below, cooking, when Ernest shouted, 'Whale!' I was just in time to see it spout and the tremendous disturbance of birds and fish that it left in the water. We hoped that it would come our way but watched sadly as its spouts fell astern. On that same day Ernest saw a tropicbird and two terns, so we knew we were nearing land, but we never caught a fish on this passage at all.

We had hoped to make good enough time on the last two days, to reach St. Helena in daylight, but at noon sight on the day of our landfall we still had 44 miles to go. It was cloudy over St. Helena and it was mid-afternoon before we saw the island. By suppertime our wind was only force 3 and we were, as Ernest said, 'Slowing down fast.' But we were content to dawdle until after supper. As the sun set we were rewarded for our patience by a glorious display of golden dolphins, both right around the horizon and close to *Tryste,* jumping, twisting, spy-hopping, doing straight up jumps then a tail twist and flop back in, up and over in pairs, and all other possible gymnastic permutations.

When they left, Ernest started the motor and we motor sailed with main and mizzen set, to pass Saddle Point, and then handed the sails to round the Sugar Loaf and head into James Bay on a beautiful calm moonlight night. As we came into the anchorage and played our spotlight over the four yachts already there, one of which was *Chianti,* a speedboat zoomed up; a young man called Chris jumped out and took our stern line, which he ran out to the 'span'—the end buoy from which a string of local boats and buoys were attached to shore—while we dropped the hook off *Tryste's* bow.

It was not a totally successful operation as we were banging on the small but heavy local boats, but once we had a bit more stern line out we were fine till morning. John and Sue came aboard with Chris and two others and drank wine and scotch until after one in the morning. When they all went away, we were grateful to turn in. It was Monday January 24th, 1983 by then, the first month of the last year of *Tryste's* cruising life, the year of the unexpected end to our second circumnavigation.

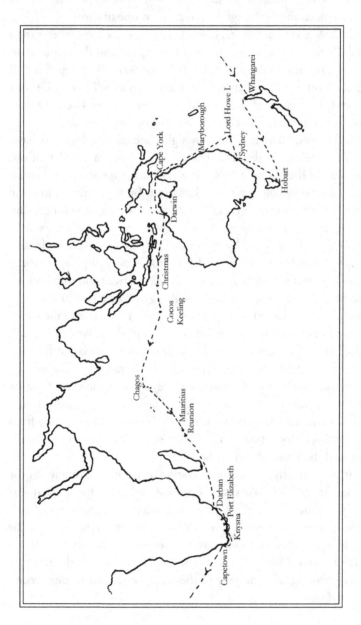

Indian Ocean. Tryste's route from Whangarei, NZ to Cape Town, SA.

Julia checking her anchor aboard *Jeshan* at Direction Island, Cocos Keeling Group.

Orange dust flying over the yachts, as potash loads in Flying Fish Cove, Christmas I. Indian Ocean.

Manager's House in deserted settlement on Boddam I, Salamon Atoll, Chagos Archipelago.

A small example of the rollers which can be a problem at harbours on Réunion in the Mascarenes.

Ernest bottom-painting on the sand and mud in front of Point Yacht Club, Durban.

l to r. Bernie, Steve, Marsh, Gary and Ernest aboard *Tryste* at Mossel Bay, South Africa.

Julia and Ernest, Cape Province Reserve, Cape of Good Hope.

Val on the 699 Jacob's steps, up from Jamestown, St. Helena below.

CHAPTER TWENTY:

A FISH CALLED CHARLIE

St Helena looked craggy and attractive when we surfaced next morning, but before we could go ashore we had a long exhausting session in the hot sun lifting our anchor. We hauled and heaved and struggled and when it finally broke surface we found that it was tangled with another one, an old coral-encrusted anchor wrapped in cord, some of which had also become wound around the point of our CQR. Later we were able to lie between two buoys in the span to shore and stow our anchor.

One of our main reasons for returning to St. Helena was to visit Cliff Huxtable, now the island's Superintendent of Schools, and his wife Delia. We should not really have been surprised, since everyone on the island was inclined to know everyone else, when we asked the Postmistress where we could phone Cliff and she said, 'I'll phone him for you—I think he's in his office.' Then she disappeared into the back room to phone and came back saying cheerfully,

'Yes! I'll take you to the Education office.' Simply abandoning her Post Office and walking out, she led the way up the street, up the stairs of one of the colour-washed houses built right down on Main Street and then, after looking in a couple of offices, located Cliff and handed us over. It was the last week of January.

'We were not expecting you until February,' Cliff said with a broad smile, 'but I just looked out of the window and I *thought* I saw you going into the Post office!' He seemed the same as ever, but when he stood up, we saw that he had to use a cane, and he told us that about four years earlier he had been knocked off his motorcycle by a drunk driver and had broken his femur, and that it had resulted in such complications that eventually he had to go to England to have a metal pin inserted right through the bone.

Delia too had been hospitalised, more recently, in her case having to go to hospital at the Cape. The good news was that they were delighted with life at their new property at Lufkin's Spring which we had seen on our last visit when they had just bought it; and that Cliff was looking forward to an active retirement, possibly making furniture there. We had been lucky enough to arrive on his last day of work as head of St. Helena's fourteen schools.

'I'm going round them all to say goodbye tomorrow,' he said. 'You can come with me if you like. It'll probably take most of the day.' Next day we visited twelve of the schools, with Cliff driving us up and down the extraordinary steep and winding roads built by local labour and paid for by the British taxpayer. We travelled all round the island to schools with evocative names like Blue Hill, Green Hill, Level wood, Sandy Bay and Longwood (where Napoleon was imprisoned and died), past large areas where before there had been fields of flax, and where now the flax was grown only in strips for soil retention between acres and acres of rows of reforestation.

In the bright green farming areas in the interior of the island we met some of the friendly, smiling, mostly dark-skinned children and teachers, and stopped at Cliff and Delia's house at Lufkin's Spring for a late lunch of fishcakes and home-grown tomatoes and bread and comb honey. To finish our tour Cliff drove us round the long, imposing carriageway past the Governor's massive, colonial–style mansion, white walls picked out in glistening black, with its big Union Jack flying, before dropping us off at the jetty.

The day after we arrived we were invited to join *Chianti*'s Sue and John at a dinner party aboard the mini-tanker, *Bosunbird*, which now lay permanently in the Jamestown roadstead for bunkering, and for selling gas and diesel to whoever could pay for it. Another small ship also lay there semi-permanently. This passenger ship, the *Arogonite*, had replaced the *St. Helena* when she went off to the Falklands war. Bob, her captain, told us that she was fully booked and just waiting for him to name sailing day.

Sue had been toiling over the meal aboard all day. It would be our first ever meal on a tanker but, to our later surprise, not by any means our last one that year. Bill, the captain of the *Bosunbird*, showed us over his ship, dwelling lovingly on the gleaming engine-room where we met Tim, the engineer, who would also be at the party. Later we met the South African couple Keith and Marion from the yacht *Tenacity*. Together with John and Sue from *Chianti*, and us from *Tryste*, we were only nine souls altogether, although later, when it became too cool to be on deck and we all moved into Tim's cabin, there seemed to be rather more of us at times.

The dinner Sue had made was delicious. There were battered shrimps for starters then curried chicken with rice and large quantities of bright yellow dhal (John's favourite, but definitely not ours). Then, as a yachtie's special treat Sue had made a dessert of fruit salad with both cream *and* ice cream. Wine and beer flowed freely all evening and after we moved into Tim's cabin, the conversation at times became a little heavy. To quote from my diary remembered next day

> 'Keith got intense and uptight and Ernest became repetitive. Bob got annoyed, but not for long, and Marion got passionate about nuclear waste, and then she and Bob argued about how long, when the conflict started, before the nuclear bomb would be used. Later Ernest and Keith (and I) tried to make Bob (deep sea Captain of the *Arogonite*) understand that as yachties we wanted the freedom *not* to call for help if we got into trouble. Chief engineer Tim made a few quiet and pithy comments, Sue went to sleep, having worked so hard all day, and I gave the men a hard time for throwing beer cans out of the porthole. John then entertained us all by giving an amazing imitation of a completely boneless man.'

At 4 am, when Sue and I wanted to go home to our boats, Ernest was on his third or fourth *gin* and didn't want to leave. 'But you take the dinghy and GO!' He said belligerently to me, 'I'll swim!' The tanker was way too dangerously high off the water for that; but in the end he came quietly, and the next morning we none of us felt at all well and settled for a quiet day of little accomplishment.

Our last full day lying off Jamestown, we saw a small Norwegian cruise liner, the *Vistafjord,* with only 300 passengers aboard, come in around 0800 and anchor. Around mid-morning the passengers, many of them of pensionable age or older, were gradually brought ashore in the ship's covered launches, seventy at a time.

We had gone ashore after breakfast to climb the 699 steps of Jacob's Ladder. Susie and Nicola had done it when we were all there before, but not us aged parents. Now we felt the urge to try it. Ernest set off up at a fine lick while I followed, uncommitted, at my own (slow) pace— 20 steps straight up then sit and rest a minute and then off again. I had no trouble at all, even if it did take me half an hour. I was delighted. At forty-eight the family thought I was too old: at fifty-six I did it fine.

Once back aboard we were in a good position to see how the passenger transfer was safely accomplished, remembering from before how dangerous going ashore at the steps could be when there was anything of a swell running.

In one of the spans of the line of buoys, in which *Tryste* was now tied astern of the French singlehanded ketch *Jonathan,* there was one of the solid local open boats tied fore and aft. As each passenger left the liner's launch amidships he or she was handed into this stationary boat by a pair of strong St. Helenians (or 'Saints') and then, after walking across the thwart, was handed into the island boat that would take them ashore to the jetty, where yet another pair of strong arms whisked them ashore and started them up the steps. It was a smooth operation that no doubt worked just as well in reverse.

To our surprise we received visitors from the *Vistafjord,* a pair of ship's entertainers, Doreen and Michael, who had seen our flag and, since Doreen was Canadian, had thought that they would come and say hello and bring us a bottle of Champagne that someone had given to them. This made them most welcome and we had a pleasant visit and were able to gloss over Michael's abysmal ignorance of all things nautical; after all he hailed from New York. Perhaps he would pick up a little more during the rest of his 10-month singing contract aboard.

Later that afternoon we snorkelled over the wreck of the *Papanui,* a passenger ship which in 1911 caught fire when lying at anchor in the roadstead off Jamestown. Chris, the 'Saint' who had helped us moor *Tryste* on our first night, had told us the story—apparently the Captain had wanted to fight the fire out at anchor, but was overpowered by the crew who ran the ship ashore and thus saved the lives of all the passengers. Chris told us that he was himself looking for artefacts there and suggested we would enjoy swimming over the wreck in such unusually calm weather. The wreck lies close in, in fairly shallow water and he pointed out the buoy that marks where she lies.

'There are still some Silver Jubilee trinkets and little boxes of sweeties to be found,' he told us. As we snorkelled over the open wreck, admiring the huge boilers and enormous anchor, a large green turtle, that apparently lived there, joined us. Although we enjoyed being able to swim over the *Papanui* we did not want to stay too long. There was something rather eerie and corpse-like about it. We did dive down where Chris told us, but we never found any of the trinkets.

We never managed to find our way back to Dot's café, either, which we had visited with Susie and Nic, and Katie and Mo from *Nanook*, on our previous voyage, but after our quiet day of rest we decided instead to try dinner at 'Ann's Place' close down by the water, which had become the favourite feeding place for boaters.

Like Dot, Ann too called everyone darling, and although in our delicate condition we said that we would not have either soup or fish course, Ann overrode us on the fish,

'I just made you a little bit darling.' She said. We had tired of tuna on our voyages but had never tried it deep-fried before. Cooked in a crisp batter, with salad on the side, it was unexpectedly tasty. We were dining, rather to our surprise, with six South Africans, two couples from the yacht *Finesse*, and Keith and Marion from *Tenacity*. We assumed they had all started their dinner with thick bean soup, since it was a hearty Afrikaner speciality.

By the time John and Sue turned up looking for food all the fish was gone, but they soon joined us for fried chicken, roast potatoes, carrots, beans, gravy and more salad. Ann did not have a liquor licence but some beer was procured from the hotel and we all enjoyed that, as well as a dessert of fruit crunch offered with thick British-style custard served in a gravy boat. Although we still felt a little frail, this wonderful home-cooked meal set us up. It cost only two pounds, twenty p. each.

Our last evening on St Helena Cliff and Delia insisted on having us to dinner. We went ashore around six, after the last of the passengers had gone back aboard the *Vitafjord*. We had cold showers ashore, watched the liner sail and then wandered around waiting for Cliff to collect us.   Although he was late, his first words were, 'I'm early by St. Helena standards,' with a big smile, then up to Lufkin's Spring for dinner, feeling a bit that our time on St Helena had been all take and no give. Were we at heart 'bludgers', we wondered, that beautifully expressive antipodean word?

Bludgers or not, Cliff and Delia gave us another superb island dinner, this time of roast pork, new potatoes, pumpkin squares, green beans and gravy, followed by lemon meringue pie and home-made ice cream. Later they drove us home together and we all parted with sad farewells, hoping to meet again when they visited Saltspring in a year or two.

The next leg of our voyage to the West Indies, or to Nicky in Barbados, as we tended to think of it, was almost a replica of the previous one, since the wind remained light and in the southeast. We enjoyed day after day of *Tryste* sailing calmly on over a near flat sea in the sunshine, unbelievably easy. If Ernest sometimes felt frustrated with our slow progress, knowing that Nic had her flight booked for March 4th, he more often relaxed and enjoyed it, closing his mind to the possible doldrum delays that lay ahead. For ten days out of this two-week passage we sailed with our tiny chute set and only the fact that one or other or both clews had ripped, and it was once again being mended, stopped us.

We never found out how long after we sailed, John and Sue left St. Helena. The only time we heard any news of *Chianti* at all was on February 8 or 9 when we were approaching Fernando de Noronha, and I picked up the UK ham net run by one, 'David', and faintly heard Sue signing in. She reported that they had SE 15 (force 3-4) winds but were still 900 miles from Salvador, their Brazilian destination north of Rio de Janeiro, where they had hoped to celebrate the Carnival, but had little hope now of being there in time. Aboard *Tryste* we were then 600 miles north of Salvador, only 2 or 3 days from the islands of Fernando de Noronha, almost on the latitude of Fortaleza.

That same day we were feeling a little anxious, since we had picked up a news item about a Russian satellite (possibly with nuclear power for the systems but not for propulsion) that had failed to burn up on re-entering the earth's atmosphere and was scheduled to land 'somewhere in the South Atlantic off Brazil,' with no date, time, or coordinates given. We heard later that day on the radio, that it *had* come down, some miles off the Brazilian Coast in the South Atlantic, and that the

Americans were going to check on radiation levels. We were relieved and intrigued, wondering if we would suddenly see the US Navy appear on our horizon but it never happened. This was also the day that we tuned in to WWV, both to get the regular weather information and to try and find out where that year's doldrums were, and found that they had discontinued the weather!

'For comments please write to Box so and so.' Apparently enough people commented forcefully enough to have the service returned.

A week after leaving St. Helena, as we winged our way up the South Atlantic, *Tryste* joined or was joined by, a school of small tuna, only three or four pounds each. We had often wondered, when we sailed through seemingly endless schools of fish in the open ocean, if we were (as it appeared) sailing through a vast shoal, or if the school was merely keeping station with us for some unknown reason of its own; for safety perhaps? Certainly these fish were partly protected by *Tryste* from the frigate birds flying out from Ascension Island, as they did not swoop down that close to the boat. It took us only half a day to confirm that this particular school was definitely travelling with us.

'Look,' Ernest said, 'they're different tuna! They've got red patches!' But we soon realised that only one specific fish, called Charlie, had a red patch. He had been attacked, by either a frigate bird's hooked beak or a big fish's spear, and had a patch of raw orange-brown flesh cut almost to the bone about two inches by two on his back just over the pectoral fins, making him easy to identify. From then on we often stepped out on the bow to check that Charlie was still with us, and to watch *our* fish, flashing blue underwater, hurrying along in a school just ahead of the forefoot or chasing the tiny flying fish up out of the waves.

On the second afternoon of travelling in company, a flock of Sooty terns who were feeding around the boat, suddenly screeched a warning and flew away, and within moments all our fish seemed to have disappeared. Ernest investigated and found them swimming in tight formation, close to the starboard float. At almost the same moment he saw a tall scimitar fin cut across in front of *Tryste*. Soon after that we both watched a huge fish take up position just astern of the self-steering gear, his long spear, wide pectoral fins and crescent-shaped tail outlined by the water-flow in brilliant blue. He looked enormous compared to Charlie and Co, somewhere between 8 and 10 feet long, with fins roughly a foot each. He followed the boat for about five minutes and then as Ernest said, 'Put it in overdrive,' and just zoomed away without a quiver. A few moments later the tuna broke ranks and started feeding again, spread out around the boat. Our monster returned the following day, and we saw his magnificent barred back, and were able to identify him as a marlin, our fish book confirming that Atlantic marlin are striped, and also mentioning their habit of stunning prey with a blow of the spear. Poor Charlie, his chances did not look good.

From then on the marlin rejoined *Tryste* and took up station astern several times, once after a hundred miles and each time the tuna took refuge close to *Tryste*, but each time after he left their numbers were diminished. Altogether they stayed with us four days, gradually becoming fewer and fewer. On the afternoon of the fourth day Charlie disappeared and next morning I wrote sadly in my diary, 'Our fish really have left us.'

Four days later we were approaching the island group of Fernando de Noronha and still had not reached the doldrums. Our noon position that day was 4°15'S, 31°15'W, only 80 miles from the islands. A rainsquall came up and enveloped us and from then on we were sailing fast for the first time since leaving St. Helena. Ernest picked up the primary navigation light on *El Pico*, a spectacular pointed rock that attempts to pierce the sky, about 0200.

Two hours later, when he had identified three navigation lights from about 4 miles off, he handed *Tryste* over to me. We lay off and Ernest, who had been on watch all night, had a nap while I watched the dawn break and the grey-shouldered lumps that were Fernando gradually emerging from the dark. Finally I woke Ernest saying, 'Shall we be on our way?'

We started sailing in with genoa and main set, and soon picked out the *Espigoes*, a group of breaking rocks to the north to avoid. Suddenly a school of about 10 dolphins broke from the water in such a flurry that I thought it was a reef, then rushed around for a few minutes, showing themselves off and welcoming us in. As the sun rose, a dozen or so frigate birds circled above us, while flocks of Blue-footed boobies passed overhead on their way out fishing. We sailed on, identifying *Ihlas Rata, do Meio* and *do Frade* and were soon speeding in with the wind and swell behind us, through a passage between gorgeous rocky islands, all undercut and volcanic, covered in green bush and low trees and lots and lots of nesting boobies.

As we came through the pass into *Baia Antonio* we saw the ketch *Spirit of Dani*. We sailed in, dropped the sails and anchored a little inshore of her in 33 ft. of good holding. It was 0730 on a Sunday morning. In the centre of the beach was a white building with a sandy roof, which said *DIVISAO DE PESCA*. (Fishing division?) There was a fat yellow wooden boat behind it and on the hill above an oil tank, an official-looking office in tarpaper and what looked like a store and a water tank. Further along was a tiny white church with a slightly Moorish tiled look and a cross on top, and then halfway down towards the point was the remains of a fairly large stone or brick building. There were more buildings to the east, perhaps left over from the original 19th century penal colony.

Ernest went over to talk to *Spirit of Dani* who had been there two and a half days, and found out that officialdom insisted on taking your passports ashore until you left, and charged you $4.00 per person per day. We had intended to go ashore and buy fresh fruit and vegetables but it seemed there were only green bananas and green tomatoes to be had, and that going ashore was extremely tricky in the surf. *Spirit of Dani's* crew had been rolled in their dinghy with the outboard on, and the Captain, Walter, had a badly banged-up knee. All in all we thought that as we had arrived at the weekend we would forget about going ashore and probably try and slip away on Monday morning before the officials were around, provided we could scrub *Tryste's* bottom satisfactorily before then.

On Sunday morning Ernest made an early start on the scrubbing, and had done one whole float before I slipped over the side into the warm shallow water to help him. Before I started on the second float he had to show me *Tryste's* incredible garden growth on the main hull. As well as a scum over the whole hull and long trailing green weed, there were groups of gooseneck barnacles clustered as tight as pins in a pincushion. My float was bad on the outside but not so bad on the inner surface. Before long a swell and surge came in and it became hard work even to hold oneself in place, not at all the flat-calm bay conditions we had sought for scrubbing. We did have one little rest, but it was obviously not getting any calmer so we pressed on to finish. Ernest did the whole main hull after doing the first float, no wonder his head was dizzy and bothered him for a few hours.

Next morning we were ready to leave at 0700, which was the earliest we expected officialdom to come to work. Just before we left we saw a mini-bus drive up and one man jump out and hurry down to the *Pesca* building where a dinghy lay, but he disappeared into the building and had not set out to see us by the time we had the hook up and had motored out of the bay.

As we passed the island of Fernando de Noronha on the way out we caught a strange grey coastal fish. Although we had never seen anything quite like it before it could have been some sort of cod. We ate it anyway, and it made us four or five tasty meals.

As we left the islands behind, flocks of noddies were feeding round us, and a few dolphins visited us briefly to say goodbye. We set the chute again with a sigh, since we still had only a light SE breeze. But though we sighed at the direction and strength of the wind, we were delighted by the increase in our speed made by having three clean hulls. By noon the second day we had reached 2°40'S, still with the chute set, but on the third day that changed. At noon we had been at 1°36'S, only ninety-six miles south of the equator. At midnight I had just finished updating my diary when I became aware that we were slopping about with very little wind. Our course had been 325°, but now we were swinging round to 270° and the chute was hanging limply useless, as faint puffs came from every which way. I waited awhile in the nothingness to be sure and then called Ernest,

'I think we've arrived,' I said, meaning the dreaded doldrums. By then a bit steadier breeze seemed to be coming in from the northeast. We handed the chute and set the main, genoa and mizzen sails. Ernest refused to go back to sleep, which was a good thing since for the next four hours the wind came from each and every direction with heavy rain showers. Every time I looked out (having been told to go back to my bunk once I had made up the log) he seemed to be crouched naked on the foredeck in the pouring rain fixing the pole onto or off the genny as the wind swung around.

When I took over at daylight, things were improving. Although ugly squalls kept building behind us, they passed through with nothing more worrying than a 10 or 20° change of wind direction, while behind us lay an elongated, sausage-shaped cumulus in all shades of purple, blue, grey and white, with rainsquall towers at intervals all along it. By the time we reached 1°S that evening we were doing 5 knots with a good breeze that, though still a little changeable, continued to be northeasterly. We scarcely dared breathe. Could the doldrums possibly be such a non-event? Ernest's next log entry said simply, 'Perfection!' It was true. We really were in the NE trades. Our 38 gallons of diesel-to-motor-through-the-doldrums remained intact. For the next ten days we averaged a delightful 155 miles a day, our best day's run being 179.

The northeaster gradually increased and the waves built up and it became glorious blue-water sailing. We caught a long slim 25 lb. Dorado with two healed marlin-spear-holes in its side, an exceptionally yellow-gold fish that gave us the most spectacular colour display in dying. As its gold faded away to almost white, its fins and back fin turned spotted brilliant blue, and finally the whole fish became an amazing deep olive green.

We passed the mouth of the great river Amazon, too far off to see any outflow evidence in the colour of the water. Day after day the sea remained a deep ultramarine blue, while white-capped waves covered the whole ocean surface and the clear line of the horizon became a white line of foam.

One morning we saw a Sei whale which was the highlight of the passage. (Sorry Charlie.) It came up rather far away at an angle of 45°, but we could clearly see it's markings of dark above and white below and that it was thin in section. Terns dived around the splash area where it was feeding. The Sei, we read, is the only whale that both skims and swallows. This one kept coming up with its mouth open and we persuaded ourselves that it was scooping up *something*, but whether it really was or not, we shall never know.

The next day was February 24th, and we celebrated Carol's thirtieth birthday, drinking her health in rum and orange. The date meant that in only eight days Nicky was due to fly in to Barbados; with little more than 500 miles to go, we no longer worried about not arriving in time. As we neared the island the wind became more easterly and we changed to running sails. Three days later we were only 75 miles off. Ernest's afternoon sight suggested that we were experiencing a favourable set. That evening a round of star sights confirmed Ernest's earlier sight. I went on deck to look and shouted,

'Oh, Ernest, there's…!' At the same moment he, still checking our position on the chart, called up, 'You should be able to see lights!' I could indeed, a line of orange lights and a flashing white one. We must have had a tremendous push from the current. The orange lights were not marked on our out of date chart, but we found an airfield marked in our National Geographic Atlas and then Ernest saw a plane land behind the lights, in confirmation. We were looking for a light on South Point to round, but the single intermittently visible flashing light seemed to be in the wrong place.

Suddenly Ernest shouted, 'We're in soundings! We can't be!' But we were. We eased sheets and I tried to steer parallel to the land while he scrutinized the chart again. To be in soundings we had to be dangerously close in, which we realised we were when we suddenly saw the actual South Point light tower ahead, outlined against the night sky, apparently with a candle in the window. At least now we knew where we were, and we were able to scrape round it and head towards Needham Point and the lights of our anchorage in Carlisle Bay. We had been doing five or six knots all this time with only genny and mizzen set. Now Ernest took the twin-pole out of the genny, to make it easy to drop the sails, motor in and drop the anchor.

As we rounded Needham Point we passed a big hotel that wafted out to us the delectable smell of a steak barbecue and the cheerful music of a steel band. Civilization! In brilliant moonlight with excellent visibility we came in to Carlisle Bay and anchored not too far astern of *Kiskadee*. In a day or two we would be drinking rum with Harold and Wendy, last seen five years ago in the Fijis where Wendy was awaiting the birth of their third child, Jennifer. In four more days Nicky would arrive. As usual with such worrywarts, we were in plenty of time.

CHAPTER TWENTY-ONE:

ERNEST'S EXTRA WIVES

On our first Panama Canal transit, after we had almost crashed bow-on into one of the concrete lock walls, I had said to Ernest, 'You can do what you like. Next time I'm going round the Horn.' That, of course was just bravado and now, in a couple of months, we would be facing our second transit. But first we would enjoy cruising the West Indies with Nicky.

The four days we had in Barbados before she arrived were enough for us to catch up with Wendy and Harold and the Goddard family of *Kiskadee*. When we saw them in the Fijis in 1978 Harold was a relaxed cruiser with a glass of rum in hand and wearing only a pair of shorts and a tan. They had left the Fijis when their new baby Jennifer was only six weeks old, and continued their round-the-world cruise to reach their Barbados home in 1982. Now here was Harold sitting behind a desk in an office in Bridgetown, looking highly respectable in shirt and tie. Luckily rum still played a part in his life. He and Wendy had held our mail for us and we were able to collect that, as well as catching up on boat chores like stocking up on diesel and stores and filling our water tanks.

Of the awaited five daughters' letters, only Carol's was there, started December and mailed in January from Saskatchewan where she and Gerry, Rhiannon and baby Christopher, had spent Christmas with Gerry's much-loved grandmother.

'Oh, of course,' I said, after we had read it, 'Nicky'll be bringing the rest.'

Wendy was very kind to us, doing our heavy bedding laundry, and driving us around Bridgetown. She also took us to meet her parents for supper, where we were introduced to battered flying fish—in a hamburger bun—an interesting, and filling, local delicacy. The day Nicky arrived Wendy drove us out to the Sir Grantley Adams airport to meet her. As we drove up the last hill a plane flew over us, a red maple leaf on its tail.

'That's Nicky's plane!' Ernest said, excitedly. From the viewing deck we looked down at the arrivals lounge and saw her moving slowly up to the immigration check-in desk. We hurried down to arrivals, but as we waited impatiently crowds of other people came out but no Nic. Wendy, who worked as a travel agent, was all prepared to go and find out what had happened to her but suddenly she appeared, beaming, but looking pale to us, compared to everyone else around. Once she was with us she assured us, between hugs, that as she flew in to the airfield she suddenly 'knew' we, and *Tryste,* were safely there to meet her. I had been right about the mail: she had letters for us from Janet, Anne and Susie, who were all well and all working.

Once aboard *Tryste,* she also handed us a small cardboard box; 'Spring' she said simply. It was the beginning of March and from our Saltspring garden she and Carol had picked violets, primroses, snowdrops, hyacinths, daffodils and the first tulip. They looked, and smelt, heavenly. To celebrate her arrival we had bought a crayfish—a local lobster—which I had already cooked, and with it we drank the bottle of bubbly that the entertainers on the *Vistafjord* had given us in St Helena. Nicky soon turned in to her allotted bunk while Ernest and I revelled in having family crew aboard and family mail to read.

The following day Harold and Wendy and the children collected us at 10 o'clock from the dock and took us all around the island. We soon headed up over the hills, passing picturesque villages with brightly painted little houses built on blocks of limestone, amongst flowers, bushes and palm trees. We passed brilliant green sugar cane plantations and a few small stands of mahogany trees before reaching pastureland with black-bellied sheep that looked like goats, and the handsome St John's church that had a tantalising view down to the sandy beaches below.

'I'm taking you down to the main fishing harbour on the east coast first,' Harold told us, smiling. We were entirely taken in, expecting a large harbour with at least one or two big crewed fish boats or charter boats, but there were only two or three small boats on moorings inside the reef and some others pulled up on the beach by tractor.

'Watch that boat coming through the pass!' Harold said. As we watched in amazement, a small one-man open fish boat, with a dark blue hull picked out in red, came through a tiny gap in the reef. It was very low tide and the boat broached as it entered, then turned and came in alongside the reef, rolling in the breakers until it was in nearly flat water. Leaving the engine idling, the fisherman slipped over the side to where he could stand then walked casually ashore with a giant paint bucket of tiny fish, perhaps flying fish. He dumped the bucket on the shore, waded back to his boat, which was turning in the tide towards a clump of coral, clambered back aboard and motored in to pick up his mooring amongst the other similar boats.

By this time we already needed to be out of the hot sun for a while and Harold drove us further north to a long beach with a lifeguard tower and—this being the cricket-mad West Indies—an intense cricket match going on (with lots of laughter) on the beach. Harold backed the car into a clump of shade trees, disturbing some honeybirds, and we had a delicious chicken lunch which included bread that Nicky had made that morning. Later we drove back to the west coast, looking for a quiet swimming beach for Nicky and the Goddard children, but by now it was sweltering in the car, and we soon gave up and drove straight to the Yacht Club in Carlisle Bay where we all had long swims at a more crowded beach, but with a good view of *Tryste* and *Kiskadee*.

Back at the Goddard's house we had showers and assorted strengths of rum-based 'brown juicy' before Wendy drove us home to the wharf and our dinghy. As the three of us aboard *Tryste* enjoyed a light supper of boiled eggs before early bed we all agreed that it had been a great day but, as Ernest said, 'It's *exhausting* enjoying yourself.'

Next morning we tied to the harbour wall for Customs and clearance. Ernest collected our new depth sounder from Customs and was able to install it before we left the dock. We had said our sad farewells and many thanks the night before. Now we were ready to cruise the Caribbean, this time the Windward Islands, with family crew aboard *Tryste* as we had done in the Grenadines nine years earlier.

In the next three weeks we sailed 500 miles through the islands, a haphazard progress by plebiscite although, as with the best democracies, the Captain had the deciding vote. In general we went where he suggested, being happy to see as many islands and different anchorages as we could; Nicky wanting more than anything to swim, sail, and walk on beaches in the sunshine.

The Windward Islands, from Barbuda and Antigua north of Guadaloupe, and those south to St Lucia and St Vincent form part of a huge volcanic arc. We did not visit the two more southerly islands but from Barbados set out directly, on an overnight passage of 200 miles, to start our cruise in Guadaloupe, the largest of the islands. Ernest and I shared this, the only overnight sail we made in the West Indies, with Ernest as usual taking the lion's share of the dark hours. It was a wild bumpy ride with a fresh NE trade wind. Since Ernest and I had long since pre-empted the wing berths, we had made up what used to be our bunk in the after cabin, for Nic. She told us next day that it had been like, 'Being in an enormous comfortable bed with someone jumping up and down on it.' In spite of which she seemed happy to be back aboard *her* boat.

We passed Martinique at 0800 next morning. As we had not made better time towards Guadaloupe, we decided to aim for the harbour of Grand Bourg on the nearer island of Marie Galante instead, which would be an easier approach after dark. At 1800 we were only nine miles off and as soon as the sun set we picked up the flashing light on the end of the jetty and the red and green fixed lights either side of the pass. We closed with the coast under sail, waiting for our new sounder to show us some depths, which, just as we began to doubt it, it eventually did; then we motored in through the easy pass and anchored.

After breakfast next morning we all went ashore to find the local gendarme, it being obvious that at this small place there would not be immigration officials. We found the *Gendarme Nationale* up beyond the old church whose spire dominated the small town. A charming officer with not much English to match our not much French, took our particulars and laboriously typed them out on an old typewriter. He told us we were now free to go to Isles des Saintes, Guadaloupe and '*peut-être*' Martinique, and although we had no stamps on our passports or papers to prove it, no one ever bothered us.

Grand Bourg proved as charming as the gendarme and the people friendly, with tiny houses on the waterfront and a few open boats with outboards, and with little Réunion-style shops and even a small supermarket. The highlight of our visit was eating ice cream cones on the jetty. We soon moved on to the historical Isles des Saintes, to the west, a perfect three hour sail in the sunshine with main and poled-out genny set wing and wing with a force 3-4 east southeast wind.

In Bourg des Saintes Bay we anchored with about 30 other yachts, spread over three little bays; mostly European cruising boats with some local charter boats. Ashore little red-roofed white-painted houses among palm trees, bougainvillea and hibiscus bushes, were shining in the sun, all dominated by a church tower, and to the south an enormous Crucifix. The imposing Fort Napoleon and the stone prison buildings stood on the headland to the north.

Ernest loves naval history, and here at Fort Napoleon the next day he happily absorbed the story of the famous British victory of the Battle of Les Saintes in 1782, when 36 British warships commanded by Rodney and Hood faced off in line of battle against a French fleet of 30 commanded by De Grasse. In the battle which followed, Rodney took advantage of a wind shift to break through the French line twice, firing broadsides, a tactic which had not been tried before and was simply 'not cricket.' Models of the ships were all laid out in battle order on an over-sized table. When Nicky and I became tired of history we walked the battlements of the huge fort and then on a lower level discovered and photographed a tame iguana, posed on a piece of ordnance by its owner, a small, entrepreneurial boy, who appeared from nowhere with his hand out.

The small island of Barbuda was as far north as we went. Here we anchored inside Spanish Point and walked inland through what seemed to be white volcanic rock, very jagged in places like Galapagos lava, with areas of sandy wastes scattered with old skeletal conches. Although there seemed to be no soil, there were fat little cactus that shed their spines (which got in our shoes) creeping vines and low bush, as well as plants in holes in the rock. We walked and then snorkelled for hours until we were worn out, and all agreed that we were too tired to look for the many wrecks of various vintages reputed to lie along the coast.

A day later we were in Guadeloupe's Baie Deshaies, where Nic ignored all well-meaning advice (again) and became more sunburnt. We had enjoyed an exciting sail past steep mountain valleys, where williwaws suddenly screamed out at us as we passed, and then left us almost becalmed a few miles further on. Altogether we spent three days admiring the island, anchoring in different bays, before sailing down towards Dominica. On the spectacular southwest coast of Guadaloupe, the verdant mountain of *La Soufrière*, highest volcano in the chain, towered over the island at 4,812 ft. and Dominica too was dramatic, boasting four volcanoes of such green mountainous beauty that we thought we must be back in the Marquesas.

Earlier we had spent several days in Antigua, where we had sailed in to English Harbour's pleasant outer Freeman Bay just as another Canadian yacht was leaving. Ernest put the binoculars on her.

'It's Honnalee!' He said. We soon saw them turning back, and in no time at all they were anchored near us. We had first met Roy and Rika Gingell in Tahiti's Papeete Harbour in 1970, and had enjoyed their company in many island groups across the Pacific and in New Zealand.

Once we had been cleared they came aboard and joined us for coffee and the buns which Nicky had baked, and both talked at once for a couple of hours. It was really great fun to see them again. Once they had sailed on their way, we moved over to Ordnance Bay, closer inshore, where we dropped the hook and tied two stern lines to the mangroves ashore. Here in company with several other overseas yachts, it was much quieter than nearby Nelson's Dockyard.

The next day Nicky and I took a local bus to the commercial harbour of St.John`s, on the northwest coast, to shop, since it boasted both a supermarket and a local market where I bought lots of fresh fruit and vegetables from friendly, helpful, local people.

'Got all you want now, darlin?' asked an older lady who had watched my perambulations through the market; and while we waited impatiently for the bus home, others reassured us, 'Bus soon come!' These mini-buses had fold-down seats through the aisles which led to complete gridlock when some of the big ladies settled down on them, but it was all cause for good-natured chaff and lots of laughter.

On our return Ernest told us that he had met another Nicky, this one a big surprise, being the sister of my Saltspring friend Sanchia Seward. She had seen our dinghy with Haigh, Ganges, B.C. on it and excitedly accosted Ernest. She was crewing on the boat next but one to us in Ordnance Bay. We soon had her over for tea and talk. Next morning she joined the three of us from *Tryste* in a long uphill walk past Clarence House to Shirley Heights, high above our anchorage. After we had wandered around the remains of gun emplacements and foundations and the old stone buildings on what was the site of the British garrison in the late 18th century, we sat on a rock wall and shared the coffee and tea and bread and jam that we had brought with us, and admired the breathtaking view over English Harbour and Nelson's Dockyard, and all the bays and inlets right across to Falmouth Harbour.

We visited back and forth with Nicky and her captain, Mickey, and also joined the throng at a rum-up at Nelson's Dockyard, meeting many other offshore cruisers, before leaving Ordnance Bay a day or two later. Sailing north up the coast we discovered smaller, less populous anchorages. In a bay at either Five Islands, on Antigua's northwest coast, or Green Island on the east, Nicola discovered three lobsters under a ridge of coral when she was snorkelling and Ernest harvested the largest of them with his spear gun. Later we learnt that it was out of season, but by then it was too late for anything but memories of a good meal, and a twinge of guilt.

It was in one of Antigua's quiet bays, on a second visit, that we met three young men aboard the Danish Westsail *Parma*. Ernest invited them over for coffee and they stayed on for wine, but when we asked them to stay to lunch as well, Peter, the captain, insisted that *we* come to *Parma*. We swam over and were soon enjoying salmon mayonnaise with fresh home-made bread. Once we had eaten heartily of what we thought was a delicious lunch they brought out the next course and we had to struggle to do justice to rice and meat in tomato sauce. It was not that hard with the help of their two or three bottles of *Rocher Bois*.

'These rice are a little very strange,' Peter said, 'But I do not think they are overcooked.' Their English was good, so we learnt that in Danish rice are plural. After lunch they had insisted we stay for coffee and more conversation. To our amazement, when we finally swam home we found that it was four in the afternoon.

From Antigua we carried a fine healthy trade wind almost all the way to Martinique. Our landfall on the northwest corner of the island was *Mont Pelée*, an active volcano that erupted in 1902, engulfing and destroying the coastal town of St. Pierre and killing the entire population of roughly 28,000 people.

Although the wind turned flukier in the afternoon, as we sailed down the west side of the island, we anchored that evening soon after six, in the big southwest bay of Fort de France. From here in Martinique our beloved crew was flying away, back to her own life and her job as a cook on Saltspring, even though we had offered her a berth all the way home aboard *Tryste*.

After two days in Martinique, while Nic was still aboard, Ernest discovered a broken backstay tang at the top of the main mast. Having been given the name of a welder by veteran sailor Peter Tangveld, he struggled to remove the fitting from the masthead, but found it impossible out at anchor. A fresh southerly breeze was blowing in, and as well it was the start of a four day weekend. Outboard-powered dinghies from cruising yachts were racing in to shore at great speed; their disruptive wakes criss-crossed by those of the launches of the Italian cruise liner *Carla C* disgorging her passengers. The mast was never still.

In such a situation Ernest always becomes stressed, but at the same time remains excruciatingly persistent. The sensible course would have been to relax and stay a few extra days, but instead we were soon heading into the careenage, where the water was calm and we were within walking distance of the commercial area. The downside was that the docksides were crowded with fish boats and pleasure boats. In the end we found a boat to tie alongside, Ernest's doggedness was rewarded. He wrestled the masthead fitting off, found someone to weld it at a miniscule cost and even had some holes drilled for free. It was blisteringly hot and the fish boats were putting on ice, which was chopped up in a machine with a hideous noise like a broken-down compressor. The best contribution Nic and I made, apart from tending the lines to the bosun's-chair, was to buy ice-cold beer for the three of us.

The day after Nicky flew home we sailed sadly out, heading for the Atlantic end of the Panama Canal. Eleven days later we were in Cristobal, tied up to a dock at the Yacht Club. When we were last there, the Canal had been US run, but since then the Torrejos Carter Treaty had been signed, and the Canal was gradually being handed over to the Panamanians.

We had known that we would need to find at least three line handlers from somewhere; last time, with Susie and Nicky aboard, we had needed to borrow only one, a girl from another yacht. We discovered that now common practice was to phone a contact person for the US servicemen still stationed in the Zone, who together with their wives were eager to experience the thrill of transiting the Canal as a change from their mundane lives at the camp. I could see that Ernest hoped that our crew would be wives.

Carol Nelson, we were told, organized the volunteers. On the second evening that we were at the Yacht Club I was elected to be the one to phone. The pay phone was in the noisy club restaurant. I stood at the phone with the sweat pouring off me in rivulets as I wrestled with the vagaries of the Panamanian phone system. As I gradually mastered it I discovered that 1. You could not dial direct from the Canal Zone; you had to dial 101 to access the operator. 2. You asked, 'Do you speak English?' and they put you onto an operator who did. 3. That getting an operator at all required patience. 4. That some operators would tell you that you could dial direct by leaving out the two, but that it did not work, and 5. That it was a good thing that I had the job and not Ernest.

I did not get through at all that first try, although I finally got an operator who was smarter than the rest who said, 'That number must be wrong,' and told me that one of the numbers that I was using had to be a four. I looked at Ernest's note again of the number he was given by the yacht *Gemini* and decided that the one I read as a seven had to be a four. I finally got through on that number but it was engaged and when I tried again there was no answer.

Next day I successfully reached Carol Nelson and she said, 'No problem, I have a long list.' We agreed to confirm the three line-handlers' availability next afternoon when our transit date and time had been confirmed. We also had a volunteer line-handler, bearded Mark, who wanted a ride to Balboa at the Pacific end of the Canal to look for news of his girlfriend, Bernadette. He had been travelling in South America with Bernadette and another girl. They had split up to get to Cristobal earlier and the two girls had found crewing jobs on two yachts and left to transit the canal. Mark soon proved his worth, helping us with the Spanish, writing a re-direction request to Puntarenas Post Office where we had told everyone to send our mail, and where we had decided that we were not now going.

Obtaining all the necessary papers included the actual transit, which in 1974 had cost only an incredible $11. We assumed that now it would be considerably more, but although they said 'Fifty-eight dollar,' in the office, this was adjustable, and in the end cost only US$23.36. Because the handover was not yet finished, the offices were often doubled up and thus necessitated hot visits to *two* Harbourmaster's offices, Immigrations, and Admeasurers, as well as to the one yacht club office to pay for our five night's moorage.

One of the places we went together was the Panamanian Admeasurer's office. This we finally found at the Harbourmaster's office in pleasant, clean, downtown Cristobal. We were taken there by the cleaning lady, who led us down several passages and then said, with a big smile, as she pointed to a door with her mop, 'Ad. Mes!' In the air-conditioned office we found Mr Cecil A. Small, a dark-skinned Panamanian with an excellent command of English but a machine gun delivery which, combined with a slurred effect, made him hard to follow. He impressed us by easily finding our *Tryste* transit booklet from 9 years ago.

Having been warned over and over on our first visit to Panama to be vigilant at all times, clutch our possessions feverishly and wear no watches to be cut off our wrists, these warnings were now reinforced by a tale that Cecil told us. He himself, although a local inhabitant living across the tracks in Colon, and fully aware of the number of thieves there, had had his wallet cut out from his back pocket by a thief so skilful that he, Cecil, had felt nothing.

Since we found that we also had to have a cruising permit for the waters and coast of Panama, Ernest tramped again from office to office in the heat. But this time he did obtain our *Zarpe*, our clearance. When we went to confirm out transit we found that it had been put back until Friday. In spite of the delay Mark remained cheerful and moved aboard on Thursday, to be ready for a 4 am start on Friday. In the meantime it gave us more time to shop for stores and diesel (luckily taxis never seemed to cost more than $2) and to make new friends, in particular Zac and Jeanette and their small son Robert, on the Australian yacht *Solcyon*.

We neither of us slept well the night before transit, although we had a few hours. We could not rid our minds of the harrowing memory of how close we had come to losing *Tryste* in the locks in 1974. Only Mark, who came home from the bar about midnight, slept well, though only until 0330 when the alarm went off for transit at four. He did get a cup of coffee in his bunk though, to help him wake up.

I had confirmed our 4 a.m. Friday transit with Carol Nelson and she had confirmed that our extra crew, the wives of servicemen, would be there, and they were. Marie, Meredith and Irene arrived, all smiles, in a gleaming Land Cruiser, just before 4, driven by one of the N.C.O. husbands, with a small son asleep in the back. They brought a flight bag apiece, as well as plenty of soft drinks and ice, while dark-haired Meredith, who was a nursery school teacher like our #3 daughter, Anne, also brought some home-made cookies.

Our pilot, Dennis, arrived ten minutes later by launch, having been misinformed as to where we were and looked for us in the anchorage, 'Out at the Flats'. It was then too late to go through with our scheduled big ship so we had to wait an hour for the next one, which turned out to be a mini-submarine belonging to some Central American country. I had warned Dennis that it might take five minutes for *Tryste* to extricate herself from the tight-fitting dock we were in, and it did, but we were ready to leave when our sub came past and we followed it out. We were a little early so we were oozing forward very gently when we saw our first-ever sloth hanging in a tree; an unexpected thrill.

In the hour that we had to wait, Dennis had given the wives and Mark a long serious how-to-do-it lecture on line handling. I was to be on the bow assisting Meredith on one critical line while Mark was allotted the other, starboard one. Marie and Irene had a line each astern, where Ernest at the helm, and Dennis in charge could keep an eye on them.

As we entered the first Gatun lock the water seemed to be boiling in. Four monkey's fists came whistling down from the line handlers on the dock above and were quickly snatched up and tied to the big loops we had ready, which the line handlers high above us hauled up and looped over enormous bollards. Then it was up to us aboard *Tryste* to haul our lines in quickly and steadily as the water poured into the dock and we rose. For a moment wind and current combined to keep the port side lines super-tight, and we looked like getting too close to the wall, but soon the eight minutes that it took to fill the lock were over. We hauled in our ropes to where they were attached to the heaving lines and held on to those, tight around the cleats, as the Panamanian line handlers walked us along, following the sub into the second Gatun lock.

The three going up locks were not easy but the girls and Mark handled the lines well and no disaster befell us. Then the time came to bid our sub companion farewell, and to take the first short cut through Gatun Lake. The wives were happy to have done three locks successfully and were able to sunbathe and to talk to their hero, Captain Ernest, at the helm, which of course pleased him. The lake was fascinating with drowned trees and tree stumps and glassy watery wastes of jungle and palm trees and birds and finally the excitement of Denis, pointing and saying, 'Was that an alligator?'

Dennis had a big smile and a nice sense of humour and with his dark hair, tee shirt, shorts and baseball cap he had an all-American college-boy look, but he had been born in Panama and was therefore Panamanian and eligible to work on the Canal.

We had been told to bring lots of food for our line-handlers, as well as ice, soft drinks, beer and water, so I had laid on cold chicken and other meat, potato salad and green salad as well as cheese and three sorts of bread, but as we took turns below to collect our food, I saw that Ernest's extra wives ate like mice. I was too stressed to eat at all, but Ernest and Dennis ate well, while Mark made up for the rest of us and made it all worthwhile. The heat made us constantly thirsty: in all we drank eighteen bottles of beer, twenty of Coke and Sprite and two big bottles of Pepsi, as well as gallons of ice water.

We kept meeting ships and tugs going the other way, and once a bow wave washed over the foredeck where the girls were sunbathing and soaked them and their towels as they squealed with delight. It quite made their, already wonderful, day. We kept thanking them and in return they kept thanking us (especially Ernest) for letting them have this wonderful experience. 'It's usually only the officer's wives who get to go!' Marie explained.

As we had motor sailed most of the way across the lake and made good time, when we reached Pedro Miguel for the first of the down locks we had to tie up alongside a dock to wait. The dock, we saw with horror, was lined with what looked like two inches of molten tar or rubber. Dennis, who was very energetic for a Pilot, intended to jump ashore, but at the last minute he changed his mind and we were blown sideways, resulting in the only almost-cross words of the transit, but we did eventually get alongside relatively safely and cleanly, and then waited for the bulk carrier that was going to share the lock, to appear behind us.

Motoring into this first lock, wind and current made steering difficult for Ernest, although Dennis, unlike our Pilot Robbie, on *Tryste's* first transit in 1974, let Ernest handle the motor in his own way, only telling him where to go and when. We went right up to the very head of the lock, caught our monkey's fists okay and sent back the lines and took turns on our cleats and then watched in horror and amazement as two big tugs edged the enormous Greek bulk carrier *Archangelos* into the dock behind us.

We wondered if one tug was going to be squashed and could hardly believe that *Archangelos* would really fit. She was, we learned later, 106 ft wide to the lock's 110, and she was 850 ft long. (The beamiest ship ever through at that time was the 750 ft. long New Jersey, who scraped through at 108 ft.) As she started to bear down on us, slowly and inexorably, Dennis said quietly, 'We'll let the stern lines out a bit, I think,' and we moved up past the 850 ft mark; only 150 left before the big steel lock gates.

Now the mechanical mules pulled *Archangelos* forward until a bell rang, then the front mules came forward, letting out cable, until they were in position to keep the Archangel from slipping astern. It almost looked as if the cables might tangle with our rigging if they came forward any more, but they apparently all knew what they were doing, so I tried to stop worrying. Since the stern lines were now the all-important ones Mark and I were allotted them, while the three girls shared the forward ones.

The lock had soon emptied and we freed our lines and positively sped out of Pedro Miguel lock and motored down the straight stretch of less than a mile to the first of the two Miraflores locks of dread memory. We went in very fast, because the current was really running and pushing us over one way. We prayed that the line handlers would be on the ball and not muff it, because the wind was right behind us. Three monkey's fists were secured, three lines safely returned and over bollards, then the fourth handler dropped the line short and lost his nerve. Twice he tried to get the monkey's fist aboard and twice he missed, then another man took two tries and finally managed it. So much for knowing what they were doing, we could have been in real trouble. Dennis was as furious as he ever could be and sounded very racist about the line handlers.

'You're dealing with real sub-standard humans,' he said angrily. We were shocked for a moment then Ernest said, 'I don't suppose they're paid very much, are they?' and Dennis gave his big wide grin and admitted that maybe that explained it. The dock-master came along, outwardly quite unperturbed, saying that when they were practicing throwing the heaving lines the other day, down at a nearby dock, one of them put the monkey's fist through his car windshield.

When the line was finally successfully thrown, all the handlers (and there seemed lots of them all of a sudden) cheered and the girls cheered too, light-heartedly, having no idea how quickly disaster could strike in the locks. In came *Archangelos* and snuggled up to us. Ahead we could see the last lock and the Pacific. The gates closed behind her (presumably, since we could see only her huge bulk looming over us), and the water started to go out. This time we were even closer to the gates, with extended lines out astern. Even Ernest was worried. He tied a line onto our spare fender tire and took it forward. Dennis gently ribbed him for that, but nothing went amiss except that Meredith lost her sun visor overboard, never to be seen again except as a sad blue piece of plastic behind the lock gates.

The gates opened again and we moved into the last lock, tying up as close to the gates as Dennis dared with, again, long lines out astern; but this time our guardian angel did not come so close. It seemed in no time our level had dropped right down and we were casting off our lines as the gates opened and we were through! Jubilation, then sudden alarm as the current grabbed *Tryste* and swirled her off to one side, but Ernest quickly corrected and we held off cheering until we really were fully out.

Then we were back in our home Pacific Ocean and it was hooray! We were all really thankful. Dennis was one big grin of achievement. He knew that we (and especially I) had been worried, and with reason, and he had worried too, about the inexperienced young wives; but was favourably impressed.

It was time for us to say, 'Thank you Dennis, thank you Mark and thank you, thank you, girls.'

'No, no,' chorused Meredith, Marie and Irene, 'Thank you!' and Marie brought out a bottle of *Liebfraumilch* which they had hidden in one of their bags, and presented it to Ernest. Both Meredith and Irene were a little sunburnt, but Marie (who joked that she was part Indian) was not. Their hands, unused to rope work, looked a bit sore and their sunburn might have been worse next day, but they had not got tar or oil on their clean bright clothes. We had been strictly instructed to pay the cost of the three girls' fares back to Cristobal, but the most they would accept was $5.00 for a taxi to where they were meeting one of the husbands. It was the same with Mark. We had hoped to pay his train fare back to Cristobal but he refused to take anything. 'I enjoyed it enormously,' he said.

'But you did so much for us,' I said. I felt that I had taken him for granted and used him like one of our own family, as he had frequently offered to hand round drinks and to fetch and carry. 'But you did so much for *me*,' he insisted, 'that lunch was the best meal I've had in six months!' We were all extremely happy. We soon motored out under what used to be the Bridge of the Americas and is now the Thatcher Ferry Bridge, a much less romantic name, before putting them all off at the Balboa yacht club with more good wishes. We were pleased to learn later that Mark had been re-united with his Bernadette.

Less than three hours later we anchored with a few other cruising boats at the offshore Panamanian island of Tobago where we eventually slept ten hours, to wake aching all over, very glad that the Canal was behind us.

CHAPTER TWENTY-TWO:

EL NINO

After one full day in the anchorage off Tobago, where *Solcyon* caught up with us, we headed out with a light breeze to see what the Gulf of Panama had to offer us. The answer for the first day was heat, humidity and not much wind, but also a wealth of bird and other wildlife.

Somehow, when we popped out of the Canal at the beginning of April 1983, we had not realised that our world was still to be dominated by a continuation of the 1982 El Niño that had caused the cruising fleet so much grief rounding the Cape of Good Hope. Although we had heard of the trades failing in the Eastern Pacific we thought all that was in the past, not something which would affect our passage and our lives. Now we found that our world was a humid hell, where every evening a near-invisible sun set as a fuzzy red ball of fire behind a strange heat haze.

But at first, to our delight, there was wildlife everywhere: skeins of pelicans, dive-bombing formations of pelicans and crawling maggot piles of pelicans, mixed with other seabirds at the ocean surface, where small fish skittered and rays leapt from the water and smacked back. A small whale came up behind the boat just as Ernest was going for a swim, so he left it for a while. Later we slowed the motor to 1 knot and, as we loved to do in the searing heat, both dragged behind the boat hanging on to the swim grid.

'Look out for sharks,' I said, as I climbed back aboard. Ernest soon joined me and shortly after that *four* hammerhead sharks lined up in our place.

Our first anchorage was Chapera Island in the Las Perlas archipelago. Anne's husband Russ had sailed around the world with *his* parents, John and Maxene Hohmann, aboard the American yawl *Uwhilna,* and Russ had copied out their useful notes for us on the coasts of Panama and Costa Rica. For them, when they sailed this way in 1974, the Perlas had been memorable, with verdant islands, golden beaches, fresh running watercourses, and plenty of fish and fruit. We hoped to find the same.

Anchored off Isla Chapera aboard *Tryste,* after failing to catch any fish on the way, we thought we would try Russ's recommendation of limpets for lunch: 'Very good pounded and fried in butter.' We collected, cleaned, pounded, got covered in limpet glue, fried some in butter and ate a few—and decided that they would make good fish bait. They did, although all we caught that evening was a puffer fish and a trigger fish; neither of which were really edible. Luckily we *liked* corned beef.

That afternoon we had scrubbed *Tryste's* bottom ready to paint, and next day we started painting fairly early, as soon as the water went out in the shallow corner where we had tucked *Tryste* up to dry out. When we finished painting a few hours later, Ernest said, 'Easiest bottom painting ever.' I thought that was putting a very positive spin on it: we had nearly melted working on the beach, although the haze lessened the sun's intensity slightly. Once we had finished all three hulls, the hardest part was waiting for the tide to come back in and float us off.

Solcyon arrived and anchored off our corner of the bay and later they came ashore and invited us to come to dinner—when we finally floated off. There was no pleasure for anyone in being on the burning beach and Zach and Jeanette soon took Robert back to the sanctuary of *Solcyon*, where it was slightly cooler.

For us there was no cooling breeze at all, and the excruciating local biting bugs, as bad as Kiwi sandflies or Marquesan *nau naus,* soon found us where we alternately sat or lay in the warm water to try and escape them. In the late afternoon in desperation we tried rowing the dinghy well out into the bay. We took drinks with us, but there was still no breeze and the bugs soon found us, even there. Finally *Tryste* floated off and at last our agony was over. We re-anchored and were soon aboard *Solcyon* enjoying conch fritters followed by a chicken casserole with rice, and—nectar of the gods—ice-cold beer.

From Isla Chapera we moved to a bay on Isla Viveros, where the golden sand of the beaches was polluted with oil. Russ's notes told us of wild pigs, parrots and iguanas as well as fresh water, but it was a different world for us, and at last we began to recognise the impact of this extreme El Niño year. There was no fresh water, the land was parched, the heat and humidity sapped our energy and we had no inclination to go inland in search of animals or fruit.

'Too Hot To Read!' My diary complained. We swam off the boat about every ten minutes in water whose temperature was itself 90° F, and which cooled us only briefly.

Two islands and three days later we anchored off slightly greener, bigger and junglier Isla San Jose, where Russ had mentioned a useful stream, but we found only a 'non-running brackish watercourse.' Here we met the *Solcyon* family again, for the last time this voyage. We invited them to dinner that evening. Robert behaved perfectly and soon fell asleep in the shade of the cockpit, as the adults talked and sipped. Next morning we said farewell and the two yachts set off in different directions. We would not meet them again until 1996, in Neiafu, Tonga, by which time they would have three sons, and both families would have new boats.

After a pleasant overnight passage, with enough wind to sail much of the time, interspersed with patches of motoring and a short spell of welcome warm rain, morning found us sailing up the green coast of Panama, where high hills and low mountains, dotted with thatched houses, ran down to open sheds on the beaches below.

We had managed up to here with a sometimes unnervingly small-scale chart. After passing Punta Mariato we were into waters covered by our Pilot Book for the West Coast of Central America and United States—all the way up to Cape Flattery, at the entrance to the Strait of Juan de Fuca which, two years earlier, had been our last sight of land.

Heading north from Panama, cruising sailors with deep pockets and big motors often decide to motor straight up the coast against both wind and current. For us aboard *Tryste*, choosing to use the wind to sail whenever we could, there was no question of that. Once we reached Golfito in Costa Rica's Golfo Dulce, we would be heading off to the northwest to Hawaii and the easier sailing route home. Until then our coastal navigation would be more straightforward now, having the Pilot Book.

Although we anchored most nights in open bays along the coast of Panama, or behind small islands, the only landlocked bay we entered was Bahia Honda, about which the Pilot Book was unusually enthusiastic:

'Deep, safe, capacious, and very easy of access.' We approached the area in an electrical storm whose flashes and rumbles came nearer and nearer. Ernest had been making a chart of the bay, and all its complexity of off-lying islands, from the Pilot Book, but the imminent thunderstorm beat him to it. Luckily he had done enough to sort out what we were looking at and to identify the pueblo ahead as being on big Isla Talon.

We were soon sailing down the western arm of the bay, past the island, whose brilliant green hillsides shortly disappeared in rain, along with the range of mountains at the head of the bay. As the thunder cracked overhead, the rain came down in torrents, and the wind tossed the water of the bay into mad whitecaps as we hurried in under motor and genoa. Ernest scrambled to hand the genny and take down the small shade tarp over the helmsman, together we secured (rain-catching) buckets and closed hatches, I hung the anchor out, and we headed in to the northwest corner where, behind a small island, we dropped the hook in 5 fathoms of good-holding brown sand off a beach lined with mango trees and palms.

The pueblo on the big island consisted of 20 or so rough houses, nestled right on the water's edge among palm trees. As the thunder rain ended, an intense golden light lit up the emerald hillsides, the water of the bay shimmered over its brown surface, the sky turned to a clear deep blue and everything seemed limned in gold.

Before long a swarthy young Indian with dark eyes and a small moustache approached, along with two boys, in a large dugout with beautifully finished gunwales and a new-looking outboard. One of the boys was near-naked and shivering, but the other sported a shirt and hat, a bright lad who picked up our sign language and skimpy Spanish much more quickly than either of his companions. We gathered that theirs was the only settlement in the huge green bay, and that they grew no vegetables or fruit, other than mangoes and coconuts, although we understood that they did grow vegetables on some of the other Panamanian islands. They asked for cigarettes, which we never carried; but we did manage to find them three cans of Coke and some chocolate and a tin of corned beef. There was nothing in the canoe but a flat bladed paddle and some hand lines.

By the time morning came we had decided to press on to Golfito, 140 miles ahead, with perhaps only two more stops. Initially we had intended to cruise the Panamanian coast and islands fairly extensively and then the southern coast of Costa Rica. We had not expected that El Niño would have such an extreme effect on us. Now we planned to call in only at Isla Brincanco in the Contrares group and then perhaps anchor next day in the big open bay of Isla Cavada in the Secas.

Sailing north up the coast from Bahia Honda we were caught in a rainsquall so blinding and with so much wind that Ernest, at the helm, could see nothing ahead but a curtain of rain, and felt that he was not in control. I had to hand the main in a hurry by myself, much harder work than I was used to. Once we were anchored in the western corner of a quiet bay on Isla Bricanco the weather calmed and we decided to stay overnight. Here, at last, we found a pool of running water. It would even have been enough to wash our bedding in if we had still needed it, but we did not, since the Lord had provided so much rain with the thunderstorm the day before. After a quiet night we scrambled up a small hill to gaze down on blue and white waves crashing on the outer shore. If only it had not been so hot and humid, it would have been a beautiful place to explore.

On the following day, we were anchored off Isla Cavada in the Secas Group. An old unpainted leaky dugout came alongside and we met Jeremiah and Manuel Garcia. Jeremiah had a little—'*poquito*'— English, which made conversation easier. Manuel was an agreeable silent partner. They brought us a present of some limes—and a radio for Ernest to mend. He established that there was something wrong with the local band, but was unable to fix it. They came aboard and had a whisky anyway, and told us that they grew corn, beans, sugar cane, cassava, yams and fruit on the island, spending 45 days there and 25 at home, mentioning Bahia Honda as one of the places that some of the workers came from. There were only two others there that day but sometimes at harvest time there were as many as seven.

We hoped to visit their plantation next morning but in the night it began to blow northwest, right into our anchorage. It was not nice. In the pitch black darkness we stowed tarps and seat cushions, shoes, masks, flippers and spear gun, upped the anchor and crept out. By

0800 next morning Punta Burica, the last Panamanian headland before Costa Rica, lay visible ahead.

During the day we gradually closed with it, in light switching winds. The only log entries were: '0800 Hot, 89°', '1200 Hotter, 93°', and '1500 Hottest, 95°.' By 'Hottest,' *Scrabble* time, we were abeam the point and counting coconut trees slowly passing on the shore. By 1800 we were finally past and heading for the next landmark of Punta Banco, the western arm of big Golfo Dulce. It took us all night to pass this unmemorable headland and to do some quiet tacking over towards the mouth of the Coto River in a gentle headwind, helped by the light of a quarter moon partly obscured by clouds.

We motored the last three miles into Golfo Dulce and anchored off hot and steamy Golfito midmorning. It was May 1st, in not much more than a month we hoped, we would be in Hilo, Hawaii; in two months we might well be home.

That afternoon we rowed ashore in the humid heat to clear in and to find the bank (Air conditioned thank God!) where we changed our US dollars to Costa Rican pesos. In the evening we went ashore to Cap'n Tom's hospitable house/club and drank cold beer with the young, mostly American, cruising sailors we found there. It was our first visit to the legendary one-legged Captain and his family and we found him bluff, welcoming, fat, white, grey-haired and extremely kind. Like other cruisers we marked up our beer in the drinks book, paid before we sailed, and signed the guest book—his sixth.

On the streets and in the market the people were friendly and greeted us usually with a cheery '*Hola!*' With over four thousand miles ahead of us to Hawaii, I wanted to stock up on as much fruit and vegetables as possible: a typical cruiser's list of several hands of the famous bananas, 15 grapefruit, 24 oranges, 20 limes, 5 kg of small cabbages, 5 kg of potatoes, 3 kg of onions, 4 kg of tomatoes, 1 kg of cucumbers, 2 dozen eggs and 1 kilo of (what turned out to be) awful goat cheese.

The heat in Golfito was unbearable; we could not wait to get away. We weighed anchor before 0700 next day to escape it, and after a few attempts to sail into a light headwind, gave it up, and motored for ten hours to make a reasonable offing from the coast before midnight.

'I'll be happy when I can't see land,' Ernest said. I felt the same way.

We seemed to be crossing the steamer lanes, seeing ten ships in those daylight hours, including a large navy ship, probably US, heading for Golfito.

'Aha!' We thought, 'an international incident in the making!' We had seen an enormous fishing boat, *LOUISE V*, that we thought was US registered, lying in the harbour with Costa Ricans aboard cradling machine guns. Apparently some guns had actually been fired when four or five boats were caught fishing illegally in Costa Rican waters. The others scattered, but *Louise* was still hauling her nets and was caught red handed.

When an electrical storm caught up with us that night it brought only a single one degree drop in the temperature of just under 94°, but gave us almost four hours of usable wind from the west southwest. The associated shower also brought a poor bedraggled swallow aboard. Ernest grabbed him and put him in the doghouse to rest and dry off. Two other passing land birds that chose to settle briefly on our floating way-station in the heat, were an Eastern kingbird and a shore bird with strikingly handsome brown and white markings, which stayed just long enough to be identified as a Ruddy turnstone.

Now that we were safely offshore we expected to pick up some assorted wind to help us on our way, but day after day the breeze failed to be anything more than force 1,2, or at best 3 (up to 10 knots) usually from north or northwest, the direction we wanted to sail. At the end of the first week we had made good only 652 miles, less than 100 miles a day, in spite of having one glorious teaser day of perfect (NE) sailing of 150 miles. The next week was to be worse, only 578 miles, with conditions made more miserable by a constant sultriness. A strange characteristic of this El Niño was a thick murky grey-brown haze all around the horizon. This haze obscured the cumulus clouds when there were any, so that only their tops showed, and each morning the sun rose invisibly somewhere behind it, only to break clear finally above it. At first it seemed that the haze ended about ten degrees above the horizon, but after a week Ernest measured it with the sextant and found that the sun by day, and the first stars by night, appeared at 20° altitude.

Comparing temperatures with our first circumnavigation in 1974, when we had sailed direct to Hilo from Tobago Island, we found that we averaged about four or five degrees hotter overall, and by the middle of the second week heat exhaustion had taken such a toll on us that I had diagnosed myself as having a touch of *Le Cafard*, and Ernest as going stir crazy. As such we complemented one another nicely.

However I was beginning to become seriously worried about Ernest's state of mind. He was so infuriated by day after day of windless weather that he was finding it hard to sleep. Usually we did not need to steer, even in these windless conditions, since our small auto-pilot, the Mini-Seacourse, did a surprisingly good job of steering *Tryste* with the motor or under the light weather sails. This was good in keeping us from being at the helm in the burning sun, but bad in that the enforced idleness, the feeling of doing nothing and going nowhere, was anathema to a man who was used to being busy all the time. We had not intended to motor more than an hour or so a day to charge the motor, so we did not have the diesel, and were, as always, at the mercy of the wind (or the lack of it.)

The heat bore down on our world. It was so extreme that even the boobies had their beaks open and were panting. Thinking back to our farming days we remembered chickens as well as dogs doing that. On our first week out we had been visited by groups of immature boobies with orangey-red feet, either Red-foots or Blue-faces. Sometimes they tried to land on the masthead or the radar reflector, both of which were too difficult as they jerked violently as *Tryste* rolled in the swells, but one day a booby finally managed to settle tenuously on the mizzen mast. Ernest, after several ingenious angry attempts, managed to dislodge it; after which I had to scrub the surrounding deck.

Shortly after that an immature booby that had not learnt any better, tried to land on our temporary clothes line and ludicrously hung itself up briefly by the neck instead—more scrubbing. Another group, of about forty, kept station for much of the day on the water. They would let *Tryste* get almost out of sight and then fly back to us, have another try at landing on the boat, then settle on the water ahead again and wait for us to pass them.

A few days later we had our hottest day of unbearable weather at sea, close and ominous and drippingly sultry, the sky overhead hot and bare and blue with no promise anywhere of a breeze, yet a sloppy sea infuriatingly suggesting wind against current. Although our noon position credited us with 70 miles, these consisted of only 3 under sail, together with 50 by motor and 17 for favourable current; this day was capped by the next three days when we actually sailed only 25 miles altogether. By now I was permanently trying to treat Ernest gently; the soft answer diffusing his wrath a little. I was treating him, in fact, as if he were terminally ill, and that was pretty much what it was like.

To stop himself from going mad with frustration, he decided to start repainting the exterior of the whole main cabin. He began to fill and sand the forward area while I took the helm for a few hours so that we could motor into a light west northwesterly, even though the breeze took half a knot off our speed.

The windless days now passed fairly peacefully since Ernest was busy preparing and painting the cabin trunk and one twin pole, and was less bothered by the calms. Even so, from time to time, we had some pretty startling shouts and curses at the Gods.

As the heat continued to envelop us I became more and more obsessed with thoughts of ice, *cold* beer and ice cream. I remembered Susie's Russian-ship cartoon nine years earlier, of the four of us homeward bound aboard *Tryste* in the East Pacific heat, waving frantically, with a huge flag flying that asked, 'DO YOU HAVE ANY ICE CREAM?' and a colossal freighter looming over us, its decks lined with sailors, and a speech bubble saying, 'I WONDER WHY THEY WANT TO KNOW OUR CARGO; COULD THEY BE SPIES?' We needed Susie's Russian freighter badly.

One night at sunset we briefly saw the true horizon with an enormous pale-red ghost sun perched on it, ready to set. It was a superb sunset, as so many were in those strange conditions, and went on and on, filling the whole sky with crimson and grey striations long after the sun sank.

Somehow that day, with only three and a half hours of motoring out of the twenty-four, we achieved 86 miles, but the slopping and slapping and banging we endured in the light airs infuriated us both. How long can this go on? I asked myself. Ernest was still busy and reasonably content, but in a day or two at most he would run out of paint. Surely we must soon find wind, although he claimed that he would 'not be worried' until we reached 110° W. We were then only at 107°.

Towards the end of the second week, when he was putting the last coat of finishing paint on his cabin sides, and on a day when we had been motoring for 5 hours, a cat's paw came in from the north that we dared not waste, and we turned off the motor and set a large sail with ingenious lines and blocks rigged to keep it off the sticky wet paint.

It was about this time that I discovered weevils in the locker where I kept our bulk flour. Curses! This could be serious! I cleared out the locker and carried everything out on deck. The guilty party turned out to be a bag of quick-dried peas generously given to us by Howard, another trimaran owner, in Durban. Thanks to my habit of double bagging everything, they had not yet chewed their way into the flour. Peas and weevils all went overboard and the danger passed. Thanks, Howard!

By now Ernest was bored and irritated, 'I was 56 when we started this trip, I'll be 106 by the time we finish it—if we ever do finish it,' he complained. He was so fed up that he was shoving me out of his way on deck as if he didn't care if he pushed me overboard. He probably didn't at that point although I was pretty sure that if that happened he would hastily fish me out again.

Next morning, at 0610, eighteen days after leaving Golfito, we were no longer bored, and life suddenly became more intense. I had caught a snippet of a weather forecast talking about a tropical depression at 9°7'N 103°W moving west northwest with an 85-mile radius of gales. WWVH had mentioned one at 6°or 8°N a couple of days ago on the general forecast but there had been no report of it since so I had hoped that it had dissipated. I found this new mention when I suddenly thought to try the Atlantic forecast.

With this specific information, and while our breakfast cooled, Ernest plotted its likely course on the chart, and decided that to avoid it, and to steer clear of the solitary mid-ocean island of Clipperton at 10°18'N, 109°13'W, we should head southwest. With my spatial dyslexia and inability to orient myself correctly from east to west, I was happy to leave such decisions to him. Since the wind was by now NNW3 and fair for this course we were able to ease sheets and, with a rising wind, enjoy a fine sail. Transmission from WWV was not good enough to get confirmation of the storm's position but at noon we had the news that Adolf, now officially a tropical hurricane (and presumably ready to conquer the world) was moving west at 7 knots.

Since we love to try and frighten ourselves, Ernest wrote in the log in capitals, 'ADOLF 350 MILES OFF HEADING STRAIGHT FOR US'. Now we had to make a decision. Hurricanes are so unpredictable.

In the northern hemisphere it should have gone west, as it did, but then later it might possibly curve to the northwest or north, both of which it finally did, but not before giving us a scare by behaving atypically for a few hours.

Ernest turned *Tryste* away from our present course and we hurried off slightly to the south of southwest while we waited to see whether Adolf would change direction; we even headed northeast for a few hours but soon changed back to the southwest again.

That afternoon Ernest collected our lifejackets (for possible capsize) from where they were put away in a locker, stowed all spare sails in the forward cabin—and worried.

'Don't imagine that this poor old trimaran could survive a hurricane,' he said darkly. All night we continued to sail a bit west of south and Adolf continued to grow in strength with 150 knot gusts at the centre, and with 95 knot gales to a radius of 160 miles. At last at 0800 next morning came the happy entry in Ernest's hand. 'Adolf turning NW— bless him.'

Now we could go harder on the wind, due west, as our courses were diverging. By 1800 that evening, when the hurricane finally turned north, we could head back on course, slightly north of west, into failing NNW winds. Our hurricane scare had lasted only an extremely long thirty-six hour day. Ernest remarked that if only we had not known about it we could have gone on our way happily and never changed course. (My fault for listening to the radio.)

After that the wind died completely, leaving only an uncomfortable slop. Ernest had expected the passing hurricane to have cleared the air, but instead it took most of our remaining wind and for twenty-four hours we endured more fluky light northwest winds. That was to be the worst of it. Later he wrote crossly in the log, 'Back in the North West Trades.' These light on-and-off-again winds lasted for six more days before at last we had his incredulous and slightly exaggerated entry in capitals, 'THE WIND HAS MOVED EAST OF NORTH FOR THE FIRST TIME IN EIGHTEEN DAYS!'

It was true. On June 1st 1983, our 28th day out from Golfito, we finally found these vigorous northeast trades, the same day that we had earlier entered a despairing note in the log about no longer believing that they existed. For two days the wind blew mostly nor' northeast and we made runs of 116 and 117 miles, before it settled firmly into the northeast and *Tryste* began to fly.

As we celebrated the fact that we were sailing fast at last and that the humidity had gone, we caught the largest yellow fin tuna that we had ever boated, 48 lbs. Over the next twenty-four hours I successfully canned, or rather bottled, fifteen jars of first class tuna and we ate as many meals of fresh tuna as we could enjoy: dinner, lunch and another dinner of kedgeree.

The sun shone and lit *Tryste's* tan sails as day after day she danced over the ocean, and the seas built into well-formed rolling waves with cresting tops and deep troughs. On the fourth and fifth days of this *Tryste* clocked up two days running of 188 miles noon to noon under her vane self-steering. We could not remember her ever doing that before in nearly 100,000 miles of voyaging, not even at the time of her previously finest hour across the Indian Ocean with Nicky and Susie aboard, when she made her record run of 205. Immodestly we recalled that Eric Hiscock once referring to the three of us, Ernest, *Tryste,* and me, as 'An amazing trio'. As the wind rose and we gloated, the gods heard us and laughed, and marked us down for retribution later.

Suddenly, on only the sixth day of trades, we realised that we had less than a thousand miles to go to Hilo. After several more good runs, optimism was beginning to be permissible and I noted: 'The eggs from Golfito are getting definitely peculiar, never mind, unless we have bad luck we should be in Hilo within a week.' It was around this time that the BBC gave us the news that the British had re-elected Mrs Thatcher—presumably on the strength of the Falklands' War.

At 2200, on the twelfth day of trade wind sailing, Ernest thought he saw the distant loom of light that must be Hilo, just before he handed over to me at the end of his night watch. It took us until 1530 next afternoon to reach port. At noon that day we crossed our 1981 outgoing course to San Francisco, and Ernest's log entry read: 'Congratulations *Tryste* on your second circumnavigation.' After a passage of 40 days and 4,333 miles we came once again to anchor in Radio Bay, Hilo, on the big island of Hawaii, and from early in the evening slept rapturously, knowing that at last, and for a few days, there would be no reason to drag oneself unwillingly from one's bunk, after only three or four hours, to stand watch.

Tryste lies beside the metal dock with *Cautelle* alongside, across from the Yacht Club under Table Mountain, Cape Town.

Vistafjord lies in the open roadstead off Jamestown, St. Helena.

First Gatun lock in the Panama Canal with the small submarine that entered ahead of us.

Marie, Irene and Meredith on *Tryste's* bow with Thatcher's Ferry Bridge behind them.

Ernest painting *Tryste's* cabin trunk in the El Niño heat, on the way to
Golfito, Costa Rica.

Big seas rolling down to Durban.

Bottom-painting *Tryste* at Isla Chapera, Las Perlas Is. Panama, in the El Niño drought.

Ugo sails *EMTEESS* off the island of Hawaii, the day we left.

255

CHAPTER TWENTY-THREE:

THE END OF THE AFFAIR

We woke next morning to see the super-inflatable *EMTEESS* next to us and to meet super-brain Ugo Conti with his brown eyes, glasses and quizzical smile. He gave us a ride to downtown Hilo the second day we were there.

The first day Ernest had walked out to the airport, which we had been told was the new home for general delivery, and then walked all the way back again with a good load of mail. This included a delightful homemade cassette tape from our eldest daughter Janet featuring one of her own inimitable poems that started:

'Janet was thin and now she's fat,

What do you think about that?'

This informed us, in several verses, and to our delight, that she was pregnant. Now we had all the more reason to be pleased that we had decided to skip Alaska and head straight home.

The day that Ugo gave us a ride into Hilo, I decided to get my hair washed and cut, and Ernest soon finished his shopping and took a bus back to *Tryste*. I found a small backstreet establishment where I did not need an appointment, and was welcomed by the proprietor, Edna, a small, dumpy, smiling Japanese-Hawaiian. After she had washed and cut my hair and was halfway through blow-drying it, she suddenly offered to set it instead. 'Okay,' I said, since she had already told me sadly, 'No one rich in Hilo, there's no industry here.' I think really that she just wanted to do it as a favour.

'I show your husband what I can do, huh?' She said, and added, 'You come back to Hilo in a year or two years and you come see me and maybe we go for a drive, yes?'

We found the local people delightful, warm and friendly. One day, when we were hitching into town, a pair of older Hawaiian ladies passed us in an early model station wagon going into Hilo, but shortly afterwards came back and picked us up, apologising for passing us in the first place, but explaining 'We had the back seat full.' As we clambered aboard they asked, 'Have you seen the Rainbow Falls? Or the Boiling Pots?' We admitted that we had not, and they insisted on driving us to see both, then and there. When they finally let us off at the Post Office downtown, an hour or two later, they were still mourning, 'If only you were staying longer'. We felt quite guilty.

Waiting for the bus back to Radio Bay on my hairdressing day, I met another Hawaiian lady of similar vintage, sitting in the bus shelter. She had a lovely wrinkled Hawaiian face, and was wearing jogging pants, rubber boots, lumberjack jacket, pink crepe de Chine headscarf and a straw hat with a fresh frangipani blossom clothes-pegged to the brim. She suddenly offered me a box of mint parfaits, 'Take some, go on, help yourself', she said. Lovely people.

When Ugo kindly took us sightseeing in his rental car; we set out at 7.30 in the morning. He said that he did not want to be out too long because he had an appointment in the evening; but we did not reach home again until 6 p.m. He took us to the places he wanted to see himself which was great. We none of us wanted to take time out to stop for a meal or snacks, but Ugo fed us on and off all day from a large bag of 'm & m's, which for me quite made up for being a little scrunched in the back of the car. We did find it a little strange though, that he never called us by our names, perhaps he could not remember them.

We reached the Volcano visitors bureau at just the right time to see a spectacular one hour volcano film, then on we went to the Thurston lava tubes, walking through huge gorgeous wild fuchsia, then round Crater Rim Drive to see the Kilauea cauldron and endless lava fields. From there we drove off in search of a reported new eruption, and down to a lagoon on the Kona coast where Ugo thought he and *EMTEESS* might be happy, then up the Saddle Road across the island, with open country, where to our delight, we saw a Hawaiian cowboy on a horse. Finally Ugo drove us up to the 9,000-ft level on Mauna Kea where we had to turn back because we were running low on gas. When we all clambered out of the car there, it was to discover that we were at the most beautiful view of all, out over the tops of limitless clouds, just like 'the end of the earth,' that Xi finally found, at the end of his long search, in *The Gods Must Be Crazy.*

After five days in Hilo we sailed out of Radio Bay and, having fulfilled our commitment to photograph EMTEESS, headed offshore, where we found the same fresh trades that had so delighted us before we reached Hawaii. They continued to blow vigorously, and by the second day water was breaking over the boat. We were heading straight home now, north of east, so we were on the wind, beating into the seas. Ernest handed the main and genoa and set the yankee with a small headsail on the inner forestay, still with the reefed mizzen set, to ease the strain on *Tryste.*

Sunrise on that second day out had been a pale orange horror of torn and tattered rain clouds, and the day featured one of the wettest wildest rides we had ever had. Ernest was not too surprised when he pumped out the bilge to find a lot of water, but when he checked the port float, which had seemed unaccountably to be making water all day, he found that the plywood skin had broken away from the stringers in places and was flexing in and out like bellows. The bilge pump seemed to be packing up again so it was hard to tell how much water we were making. Had we pushed our luck too far? After all we had circumnavigated twice now with *Tryste.*

He fixed the leak with a major shipwright effort—bracing three pieces of 1 x 3 across the narrow forward part of the float and screwing them in—working both in the float and on deck. Before this we had to clear out eight spare 5-gallon plastic water jugs and stow them in the cockpit to make room for him to crawl in. At the best of times it was extremely difficult to work crouching or lying down in this forward skinny area of the float. With a heavy sea running it must have been excruciating.

In later years, when he was asked if our break-up had been occasioned by 'a storm' he would always deny it vigorously, claiming that the winds at that time were just regular ordinary trades. But a look back at my diary, and at the logbook, suggests that for a day or two those trades were extreme or at least super-fresh, and we were on the wind, '*Tryste's* worst point of sailing' as Ernest often grumbled.

Even the first night out he had written in the log, 'Wild ride, bashing to windward.' It had been rough enough to rip two piston hanks off the genoa luff wire. He had mended that mid-morning, leaving the yankee in its place. Later he noted that we were, 'Crashing brutally to windward,' even without the mainsail set.

Our newest logbook, which we had started for the homeward passage from Hilo to BC, featured a space for comments after each three days. Our first entry, on day 3, was:

'Repaired 2 piston hanks on genoa, repaired 2 seams on main and repaired port float (still pumping). Things may improve.'

By the time of the second entry, three days later, disaster had struck, the starboard float had broken off and broken up and floated away and the mainmast had gone overboard. The log, written up later, as we motored the remains of our broken boat north, commented laconically:

'Things didn't.'

Would it have made any difference? I asked myself later—long after the float and the mast had disappeared astern—would it have made any difference, on that dark night, when I thought I saw some movement in the forward beam, if I had woken Ernest from his watch below and told him what I had seen? He was so tired after wrestling with all *Tryste*'s problems since we left Hilo that I had hated the idea of waking him. Perhaps I should have done.

It had been just four days earlier that we had photographed *EMTEESS* just off the coast of Hawaii and then sailed away to meet our destiny, which was, unexpectedly, to see Alaska after all—under tow from the 45,000 ton USNS tanker *Hudson*—so that we did not reach home on Saltspring roughly twenty days after leaving Ugo in Hawaii as we had hoped, in plenty of time for Nicky's birthday in July, but a whole month later in August by way of a detour to Whittier, in Prince William Sound, Alaska, where ice-blue glaciers flowed imperceptibly down to the ocean and killer whales cut patterns in the still surface of the sound. Only then, tied up in Whittier's Hobo Harbour, were we able to send Ugo his film, so that eventually he was able to use some of the transparencies we took—in his Cruising World story—and to write to us his exuberant, 'Friends, you blew my mind!' letter from California.